KANT'S CR
PURE R

5000928688

 **University (**
Hertfordshi

D1610489

College Lane, Hatfield, Herts. AL1

Learning and Information Service

For renewal of Standard and One Week Loans,
please visit the web site **http://www.voyager.herts.ac.uk**

This item must be returned or the loan renewed by the due date.
The University reserves the right to recall items from loan at any time.
A fine will be charged for the late return of items.

CAMBRIDGE INTRODUCTIONS TO KEY PHILOSOPHICAL TEXTS

This new series offers introductory textbooks on what are considered to be the most important texts of Western philosophy. Each book guides the reader through the main themes and arguments of the work in question, while also paying attention to its historical context and its philosophical legacy. No philosophical background knowledge is assumed, and the books will be well suited to introductory university-level courses.

Titles published in the series:

KANT'S *CRITIQUE OF PURE REASON*

An Introduction

JILL VANCE BUROKER

California State University, San Bernardino

CAMBRIDGE
UNIVERSITY PRESS

CAMBRIDGE UNIVERSITY PRESS
Cambridge, New York, Melbourne, Madrid, Cape Town, Singapore, São Paulo

Cambridge University Press
The Edinburgh Building, Cambridge CB2 2RU, UK

Published in the United States of America by Cambridge University Press, New York

www.cambridge.org
Information on this title: www.cambridge.org/9780521618250

© Jill Vance Buroker 2006

First published 2006

Printed in the United Kingdom at the University Press, Cambridge

A catalogue record for this publication is available from the British Library

Library of Congress Cataloging in Publication data

ISBN-13 978-0-521-85315-6 hardback
ISBN-10 0-521-85315-x hardback

ISBN-13 978-0-521-61825-0 paperback
ISBN-10 0-521-61825-8 paperback

For Sophie

Contents

Acknowledgments

I am grateful to California State University, San Bernardino, for sabbatical and research support while I was writing this book. I also thank my colleague, Tony Roy, for helpful conversations, and students who allowed themselves to be test subjects for various chapters. My interpretation of Kant has been most heavily influenced by Henry Allison, Gordon Brittan, Jr., Lorne Falkenstein, Michael Friedman, Michelle Grier, and Arthur Melnick. Gordon Brittan and Lorne Falkenstein both made valuable comments on early drafts. I am indebted to Hilary Gaskin of Cambridge University Press, and three readers for the press, William Baumer, Fred Rauscher, and Lisa Shabel, for their sympathetic criticisms and suggestions. I was especially fortunate to have Angela Blackburn as my copy-editor. Finally, I want to thank Ed McCann for his encouragement.

Abbreviations

CPR	Kant, *Critique of Pure Reason*
MFNS	Kant, *Metaphysical Foundations of Natural Science*
NST	non-spatial and non-temporal (non-spatiotemporality thesis)
PD	Principle of Determinability
Prolegomena	Kant, *Prolegomena to Any Future Metaphysics*
PTD	Principle of Thoroughgoing Determinability
t.u.a.	transcendental unity of apperception
UT	unknowability thesis

CHAPTER I

Introduction to the critical project

I. KANT'S LIFE AND WORKS

Immanuel Kant was one of the greatest thinkers in the history of philosophy. Unfortunately, he was not a good writer, and his works are very difficult to read. Not only did Kant write on most major philosophical problems – concerning knowledge, metaphysics, ethics, aesthetics, religion, law, and government – he also developed views of extreme depth and subtlety. Especially impressive is the way Kant unified his theories into a larger system, called an "architectonic." Although he sometimes appears to stretch his ideas to fit them into his system, generally the unity in his views is not forced, and rests on philosophical principles.

Kant lived from 1724 to 1804, during a period of enormous change in science, philosophy, and mathematics. Kant himself was neither a scientist nor a mathematician (although he did make a contribution to cosmology). Nonetheless he shared the hopes of predecessors such as Descartes and Locke to provide a philosophical foundation for the new physics. The scientific revolution, initiated by Copernicus's *On the Revolutions of the Heavenly Spheres* in 1543, put an end to the Aristotelian worldview that had reigned for almost 2000 years. The French philosopher René Descartes (1596–1650), a contemporary of Galileo (1564–1642), was the first to attempt a systematic theory of knowledge to support the Copernican astronomy. Descartes not only invented analytic geometry, he also developed his own physics and made important discoveries in optics, among them the sine law of refraction. The power of mechanistic science became undeniable with Isaac Newton's formulation of the three laws of motion and the law of gravitation, published in his *Principia Mathematica* of

1686. In providing a general explanation for Kepler's laws of planetary motion, Newton's achievement brought to the fore questions about the foundations of science. The new physics also depended on the calculus, invented independently by Newton and Leibniz.

Immanuel Kant was born April 22, 1724, in Königsberg, the capital of East Prussia (now Kaliningrad in Russia).[1] He lived his entire life in or near Königsberg, a thriving commercial city. His father was a saddler, and Kant grew up in a working class family. Between the ages of eight and sixteen, Kant attended the Friedrichskollegium, whose principal was Albert Schultz (1692–1763). Schultz had been a student of the Enlightenment philosopher Christian Wolff (1679–1754), himself a student of the great philosopher and mathematician Gottfried Wilhelm Leibniz (1646–1716). The Friedrichskollegium was affiliated with Pietism, a seventeenth-century German Protestant movement. It emphasized the "scrutiny of the heart," and valued the active devotion of the person. Kant rejected its more rigid practices, but evidently admired its general principles. The school's curriculum emphasized religious instruction in Hebrew and Greek; non-religious subjects were less important. In 1737, when Kant was thirteen, his mother died. He was very close to her, and credited her with nurturing both his spirit and his intellect. In 1740 Kant graduated second in his class from the Friedrichskollegium, and entered the University of Königsberg. There he was influenced by another student of Wolff, Martin Knutzen (1713–51), a professor of logic and metaphysics. Under Knutzen's tutelage from 1740 to 1746, Kant studied philosophy, mathematics, natural sciences, and classical Latin literature.

Following his father's death in 1746, Kant left the university to support himself as a private tutor. In 1747 he completed his first work, *Thoughts on the True Estimation of Living Forces* (published in 1749), in which he attempted to resolve a dispute between Leibnizians and Cartesians over the formula for calculating force from mass and velocity. Unfortunately Kant was ignorant of the correct solution, proposed by d'Alembert in 1743. Nevertheless, this work, written in German rather than the traditional Latin, marked the beginnings

---

[1] Two excellent biographies are available in Ernst Cassirer's *Kant's Life and Thought*, and Manfred Kuehn's recent *Kant: A Biography*.

of Kant's lifelong interest in the foundations of physics. During the
1750s he produced several scientific treatises, the most important his
Universal Natural History and Theory of the Heavens (1755). His theory
of the formation of galaxies, later dubbed the "Kant-Laplace hypothesis," had a significant influence on astronomy. In the same year Kant
completed his doctoral dissertation *Meditations in which the Ether is
Succinctly Delineated*, and his "habilitation" treatise *A New Elucidation of the First Principles of Metaphysical Cognition*. The latter work
marks his earliest criticism of Leibnizian philosophy.

Although Kant began lecturing at the University of Königsberg
in the fall of 1755, he was practically destitute, depending on fees
from tutoring and lectures. After several unsuccessful applications for
professorships in logic and metaphysics, he received his first salaried
position in 1766 as assistant librarian at the palace library. Not until
1770, at the age of forty-six, was Kant awarded the professorship
he desired. His workload was formidable: he taught logic, mathematics, metaphysics, physical geography, and foundations of natural
science. Eventually he added ethics, mechanics, theoretical physics,
geometry, and trigonometry. Despite the stereotype of Kant as rigidly
intellectual (and punctual), he was a great favorite both in and out
of the classroom. His lectures were renowned for erudition and wit.
But he was also quite sociable, sharing long dinners with friends and
frequenting the theater and casinos. He was highly prized for his
sparkling conversation in the most fashionable salons. This passage
from a student, the poet and philosopher Johann Gottfried Herder,
should put to rest the misleading stereotype:

I have had the good fortune to know a philosopher. He was my teacher.
In his prime he had the happy sprightliness of a youth; he continued to
have it, I believe, even as a very old man. His broad forehead, built for
thinking, was the seat of an imperturbable cheerfulness and joy. Speech,
the richest in thought, flowed from his lips. Playfulness, wit, and humor
were at his command. His lectures were the most entertaining talks. His
mind, which examined Leibniz, Wolff, Baumgarten, Crusius, and Hume,
and investigated the laws of nature of Newton, Kepler, and the physicists,
comprehended equally the newest works of Rousseau . . . and the latest
discoveries in science. He weighed them all, and always came back to the
unbiased knowledge of nature and to the moral worth of man. . . . No

cabal, no sect, no prejudice, no desire for fame could ever tempt him in the slightest away from broadening and illuminating the truth. He incited and gently forced others to think for themselves; despotism was foreign to his mind. This man, whom I name with the greatest gratitude and respect, was Immanuel Kant.[2]

Until the 1760s Kant was a devotee of Leibniz through the teachings of Christian Wolff. In 1768 he published the short treatise *On the Differentiation of Directions in Space*, in which he used the argument from incongruent counterparts (objects like left and right hands) to support a Newtonian theory of absolute space against Leibniz's theory of relational space. I argue in my *Space and Incongruence: The Origin of Kant's Idealism* that after 1768 Kant developed the incongruent counterparts argument to reject Leibniz's theory of the relation between the sensibility and the intellect, and ultimately to support the transcendental ideality of space and time. His introduction to Hume's *Enquiry Concerning Human Understanding* (published in 1748), probably around 1769, crystallized his misgivings about rationalism and dogmatic metaphysics. Kant took his first step toward the critical philosophy, the theory presented in his three *Critiques*, in his Inaugural Dissertation of 1770, *On the Form and Principles of the Sensible and Intelligible World*. Here he radically distinguished the sensibility from the intellect, arguing that the former provides knowledge only of phenomenal appearances. Nevertheless, he retained Leibniz's view that the intellect has access to noumena, the reality behind the appearances.

In his February 21, 1772 letter to Marcus Herz, a former student and friend, Kant lays out the questions haunting him since the dissertation, which define the critical project:

In my dissertation I was content to explain the nature of intellectual representations in a merely negative way, namely, to state that they were not modifications of the soul brought about by the object. However, I silently passed over the further question of how a representation that refers to an object without being in any way affected by it can be possible.[3]

Kant had come to see that he needed a more systematic treatment of the intellect, in both its theoretical and practical activities. In the letter Kant outlines a plan for his work, remarking optimistically that he expects to complete the first part, on metaphysics, in three months.

[2] Quoted in Cassirer, *Kant's Life and Thought*, 84.   [3] *Correspondence*, 133.

In fact he did not produce the first edition of the *Critique of Pure Reason* until 1781, almost twelve years after conceiving the project. Unfortunately the work initially drew negative responses, both for its obscurity and its conclusions. Eventually opinion shifted, and the *Critique* began to exert its influence in Germany and elsewhere. In 1786 Kant was made a member of the Berlin Academy of Sciences; in 1794 he was inducted into the Petersburg Academy, and in 1798 into the Siena Academy.

Once engrossed in developing his critical philosophy, Kant became a recluse. This is the only explanation for his enormous output from 1781 to his death in 1804. These are the major works in that period:

1781   *The Critique of Pure Reason*, first edition (referred to as A)
1783   *The Prolegomena to Any Future Metaphysics* (an obscure summary of the *Critique*)
1785   *The Groundwork of the Metaphysics of Morals*
1786   *The Metaphysical Foundations of Natural Science*
1787   *The Critique of Pure Reason*, second edition (referred to as B)
1788   *The Critique of Practical Reason*
1790   *The Critique of the Power of Judgment*
1797   *The Metaphysics of Morals*
1798   *Anthropology from a Pragmatic Point of View*

During this period Kant also wrote many shorter essays, among them "The Idea for a Universal History with Cosmopolitan Intent" and "What is Enlightenment?" (both 1784), *Religion Within the Bounds of Reason Alone* (1793), *On Eternal Peace* (1795), and *The Conflict of the Faculties* (1798).

His publication of the 1793 treatise on religion brought him into conflict with a religious edict issued in 1788 by Frederick William II (1786–97). Under Frederick William I (1713–40) and Frederick II, the Great (1740–86), Prussia had been transformed from an authoritarian state to a constitutional monarchy. Also known for religious tolerance, it welcomed refugees from other countries, including Huguenots from France, Catholics from Eastern Europe, and Jews. Despite these progressive developments, the edict of 1788 put an end to religious liberalism. Although the theology faculty of the University of Königsberg declared that Kant's treatise was not an essay in theology, the king opposed its publication. During this affair, in June of 1794, Kant published his second treatise on religion, the ironic *The End of All Things*. In October of 1794 Frederick William II ordered Kant to desist from such writing. Although Kant defended himself against the charges, he agreed to renounce further essays on religion as long as the king lived.

Kant's last project, published as the *Opus Postumum*, was intended as a bridge between the critical philosophy and empirical science. Although he began the work in 1796, he was not to complete it. On October 8, 1803, he became seriously ill for the first time. He died four months later, on February 12, 1804. Thousands of mourners attended his funeral procession on February 28. They took Kant's body to the professors' crypt in the cathedral and university chapel of Königsberg. A plaque later installed over the grave contains the famous quotation from the *Critique of Practical Reason*: "Two things fill the mind with ever new and increasing admiration and awe, the more often and more steadily we reflect on them: *the starry heavens above me and the moral law within me.*"[4]

2. THE CRITICAL PROJECT

Kant's critical philosophy attempts to show that human reason can attain objective truths about the nature of reality as well as morality. Both types of knowledge are based on laws that are necessary but known *a priori*, that is, independent of experience. Theoretical knowledge is based on laws of nature, and moral knowledge on the moral law. Neither rationalism nor empiricism explains how we have such knowledge because both schools give mistaken analyses of the human mind. Empiricists favor sense perception over the intellect, and effectively deny the possibility of *a priori* knowledge. Rationalists recognize *a priori* knowledge, but have no coherent account of its relation to experience. Kant originally intended the first *Critique* to provide a philosophical justification for both theoretical and moral knowledge. Recognizing after 1781 that morality required a distinct foundation, Kant published the *Groundwork of the Metaphysics of Morals* in 1785 and the *Critique of Practical Reason* in 1788. In the *Critique of the Power of Judgment* of 1790 Kant broadens his project to

---

[4] *Practical Philosophy*, 269.

include an analysis of teleological judgment at the basis of aesthetics and empirical science. Although the three *Critiques* are the foundation of Kant's critical philosophy, the other works listed above on morality and science expand his analysis of theoretical and practical reason. In this section I will focus on the problems defining Kant's critical theory of knowledge in the first *Critique*.

It is not misleading to view Kant's critical philosophy as responding to the defects of rationalism and empiricism. The rationalists of the modern period include Descartes, Baruch Spinoza (1632–77), and Leibniz. In general they argue that knowledge derives from the intellect, which may be aided or hindered by sense perception. Although these philosophers differ on how the senses relate to the intellect, they agree that the intellect alone can grasp truths about reality, through innate ideas, prior to all sense experience. Descartes undoubtedly provides the most famous arguments along these lines in his *cogito* argument for his existence and his proofs for the existence of God. Although the senses can contribute to physical science, Descartes thinks sense perceptions are more likely to interfere with intellectual intuition. Leibniz conceives the relation between the senses and the intellect differently, taking sensory experience as a confused form of thinking. Although he agrees that knowledge of noumena, or things in themselves, is innate, depending entirely on the intellect, he holds that there is a correspondence between noumenal reality and phenomenal appearances. His *Monadology* (1714) is a paradigmatic rationalist attempt to base metaphysics on logical principles of identity and non-contradiction.

In contrast to the rationalists' optimism about the power of reason, the British empiricists of the modern period – John Locke (1632–1704), George Berkeley (1685–1753), and David Hume (1711–76) – emphasize the role of the senses. "Empiricism" is derived from the Greek word for experience; on their view all ideas originate in sense perception and reflection on our own minds. The intellect alone cannot know reality; at best it can operate on ideas given through the senses by such processes as association, comparison, abstraction, and deduction. In his *Essay Concerning Human Understanding* (1689), Locke argues, like Aristotle, that the mind is a *tabula rasa* or blank slate at birth; all mental processes begin with sensory stimulation, and the mind contains no innate ideas. Despite his empiricism, Locke accepts many of Descartes's metaphysical beliefs, such as the existence of God, bodies, and causal connections. Although he thinks knowledge of reality can never be certain, Locke does not question our capacity to acquire scientific knowledge, however fallible.

It is a paradox of empiricism that a commonsense theory of knowledge leads ultimately to a profound skepticism. Berkeley takes the first steps by arguing that belief in a mind-independent material world is not only unjustifiable but incoherent. Thus he rejects Descartes's substance dualism in favor of metaphysical idealism – the view that all reality consists of minds and their mental states. In his *Principles of Human Knowledge* (1710) and *Three Dialogues Between Hylas and Philonous* (1713), Berkeley rejects the existence of matter. Nevertheless, he retains Descartes's beliefs in the existence of God and minds as mental substances.

Hume, of course, argues for the most sweeping skepticism. In his *Treatise of Human Nature* (1739), Hume argues against knowledge of reality outside one's perceptions, including minds, bodies, and God. Against the rationalists, Hume makes devastating criticisms of the capacity of "reason" as a purely intellectual faculty. In place of a philosophical justification of metaphysics, he offers a psychological account of its origins. Appealing to "reason" in a broad sense, including the functions of the imagination, Hume claims that metaphysical beliefs are "natural," even if not strictly justified. Although his contemporaries failed to appreciate Hume's brilliance, he effectively put an end to rationalist metaphysics.

As we saw above, Kant was raised a Leibnizian, taught by students of Wolff. Nevertheless, in the 1760s he recognized the power of Hume's attack on metaphysics. As he explains in the *Prolegomena to Any Future Metaphysics*: "I openly confess that my remembering David Hume was the very thing which many years ago first interrupted my dogmatic slumber and gave my investigations in the field of speculative philosophy a quite new direction."[5] Kant was less impressed, however, by Hume's psychological account of metaphysical belief. So by 1769, Kant embarked on the first steps of his critical project.

Kant intends to defend metaphysics and scientific knowledge by providing an accurate analysis of human reason. His theory is based

[5] *Theoretical Philosophy after 1781*, 57.

on his discovery of synthetic *a priori* knowledge, judgments that are both informative and necessary. The problem is to explain how such judgments arise, as well as to give an account of their truth. Agreeing with Hume that experience cannot be their source, Kant takes the "critical turn," locating such knowledge in the subject. But equally unhappy with rationalism's appeal to innate principles, Kant must offer a new theory of the mental faculties. The key is his view that human reason, both theoretical and practical, produces synthetic *a priori* principles in the course of its natural activities. The *Critique of Pure Reason* argues that the necessary mathematical and metaphysical principles underlying all theoretical knowledge originate in the pure forms of sensibility and the intellect.

From Kant's point of view, all thought before him is pre-critical: he was the first to offer a systematic, functional justification of pure concepts and principles. To do this, Kant invents a new type of argument, which he calls a "transcendental deduction." His strategy is to show that a certain type of experience has particular necessary conditions. Thus anyone who accepts the "fact of experience" must agree that its transcendental conditions or presuppositions are true. All previous philosophers assumed that there were only two alternatives: either accept some substantive beliefs dogmatically as self-evident, or fall into an infinite regress of justification. One hallmark of Kant's brilliance is the way his critical method sidesteps this dilemma, by exploiting assumptions necessary to frame the skeptical challenge.

Kant's view that synthetic *a priori* knowledge originates in the subjective capacities of the knower results in transcendental idealism. This is the position that all theoretical knowledge is only of appearances, and that things in themselves are unknowable. Despite its radical nature, Kant's idealism offers solutions to two skeptical challenges. First, while it sets clear limits to metaphysics and empirical science, it explains how humans can attain knowledge of the spatial-temporal world. Second, it provides the basis for claiming that knowledge of a world governed by causal necessities is compatible with the practical freedom required by the moral law. These interwoven strands of the critical philosophy – the analysis of human reason, the justification of synthetic *a priori* knowledge, and transcendental idealism – will serve as main themes in this guide.

3. THE STRUCTURE OF THE *CRITIQUE OF PURE REASON*

As mentioned above, Kant's philosophy is noteworthy for its systematic nature. The *Critique of Pure Reason* is organized around several
fundamental distinctions. After the two Prefaces (the A edition Preface of 1781 and the B edition Preface of 1787) and the Introduction,
the text is divided into the Doctrine of Elements and the Doctrine
of Method. The first part explains the *a priori* contributions of the
mind to experience, and the legitimate and illegitimate use of these
representations. Kant further divides the Doctrine of Elements into
the Transcendental Aesthetic and the Transcendental Logic, reflecting his basic distinction between the sensibility and the intellect. In
the Transcendental Aesthetic he argues that space and time are pure
forms of intuition inherent in our sensory capacities, accounting for
the *a priori* principles of mathematics. The Transcendental Logic
is divided into the Transcendental Analytic and the Transcendental Dialectic. The former defends the legitimate uses of the *a priori*
concepts, the categories, and their correlative principles of the understanding, in attaining metaphysical knowledge. The section titled
the Metaphysical Deduction explains the origin of the categories;
in the Transcendental Deduction, Kant makes the central argument
justifying their application to experience. Following this, the Analytic of Principles contains detailed arguments for the metaphysical principles correlated with the categories. This section begins
with the Schematism, which explains how the imagination functions
in applying pure concepts to the sensible data given in intuition.
Then follow the detailed arguments for the *a priori* principles correlated with the schematized categories. The last part of the Doctrine of
Elements, the Transcendental Dialectic, explains the transcendental
illusion that motivates the misuse of these principles beyond experience. Kant's most significant arguments are the Paralogisms of Pure
Reason, the Antinomy of Pure Reason, and the Ideal of Pure Reason,
aimed against, respectively, traditional theories of the soul, the universe as a whole, and the existence of God. In the Appendix to the
Critique of Speculative Theology Kant explains the positive role of
the transcendental ideas of reason. The Doctrine of Method, which
takes up no more than a sixth of the text, contains four sections, of

which the first two are most significant. The Discipline of Pure Reason contrasts mathematical and philosophical methods of proof, and the Canon of Pure Reason outlines the relation between theoretical and practical reason, in preparation for the critical moral philosophy. Here is an outline of the text, listing the main discussions:

1. First and second Prefaces
2. Introduction
3. Doctrine of Elements
   A. Transcendental Aesthetic
   B. Transcendental Logic
      (1) Transcendental Analytic
         a. Analytic of Concepts
            i. Metaphysical Deduction
            ii. Transcendental Deduction
         b. Analytic of Principles
            i. Schematism (bridging chapter)
            ii. System of Principles of Pure Understanding
               a. Axioms of Intuition
               b. Anticipations of Perception
               c. Analogies of Experience
               d. Postulates of Empirical Thought (Refutation of Idealism)
            iii. Ground of Distinction of Objects into *Phenomena* and *Noumena*
            iv. Appendix on the Amphiboly of the Concepts of Reflection
      (2) Transcendental Dialectic: Transcendental Illusion
         a. Paralogisms of Pure Reason
         b. Antinomy of Pure Reason
         c. Ideal of Pure Reason
         d. Appendix to Critique of Speculative Theology
4. Transcendental Doctrine of Method
   A. Discipline of Pure Reason
   B. Canon of Pure Reason
   C. Architectonic of Pure Reason
   D. History of Pure Reason

4. THE SECOND (B) EDITION VERSION

The first important review of the *Critique* appeared in the January 19, 1782, edition of the *Göttingischen Anzeigen von gelehrten Sachen*. The review was originally based on a sympathetic exposition of Kant's arguments by Christian Garve (1742–98), a moral philosopher. The published version, however, rewritten by J. G. H. Feder (1740–1820), omitted most of Garve's interpretation, and emphasized three objections. First, it mistakenly assimilated Kant's idealism to Berkeley's idealism, which analyzes spatial objects as collections of sense data. Second, based on this reading, it charged that Kant's theory could not distinguish between the real and the imaginary. And finally, it attacked the distinction between theoretical and practical philosophy, on the grounds that morality is based on common sense. This misreading and Kant's own dissatisfaction with the Transcendental Deduction prompted him to publish a revision in 1787.

In his revised (or B) edition Kant separates his transcendental idealism from Berkeley's "empirical" idealism, and reworks several key arguments. The second edition Preface presents Kant's critical approach through the startling metaphor of the Copernican revolution. Kant also expands his arguments in the Introduction and the Transcendental Aesthetic. The two major changes in the Analytic are a completely revised Transcendental Deduction of the categories, and a new section, the Refutation of Idealism, added to the Analytic of Principles. Kant reworks the Transcendental Deduction to address two defects of the earlier edition: a failure to make the unity of self-consciousness the foundation of the argument, and a lack of connection to the theory of judgment. In the Refutation of Idealism Kant clarifies his idealism. Although the proof is aimed at Descartes's view that knowledge of the external world is less certain than self-knowledge, Kant elucidates the difference between his and Berkeley's idealism as well. Because of this addition, Kant also revised the Paralogisms section of the Dialectic.

In this text my main purpose is to explain Kant's arguments intelligibly to the student who has some familiarity with the history of philosophy. In keeping with the principle of charity, I attempt to give Kant's views the most plausible interpretation consistent with the texts. At the same time I indicate the main strengths and weaknesses in his views. While it is impossible to evaluate the many criticisms leveled against Kant, I point out both some clear misunderstandings and many reasonable questions raised by commentators. And since I believe it is impossible to understand a philosophy without knowing the issues engaging the philosopher, as well as the legacy, in general the discussion situates Kant's arguments in the context of his times.

CHAPTER 2

The Prefaces and the Introduction

In the first edition Preface Kant explains why a critique of human reason – the power to know – is necessary. At Avii he says it is the nature of reason to ask questions it cannot answer. Although he gives no examples, these questions are the basis of traditional metaphysical disputes Kant examines in the Transcendental Dialectic: is the universe finite or infinite in space and time? Is matter infinitely divisible or composed of simple parts? Do humans have free will or are we determined by causes outside our control? And does the existence of the universe presuppose a necessarily existent being? We can see how these questions arise in our everyday thinking. Consider the principle underlying scientific investigation: "Every event has a cause." We "naturally" ask: what caused the earthquake? What causes the earth to revolve around the sun? What caused the universe? But if these questions arise naturally, then what is the problem?

In the Dialectic, Kant describes how, in trying to explain reality, reason ends up in a dilemma: either the explanatory chain continues forever, or it must end somewhere. The temptation is to find a stopping place, to invent an "absolute" to end the series. Examples of such "absolutes" are God as the cause of the universe, and freely acting souls as the causes of human actions. The problem with such answers is that they cannot be verified by experience. Humans cannot experience the entire history of the universe, or God, or an immaterial soul as they can experience everyday events in space and time. As Kant puts it, once we have conjectured about the existence of things that are not possible objects of experience, then reason has overstepped its bounds, namely "all possible use in experience" (Aviii).

This is why the traditional metaphysical debates have never been resolved. Since the Greeks, philosophers have inquired about the ultimate nature of reality, but once they posited the existence of "absolutes," their answers could not be tested by experience. So metaphysicians could only conjecture rather than make genuine claims to knowledge. Worse, different philosophers gave opposing solutions, and thus human reason "falls into obscurity and contradictions" (Aviii). Because Kant treats these questions at length in the Transcendental Dialectic, here he only points out that the unresolved debates of metaphysics show that philosophers have been using the wrong methods. In particular, he will argue that all cognitive claims must be decidable by reference to experience. (A version of this idea gains prominence as the "verifiability principle" of meaning espoused by twentieth-century positivists.)

From Aix to Ax Kant describes the battles between dogmatists – rationalists such as Plato, Descartes, and Leibniz – and skeptics – empiricists who questioned the ability to discover the nature of reality. Kant mentions that Locke attempted a "physiology" of the understanding, but this settled nothing, since Locke wrongly assumed that the answer lies in analyzing how experience arises historically. In fact, none of Kant's predecessors identified the necessary conditions for knowledge. Until this is done, the traditional problems of metaphysics cannot be resolved.

Philosophy must start all over again by examining *reason itself* to discover what it is capable of knowing. Here as well as in the deduction of the categories, Kant uses the metaphor of judicial claims to describe his task, since he thinks of reason as having to establish its rightful claim to knowledge. As he explains at Axii, a critique *of* reason *by* reason would examine the sources, extent, and limits of our cognitive capacities. More specifically, the critique would answer these questions:

1. What can reason know independently of experience?
2. Is metaphysical knowledge possible? Are metaphysical questions meaningful and decidable?

3. What are the limits of knowledge by reason alone? In particular, Kant is concerned about whether humans can attain knowledge of things in themselves, or things as they exist independently of human perceivers.

Like many of Kant's key terms, the term "reason" (*Vernunft*) has several meanings. Kant uses "reason" in three important senses. In its broadest use, "reason" refers to all subjective processes involved in knowing. The second sense is less inclusive, and refers to intellectual as opposed to sensory capacities. The third and narrowest sense of "reason" refers to the inferential operations involved in logical justifications and explanations; in this sense reason is distinguished from the understanding as the faculty of judging. Kant attributes the errors of traditional metaphysics to reason in the narrowest sense.

At Axiii Kant makes this extravagant claim: "In this business I have made comprehensiveness my chief aim in view, and I make bold to say that there cannot be a single metaphysical problem that has not been solved here, or at least to the solution of which the key has not been provided." Now since philosophers before Kant spent several thousand years wrangling over metaphysics, the immodesty of his statement cannot fail to strike the reader. But the next sentence explains Kant's optimism. Pure reason is "such a perfect unity" that its principle supplies the solutions to all metaphysical problems. This means that the solutions to the metaphysical debates depend on what the subject contributes to knowledge. Kant will argue that human reason is governed by a single principle, that it has one and only one function. Once we understand that function, we can decide which are the rightful claims to knowledge. (In brief, reason functions to provide the *forms* of knowledge.) In any case, an accurate analysis of reason will guarantee a correct, complete system of metaphysics. Kant will conclude that some traditional metaphysical claims (e.g., "Every event has a cause") are legitimate, whereas others (e.g., "God exists") are not.

Finally, at Axvi–xvii Kant describes two sides to the deduction of the categories (*a priori* concepts), one *objective*, the other *subjective*. The aim of the former is to demonstrate the "objective validity" of the categories, that is, their applicability to objects of experience. The latter explains how *a priori* representations arise from subjective cognitive processes. Since the *Critique* first appeared, commentators have debated whether Kant's subjective analysis contains a "faculty psychology," like Hume's theory of custom and association, which would beg questions at issue in the *Critique*. As we shall see in chapter 5, although the two sides are interdependent, Kant clearly intends his account to be epistemological rather than psychological.

2. THE B EDITION PREFACE: KANT'S COPERNICAN REVOLUTION

In the 1787 Preface Kant approaches the problem of reason from a different angle. He first asks whether metaphysics can attain the certainty of science, or must continue to grope for knowledge. The model used for comparison is logic, the science of the formal rules of thought. Kant believes this system – the elaborated Aristotelian system of syllogistic inference – is complete and certain. It owes its success to the fact that it abstracts completely from the content of thought, and merely codifies the forms of valid inference. For example, the argument form *modus ponens* consists of two premises, one a conditional "If P, then Q", the other the antecedent "P" of the conditional, and the conclusion, the consequent "Q". Any argument having this form is deductively valid: if the premises were true, then the conclusion would have to be true. So, for example, the following two arguments are both valid because they have the form *modus ponens*:

1. If the Sun does not revolve around the Earth, then the Earth revolves around the Sun.
2. The Sun does not revolve around the Earth.

3. Therefore, the Earth revolves around the Sun.

and:

1'. If the universe exists, then it must have been created by an infinite spirit, God.
2'. The universe exists.

3'. Therefore, it must have been created by an infinite spirit, God.

The two arguments differ not in validity or logical correctness, but in the actual truth value of the premises. The first argument is sound, since it is valid and the premises are in fact true. Whether the second argument is sound is controversial, because the first premise is clearly debatable. In general, logic cannot decide on the soundness of an argument, since determining the truth value of claims about reality requires factual or empirical knowledge. Nevertheless, Kant thinks any discipline aspiring to be a science must aim for the completeness and certainty exemplified by logic. Now this strikes contemporary readers as ironic, since only a century later, the German philosopher Gottlob Frege inaugurated the development of modern logic by demonstrating the inadequacies of the logic in which Kant had so much confidence. Despite the limitations of his logic, Kant had a clear idea about what a formal science was supposed to do.

Although he does not complete the comparison here, Kant's point is that if metaphysical knowledge is possible, it will share some characteristics of logic but diverge in others. For Kant, any science must be based on necessary principles. If scientific principles were only contingent, one could never be certain that the theories were true. For this reason all scientific knowledge must be based on a unified system of formal rules of thought. But unlike logic, which is purely formal, metaphysics has a content because it is the science of reality. We shall see below what kinds of objects metaphysics studies.

At Bix–x Kant distinguishes theoretical from practical reason, a distinction at the foundation of his entire critical system. Kant borrows this distinction from Aristotle, although he expresses it rather differently. Essentially the difference is between representing existing states of affairs, and representing states of affairs that ought to exist. As Kant puts it, we may know objects in two ways. In the first, we apply a concept to an object that is given or exists independently of our awareness of it. In this case the object is not created in the process of knowing. When Kant says we "determine" an object and its concept, he means we predicate one of a set of mutually exclusive concepts to it. For example, in judging that a book is rectangular, I am classifying it; my representation of it is determinate with respect to its shape. We use theoretical reason when we make claims about the properties of things we take to exist independently of us. Claims of theoretical reason are "is" claims.

By contrast, practical reason concerns the thinking involved in acting, when we decide what we ought to do. In this process, we bring objective states of affairs into existence. Consider that in making a decision (say, whether to keep a promise), one first has to appeal to some rule concerning one's values or desired goals. Kant calls such rules imperatives, because they express what one ought to do. (The highest principle of morality for Kant is the categorical imperative, but we also act according to non-moral or hypothetical imperatives.) Now practical reason consists in making value judgments – accepting imperatives – and applying them in making choices in concrete situations. For example, if I decide to brush my teeth after eating breakfast, it is because I accept a principle of the form "If you want to be healthy, you should brush your teeth after meals." When we act, we change the objective situation by bringing about a new state of affairs. In this sense the "object" of the judgment does not exist prior to the judgment. For Kant, the state of affairs resulting from the action also includes the state of our own will.

Kant believes that both theoretical and practical knowledge have metaphysical parts. The metaphysics of each type of knowledge consists in the *a priori* or pure rules originating in reason alone. *The Critique of Pure Reason* is Kant's account of the metaphysical foundations of theoretical reasoning. Kant presents his metaphysics of practical reason in *The Critique of Practical Reason*, where he argues for the validity of the categorical imperative.

From Bxi to Bxiii Kant characterizes his new critical method as his "Copernican revolution": "reason has insight only into what it itself produces according to its own design" (Bxiii). Kant accepts Hume's arguments that if theoretical knowledge depended solely on experience, we could never arrive at laws of nature: "accidental observations, made according to no previously designed plan, can never connect up into a necessary law, which is yet what reason seeks and requires." Inductive generalizations take the form "All Fs observed so far are Gs" (e.g., "All crows observed so far are black") rather than "All Fs are necessarily Gs" ("All crows are necessarily black"). If necessary knowledge cannot be derived *a posteriori*, from experience, then it must be known *a priori*. As we shall see in the Introduction, one criterion of *a priori* knowledge is its necessity.

With this point established Kant makes his famous claim to do for philosophy what Copernicus did for astronomy. Kant effects his Copernican revolution by rejecting a traditional assumption about knowledge:

Up to now it has been assumed that all our cognition must conform to the objects; but all attempts to find out something about them *a priori* through concepts that would extend our cognition have, on this presupposition, come to nothing. Hence let us once try whether we do not get farther with the problems of metaphysics by assuming that the objects must conform to our cognition. (Bxvi)

All previous philosophers, rationalist and empiricist, assumed that knowledge depends entirely on the world outside the perceiver. Accordingly, our knowledge is of things as they exist independently of us. Objective truth is independent of subjective conditions of knowledge. In Kant's terminology, this standpoint identifies the objects of knowledge with things in themselves, that is, the ultimate reality behind the appearances. Now although they disagreed about the roles of reason and perception, both rationalists and empiricists assumed that knowledge consists in discovering subject-independent truths.

Kant's reason for giving up the assumption is this: if all cognition conforms to objects (depends on subject-independent truth), then one could never establish the validity of *a priori* or necessary knowledge. As mentioned earlier, Hume proved that experience at best yields contingent truths. Now rationalists typically claimed that knowers possess innate knowledge, the intellectual capacity to intuit truths about existing things. But Kant rejects these claims. The problem with innate ideas is to account directly for their application to the world. Both Descartes and Leibniz justify innate knowledge by the goodness of God, thereby presupposing that reason can arrive at truths about reality. Moreover, Kant agrees with Hume that no knowledge of matters of fact can be obtained apart from a reliance on the senses. Knowledge through pure thought either is analytic (i.e., of relations of ideas), or concerns the general form of thought itself and does not inform us about actual existence. But a strict empiricism leads to skepticism, the view that there is no objective basis for claims to know necessary truths about existing things. Kant firmly rejects such skepticism.

The solution to proving the validity of *a priori* knowledge is to perform the same shift in perspective that the Polish astronomer Nicolaus Copernicus made in his revolutionary theory. Before Copernicus, astronomers assumed that the spectator on Earth is motionless, contributing nothing to the observed motions. Accordingly, the observed motions of heavenly bodies are in fact their true motions. On his deathbed in 1543, however, Copernicus published *On the Revolution of the Heavenly Spheres,* which replaced the Ptolemaic geocentric system with the heliocentric or sun-centered system. The Earth is not motionless at the center of the universe, but rotates around the Sun along with other heavenly bodies. Thus the motions of planets and stars apparent to a spectator on Earth result from both their true motions and the motions of the spectator. Kant believes that only through a similar shift can we explain how we have *a priori* knowledge. He will argue that empirical knowledge depends jointly on what exists independently of us and on our nature as subjects. As this reasoning implies, the features of objects known to be necessary are those the subject contributes to experience. Contingent knowledge is still dependent on our actual experience of objects.

In fact, Kant believes that the history of geometry, physics, and chemistry lends support to this shift. At Bxi–xii he remarks that geometry became a science of necessary truths only when geometers stopped measuring objects to determine their properties, and instead considered what was required to construct geometrical figures in space. Similarly, experimental results in physics and chemistry achieved a firmer footing when scientists such as Galileo, Torricelli, and Stahl followed methods constrained by causal principles. In all these cases the revolutionary shift consisted in the idea that reason provides principles that govern the scientist's demonstrations or use of empirical evidence.

But this new critical perspective has some startling implications, namely that "we can never get beyond the boundaries of possible experience," and that *a priori* cognition "reaches appearances only, leaving the thing in itself as something actual for itself but unrecognized by us" (Bxix–xx). Recall that the "thing in itself" (*Ding an sich*) is whatever exists as it is independently of our cognitive access to it. Appearances, as we shall see, are these existing things *as they appear to us*. Once we no longer assume that empirical truth is independent of our subjective capacities, it follows that knowledge does not reach things in themselves. We must settle for knowledge of appearances.

The thesis that we cannot know things in themselves, called the "unknowability thesis" (UT), is the most radical aspect of Kant's transcendental idealism and is rejected by many philosophers. But it is a mistake to dismiss Kant's philosophy because of it, especially if one does not appreciate its role in his theory. First, UT is not an assumption of Kant's method, but rather a *conclusion* (I think a plausible one) from his theory of cognition. Here Kant neither assumes it nor argues for it; he merely alerts the reader that it in fact follows from his critical theory of knowledge. So anyone persuaded by Kant's analysis of human sensibility and understanding must logically accept UT. But if these arguments are not convincing, then clearly it is not necessary to accept UT (although one might hold it on other grounds). It would be an error to dismiss Kant's system because one misunderstood the status of the thesis in his philosophy.

The real danger in reacting too strongly to Kant's radical conclusion is to close oneself off from the profound and subtle arguments he makes throughout the *Critique*. It is hard to emphasize strongly enough the care with which Kant considers his predecessors' views, the painstaking nature of his arguments, and the enormously rich and powerful theory that results. Whether or not one agrees with Kant's theory, it is worthy of serious consideration. (Not to mention its enormous influence on the history of philosophy.) The truly disinterested reader must go where the arguments lead. There are many grounds for rejecting Kant's arguments; throughout this guide I will pinpoint the areas of greatest controversy. But at this point, it is important to keep an open mind about what is to come.

Now back to UT. Kant also expresses it as a denial that we can have knowledge of the unconditioned. He says: "For that which necessarily drives us to go beyond the boundaries of experience and all appearances is the **unconditioned**, which reason necessarily and with every right demands in things in themselves for everything that is conditioned, thereby demanding the series of conditions as something completed" (Bxx). In Kant's jargon, the "unconditioned" is any presupposition of a cognitive claim, which itself has no presuppositions. For example, the idea of a first or uncaused cause is one example of the "unconditioned" since it is a cause unconditioned by any prior cause. In the case of appearances and things in themselves, Kant sees the latter as the condition of the former, since (as he says at Bxxvi–xxvii) it would be absurd to think that there could be appearances without anything that appears. In other words, the existence of things in themselves is a *logical presupposition* of the fact that something appears to us.

The claim that things in themselves exist has struck many readers as unjustified and even inconsistent with other views Kant holds. Before we can form an opinion on the matter, however, we need to be clear on what this position involves. First, it means we are logically justified in making the minimal existential assumption that something exists that has its own nature. (In terms of quantificational logic, Kant is simply asserting that we have the right to take some domain as existing, and to quantify over it.) This assumption, however, implies nothing about our ability to know the nature of these things in themselves. Some commentators claim that even the minimal thesis that things in themselves exist violates UT. But this ignores the fact that knowledge consists of true predications, and to claim that things in themselves exist is to predicate nothing about their natures. When we make empirical existence claims, such as "Cats exist," we are (according to modern logic) asserting that something that exists has the properties of a cat. In fact Kant was clear that existence is not a real predicate of things (or, as we would say, a first-order predicate), and so it gives us no information about the nature of things in themselves.

In spite of this solution, Kant's various statements about things in themselves raise a host of questions. As we shall see, although we must assume that things in themselves exist, Kant will argue not only that we can know nothing about them, but also that they cannot have features essential to appearances, i.e., they cannot be spatial or temporal, or quantifiable, or substances standing in causal relations. At the same time, Kant clearly thinks of things in themselves as the basis of appearances. His view of the relation between things in themselves and appearances has stimulated a lively debate among commentators. We shall return to these issues in chapter 3, after examining the first arguments for these conclusions. In my concluding remarks following chapter 11, I also offer a general overview of the coherence of Kant's idealism.

In any case, at Bxx Kant repeats his first Preface point about the contradiction that results when we assume that we can know things in themselves. It is an indirect proof of the critical position that the contradiction vanishes if we deny the assumption. But he then remarks at Bxxi that although theoretical reason cannot know things in themselves (the "supersensible"), practical reason, which does not depend on sensory experience, can make claims going beyond experience. In particular, Kant has in mind the conflict over free will and determinism. As he says at Bxxvii–xxix, one key conclusion in the *Critique* will be that appearances are subject to causal laws. But this principle also applies to our own actions as we experience ourselves. From the standpoint of theoretical reason, we must always understand our actions as effects of antecedent states such as desires. But if we consider the human will not as it appears to us, but as a thing in itself, it is possible to think of ourselves acting freely. This is why Kant says that although one cannot cognize freedom as a property of things in the world of sense, "nevertheless, I can **think** freedom to myself, i.e., the representation of it at least contains no contradiction" (Bxxviii). This example of the debate over free will indicates one way the critical method will resolve traditional metaphysical problems.

At Bxxv–xxvi Kant states the precise views at the basis of UT. These are "that space and time are only forms of sensible intuition," and therefore apply only to appearances, and that we can apply concepts of the understanding to objects only "insofar as an intuition can be given corresponding to these concepts." He derives the thesis concerning space and time in the Transcendental Aesthetic, which analyzes human sensibility and its capacities. Kant argues for his view of concepts of the understanding in the Transcendental Analytic. Here, again, he is only anticipating the main results of his arguments to come.

Before we go on to the Introduction, it will helpful to put Kant's transcendental idealism in historical perspective, to give us a sense of both the continuity between Kant and his predecessors, and the radical nature of his idealism. In general the issue between realists and idealists concerns the *metaphysical status* of certain entities or properties. But often these metaphysical questions arise because of views about knowledge, and so the realism-idealism controversy is often linked to *epistemological* issues as well. To begin, let us start with a baseline realist position, which I shall call "naive realism." Naive realism includes any philosophy that considers things as they appear to us (however this may be) to be these things as they exist independently of knowers. This realism accepts without qualification the assumption that all knowledge conforms to objects. Such a theory assumes that we only discover characteristics of real things, that our perceptual or other cognitive processes do not distort or conceal their real properties, or contribute new features to the appearances. So, for example, a naive realist would hold that physical objects have exactly the shapes, sizes, colors, and so on that we sense in them. To the extent that Aristotle accepted this view, his position falls under naive realism.

The first step away from naive realism is scientific realism. It appears as early as ancient atomism, but the scientific realists most familiar to Kant were Descartes and Locke. They believe that some of the properties objects appear to have are in fact properties they possess independently of being perceived. Other properties of appearances are not real properties of the objects, but result merely from the perceptual process. In Cartesian dualism, for example, things in themselves are divided into two sorts of substances, minds and bodies. With respect to physical substances, Descartes argues that every particle of matter, whether it is perceived or not, really has such properties as extension in space, size, shape, and rest or motion. Locke added solidity to this list of real physical properties. Thanks to Robert Boyle, these properties became known as "primary qualities." Other perceived properties, however, such as colors, odors, sounds, and the heat and cold we sense, were analyzed as subjective effects in perceivers caused by the real properties of the particles. Although different philosophers defined the terms somewhat differently, in general these sensory qualities became known as "secondary qualities." For the scientific realist, then, the primary qualities are real properties of physical things, but the secondary qualities (as we perceive them) are only subjective or ideal. That is, if there were no perceivers with visual organs, colors as they appear would not exist. So scientific realists maintain that some features of appearances are also real features of things in themselves, but others are not. But they also hold that it is possible to get "behind" the appearances, so to speak, to discover the natures of things in themselves.

The phenomenalism of George Berkeley is idealistic in a different sense, since for Berkeley the only things that exist are minds and their ideas. Berkeley argues that the entities we call physical objects really are nothing more than collections of ideas in a mind. Thus he denies that what we take to be physical objects in space really are material, extended things existing independently of human perceivers. Berkeley does not deny that objects such as trees, rocks, tables, and chairs really exist; he only denies that they are non-mental. In his phenomenalism, what we mistakenly consider material objects are nothing more than collections of sensible ideas. Furthermore he sees no difference in the metaphysical status of primary and secondary qualities – all are merely ideas in perceivers' minds. But Berkeley agrees with realists that we can know the true nature of the minds and ideas that constitute things in themselves.

An even more radical idealism is found in Leibniz's philosophy, since Leibniz thinks both space and time are ideal. It is no accident that this version is closest to Kant's, for Kant was educated by students of the Leibnizian Christian Wolff. Although Kant rejects Leibniz's epistemology, he borrows much of his terminology. Leibniz is a rationalist who believes that sense perception is a confused or degraded form of intellection. In his metaphysics, called the monadology, the ultimately real substances are monads, indivisible "intelligible" or "noumenal" entities of which everything is composed. Leibniz argues from basic logical principles that these entities are not themselves in space and time. Rather, spatial and temporal features emerge from the perceptual process; thus Leibniz classifies space and time as ideal or "phenomenal." Despite their subjective nature, however, spatial and temporal properties correspond to real features of monads. Leibniz expresses this in the view that space and time are "well-founded phenomena." So Leibniz's idealism is more radical than Berkeley's, although he also maintains that reason can know things in themselves.

In *Space and Incongruence* I argue that Kant's idealism resulted from his rejection of Leibnizian idealism. A key step in Kant's reasoning was rejecting Leibniz's theory that sense perception is merely a confused form of intellection. Despite this difference, Kant did maintain part of Leibniz's idealism, namely the view that objects of experience are merely phenomenal manifestations of underlying, non-spatial, non-temporal entities. Kant differs from Leibniz in concluding that we cannot posit any correspondence between phenomena and the underlying noumena, or in Kant's vocabulary, between appearances and things in themselves. In any case, Kant takes Leibniz's idealism one step further, to UT. From the epistemological standpoint, Kant's idealism is the most radical, since he ends up denying that we have any knowledge of things in themselves. From the metaphysical standpoint, Kant's idealism is less radical than Berkeley's, since Kant will argue that space and material objects are no less empirically real than minds and their ideas. In short, the history of philosophy before Kant leads to ever more idealistic forms of philosophy. Transcendental idealism is the first idealism to deny that we can draw any theoretical conclusions about things in themselves. Let us now turn to Kant's first steps in arguing for this position.

3. THE INTRODUCTION: THE PROBLEM OF SYNTHETIC *A PRIORI* KNOWLEDGE

It is impossible to understand Kant's arguments that reason supplies formal features of experience unless one grasps his technical notion of synthetic *a priori* knowledge. It is no exaggeration to say that the precise motivation for Kant's Copernican revolution is his conviction that no predecessor had explicitly recognized this kind of knowledge. Although synthetic *a priori* knowledge can provide a foundation for science, it is not obvious how we come by it. Kant's new critique of reason undoubtedly arises from his recognition of the peculiar properties of such cognitions.

The main task of the Introduction is to provide a new classification scheme of judgment, and to identify the best candidates for synthetic *a priori* cognition. Kant's account rests on two distinctions, the first between *a priori* and *a posteriori* cognitions, and the second between analytic and synthetic judgments. Leibniz and Hume offer similar analyses, but each makes only one distinction. Leibniz classifies all propositions as analytic or synthetic; Hume divides all beliefs into relations of ideas (*a priori* beliefs), and matters of fact (*a posteriori* beliefs). On Kant's view both philosophers mistakenly collapse what should be two distinctions into one. This is the reason each fails to recognize the peculiar nature of synthetic *a priori* knowledge.

Kant begins by distinguishing *a priori* or pure from *a posteriori* or empirical cognition. First he agrees with the empiricists that all cognition begins with experience, because he accepts a stimulus-response model in which all cognitive processes are triggered by the reception of sensory input. "**As far as time is concerned**, then, no cognition in us precedes experience, and with experience every cognition begins" (B1). But the second paragraph maintains that although all cognition is *temporally* dependent on experience, it does not follow that it is *logically* dependent on it. It is possible that the content of cognition is not all derived from sense impressions. This would be so if the subject supplied representations in addition to the sense impressions arising from contact with objects. Here Kant explicitly offers an alternative to Hume's theory that all simple ideas are only copies of antecedent simple impressions.

The question to be investigated in the *Critique* is whether any cognition is logically "independent of all experience and even of all impressions of the senses" (B2). Kant calls such cognition *a priori*, in contrast to empirical or *a posteriori* cognition, which is dependent for its source and content on experience. In the last two paragraphs he distinguishes two senses of "*a priori*," one relative and the other absolute. He points out that sometimes we classify cognition as *a priori* relative to some general principle: we say someone should know that undermining the foundations of his house would cause it to fall *before* he actually did it. But this is not absolutely *a priori* knowledge, because experience is required to know that bodies are heavy. The *a priori* knowledge Kant is concerned with is absolutely prior to all experience, not just prior to some particular experiences. In the last two sentences of this section, he also specifies that by "pure" *a priori* cognition he means cognition having "no admixture of anything empirical." The proposition "Every alteration has its cause" does not qualify as pure in this sense, because Kant thinks the concept of an alteration can be derived only from experience of events in time. Now in general we, like Kant, will ignore this caveat in the rest of the text. In *The Metaphysical Foundations of Natural Science*, Kant clarifies his view of the *a priori* status of the laws of physics. For our purpose we can safely equate pure with *a priori* knowledge.

Section II of the Introduction explains that the criteria of *a priori* judgments are *necessity* and *strict universality*. Unlike a judgment based on experience, which is only contingent, an *a priori* judgment is "thought along with its **necessity**" (B3). Moreover, such judgments are also recognized to have a "strict" rather than "merely comparative" universality. As we saw earlier, Kant accepts Hume's argument that inductive generalizations from experience are only contingent. And because they are based only on observed instances, they are restricted in scope. But science presupposes necessary judgments, which do not allow for exceptions. For example, the principle of causality – "Every event has a cause" – is assumed to be necessarily true of all events in time. Obviously it cannot be based on observed instances. In the last paragraph, from B5 to B6, Kant points out that the term "*a priori*" applies not only to judgments, but also to non-propositional representations such as concepts. In fact he will argue that synthetic *a priori* judgments rest on *a priori* intuitions and on *a priori* concepts. Although many philosophers reject Kant's view that there are *a priori* intuitions and concepts, the distinction between necessary and contingent judgments is generally accepted. Which judgments are necessary, and whether there are synthetic *a priori* judgments are, however, controversial issues.

Kant's second major distinction is between analytic and synthetic judgments. Unlike the distinction between *a priori* and *a posteriori* representations, which concerns the origin of cognition, this distinction is *logical* and concerns the content of judgment. It does, however, have epistemological consequences. Kant's first characterization is based on the idea of conceptual containment. Regarding affirmative subject-predicate judgments, Kant says those in which the predicate is (covertly) contained in the subject are analytic; those in which the predicate is not contained in the subject are synthetic. His examples are "All bodies are extended" and "All bodies are heavy." Kant thinks the concept "body" includes the concept "extended" but not the concept "weight." Analytic judgments are merely clarifying since, if one already understands the concepts, the judgment adds no new knowledge. Synthetic judgments, however, are ampliative, since the predicate concept adds something that is not part of its content to the subject concept.

From the notion of concept containment, Kant moves to the more general idea that analytic judgments are those whose truth value can be determined by means of the law of non-contradiction, the logical principle that a judgment P and its negation not-P cannot both be true simultaneously. At A7/B10, he points out that if the predicate is contained in the subject, then the predicate would be identical with at least part of the subject. And in these cases, one already has in the subject all the information one needs to make the judgment "in accordance with the principle of contradiction" (B12). In synthetic judgments, there is no identity between the subject and predicate, and so the principle of non-contradiction is not sufficient for determining their truth values.

Now there are several remarks to make here. First, although Kant's intentions are clear, his account is not general enough. (This is in fact a problem in Hume's discussion as well.) First, Kant makes the original distinction in terms of subject-predicate judgments. But he also recognizes more complex forms of judgments such as conditionals ("If . . . then . . .") and disjunctions ("Either . . . or . . ."). And it is not clear how "concept containment" would work for these complex forms. Second, Kant admits that he is only considering affirmative subject-predicate judgments, although he claims it is easy to apply his distinction to negative judgments. In other words, it seems we would want to label the judgment "No bachelor is married" analytic rather than synthetic, although the concept of being married is clearly not contained in the concept of bachelor. A third problem concerns the relation between analyticity and truth. Again, it looks as if the concept containment criterion works only for analytically *true* (affirmative) judgments in which the predicate is in fact contained in the subject. But the analytic-synthetic distinction should apply to both true and false judgments. Since the logical character of the judgment is at stake here, we should consider judgments in pairs, so that any judgment P and its negation not-P would fall under the same classification. That is, because the truth of "All bachelors are unmarried" entails the falsity of "Some bachelor is married," we should recognize both analytic truths and analytic falsehoods. In both cases the truth value of the judgment can be determined by the principles of logic and the meanings of the terms alone. Fortunately, there is a way to generalize Kant's distinction to incorporate all judgments, simple and complex, affirmative and negative, true and false.

Following Kant's reference to the principle of non-contradiction, we can reformulate the distinction this way: a judgment and its negation are both analytic if and only if one of the pair is self-contradictory, or false by virtue of the definitions of words or its logical form. (This is actually close to one of Hume's criteria for relations of ideas.) Thus the judgments "All bachelors are unmarried" and "Some bachelor is married" would be analytic: the first is true and the second is false (actually self-contradictory) by the definition of "bachelor." By contrast, Hume's famous examples "The sun will rise tomorrow" and "The sun will not rise tomorrow" are synthetic, since neither judgment is self-contradictory. Mere definitions of terms or logical form are not sufficient to determine the truth values of synthetic judgments. In this particular case, actual experience is required to know which of the pair will be true.

This reformulated criterion can also be applied to complex judgments. In some cases complex judgments will be analytic by virtue of their logical form, or the meanings of logical operators, regardless of the content of their constituent judgments. For example, the judgment "Either the sun will rise tomorrow or the sun will not rise tomorrow" will be a true analytic judgment since it has the form "Either P or not-P" which is logically true in classical systems of logic. And by the same token the conjunction "The sun will rise tomorrow and the sun will not rise tomorrow" will be a false analytic judgment because judgments of the form "P and not-P" are self-contradictory or logically false. In other cases, complex judgments would be analytic by virtue of the meanings of non-logical terms: "If something is red, then it is colored" would be a true analytic judgment, and "If something is round all over, then it is square all over" would be a false analytic judgment. Finally, this way of making the distinction would make all existence claims about logically possible objects synthetic, which is in fact Kant's view. This characterization, then, fits consistently with both his examples and his arguments for synthetic *a priori* judgments. Based on textual grounds as well as the principle of charity, we shall treat the analytic-synthetic distinction as reformulated here.

In principle, with two sets of distinctions, it looks as if there could be four kinds of judgments: analytic *a priori*, analytic *a posteriori*, synthetic *a priori*, and synthetic *a posteriori*. In fact, however, only three kinds of judgments are possible. At A7/B11–12 Kant discusses the possible combinations and explains the problematic character of synthetic *a priori* judgments. First he notes that there are no analytic *a posteriori* judgments. All judgments of experience or *a posteriori* judgments are synthetic, "For it would be absurd to ground an analytic judgment on experience" since determining their truth value requires appealing only to logical form or meanings of terms. Just as it is obvious how we come by analytic *a priori* judgments, it is obvious that synthetic *a posteriori* judgments such as "Some swans are white" are based on experience, both for their content and their truth value. The problematic case is synthetic *a priori* judgments, since neither meanings of terms nor experience can account for their features. Because they are synthetic, their truth value cannot be based logically on their content; nor can it be derived from experience, since they are *a priori* and hence thought with necessity. In the judgment "Every event has a cause," there is no logical connection between the concepts of an event in time and being caused: an uncaused event is conceivable. But experience cannot ground this judgment either, since it cannot confer necessity and universality on the principle. As Kant poses the problem at A9/B13, "What is the unknown = X here on which the understanding depends when it believes itself to discover beyond the concept of A a predicate that is foreign to it yet which it nevertheless believes to be connected with it?" In short, how can there be ampliative or informative judgments that are nevertheless necessarily true? This is the technical problem driving the critical philosophy.

Another approach to the problem of synthetic *a priori* judgments concerns their necessity. This point is important because it is the subject of some misunderstanding among commentators. Recall that for Kant all *a priori* judgments are necessary. Now this is easily understood with analytic judgments, since their necessity is clearly logical or conceptual. But the necessity characteristic of synthetic *a priori* judgments cannot be logical necessity. Kant admits that an uncaused event is logically possible, and yet we think it necessary that every event has a cause. So an alternative description of Kant's project is to account for this peculiar kind of non-logical necessity. As we examine his arguments we will begin to appreciate what kind of necessity this is. For now let us call it an "epistemic" necessity.

In section V Kant takes a preliminary stab at convincing the reader that mathematics, natural science, and metaphysics in fact contain synthetic *a priori* judgments. Although mathematical inferences may rely on logical principles, the fundamental propositions of arithmetic and geometry are synthetic *a priori*. First he claims that arithmetic formulae such as "$7 + 5 = 12$" are not analytic, despite their necessity, because the mere concept of $7 + 5$ does not determine the distinct individual that results from the act of addition: "no matter how long I analyze my concept of such a possible sum I will still not find twelve in it" (B15). Similarly, he argues that postulates of geometry are synthetic: "That the straight line between two points is the shortest is a synthetic proposition. For my concept of **the straight** contains nothing of quantity, but only a quality" (B16). Kant thinks the arithmetical sum and the geometrical lines both have to be constructed with the aid of sensible intuition, which adds a non-conceptual content to our cognition. Now these controversial claims are based on Kant's complex theory of mathematics, which he details only in the Discipline of Pure Reason in the Doctrine of Method. In both the Aesthetic and the Analytic, he sketches the process of construction required for mathematical knowledge. In general, the informative character of all synthetic judgments depends on the role of intuition.

Kant also claims from B17–18 that physics and metaphysics contain synthetic *a priori* judgments. The examples from physics are conservation principles: in all physical interactions the quantity of matter remains constant, and action and reaction are always equal in communication of motion among particles. Kant believes these principles are actually physical versions of the metaphysical principles "In all change of appearances substance persists, and its quantum is neither increased nor diminished in nature" and "All alterations occur in accordance with the law of the connection of cause and effect." Kant argues for these latter principles in the section titled the Analogies of Experience, in the Transcendental Analytic.

In the closing sections VI and VII Kant returns to Hume, whose arguments he obviously takes seriously. He notes here, as elsewhere, that Hume saw the problem of how we could make informative judgments that we believed to be necessarily true, but did not arrive at the correct solution to the problem. Hume concluded that our belief in necessary connections of existing things arises from a psychological association based on repeated experiences. For Kant, this is tantamount to explaining an objective necessity in terms of a psychologically subjective necessity. Thus Hume regarded metaphysical knowledge as a "mere delusion" (B20). In fact, in the last paragraph of the *Enquiry Concerning Human Understanding*, Hume writes:

If we take in our hand any volume; of divinity or school metaphysics, for instance; let us ask, Does it contain any abstract reasoning concerning quantity or number? No. Does it contain any experimental reasoning concerning matter of fact and existence? No. Commit it then to the flames: For it can contain nothing but sophistry and illusion.

Kant remarks in his preface to the *Prolegomena* of 1783, that Hume "threw no light on this kind of knowledge; but he certainly struck a spark from which light might have been obtained, had it caught some inflammable substance and had its smouldering fire been carefully nursed and developed." So although Hume showed that metaphysical knowledge could not be justified by rational insight into the nature of things, his account of metaphysical beliefs went seriously astray.

Finally, in section VII, Kant describes the critical theory as "transcendental" philosophy. The term "transcendental" is a key term, which has several uses depending on the context. Here Kant says, "I call all cognition transcendental that is occupied not so much with objects but rather with our mode of cognition of objects in so far as this is to be possible *a priori*" (A11/B25). He means that the *Critique* contains a theory about the necessary conditions for knowing objects rather than adding to our knowledge of them. If knowledge of objects is empirical (or first-order) knowledge, then the critical philosophy is a (second-order) theory about such knowledge. In general Kant uses the term "transcendental" to characterize the necessary conditions of cognition. It is important not to confuse this with the term "transcendent," which usually means going beyond experience. For theoretical reason, the idea of God is a transcendent idea.

4. THE ANALYTIC-SYNTHETIC CONTROVERSY

Kant's views about synthetic *a priori* knowledge raise questions that are still debated by philosophers. Two contested aspects of his theory concern the analytic-synthetic distinction and his theory of mathematics. Here I shall briefly discuss the first issue, treating the second question in chapter 3. Following Kant, the analytic-synthetic distinction became a staple of contemporary philosophy, largely accepted (with some redefinition) by Frege and the logical positivists. But in 1950 Morton G. White published "The Analytic and the Synthetic: An Untenable Dualism," which rejected the notion of analytic statements. Two years later Willard Van Orman Quine took up the attack in his classic paper, "Two Dogmas of Empiricism." After arguing that the defining process cannot give us an account of analyticity, Quine rejects the view that one can separate linguistic from factual components of the meaning of a statement. Because knowledge is a "web of belief," underdetermined by experience, there are no statements immune to revision in the future, including the laws of logic. Not all philosophers were persuaded by these attacks. In 1956 H. P. Grice and P. F. Strawson published "In Defense of a Dogma," in which they offer an alternative definition of synonymy to save the analytic-synthetic distinction. Similarly, in "The Significance of Quine's Indeterminacy Thesis," Michael Dummett points out that in "Two Dogmas," Quine himself defines an analytic statement as one such that no recalcitrant experience would lead us to regard it as not true. Moreover, in his later work *Word and Object*, Quine explicitly allows for stimulus-analytic sentences. Thus there are good reasons to reject Quine's argument in "Two Dogmas."

5. SUMMARY

In the Prefaces and the Introduction Kant lays the foundation for his critical theory. The Prefaces introduce the problem of metaphysics through the idea that reason naturally poses questions about reality that are not easily answered. Since ancient Greece, philosophers have debated whether *a priori* knowledge is possible, as well as what it consists in. The second edition Preface explains the problem in terms of the Copernican revolution: *a priori* knowledge is possible only if the subject contributes features to experience, so that what appears depends on the subject's cognitive capacities. This requires giving up the traditional assumption that knowledge conforms to things as they exist independent of the subject. And this, in turn, leads to Kant's transcendental idealism, the view that knowledge is only of appearances, and that things in themselves cannot be known. The Introduction presents the technical analysis at the basis of the critical philosophy. This requires two fundamental distinctions, between *a priori* and *a posteriori* representations, and between analytic and synthetic judgments. Of the three possible types of judgment, the problematic case is synthetic *a priori* judgments, since they are both informative and necessary. Kant argues that this is the proper classification of metaphysics and mathematics. The task for the *Critique* is to show that there is such knowledge, and to justify its application to experience.

CHAPTER 3

The Transcendental Aesthetic

Kant will argue in the Transcendental Aesthetic that human subjects have two pure forms of intuition, space and time, which are the source of synthetic *a priori* knowledge of mathematics and mechanics. Because these forms are part of the subject's sensibility, he will further conclude that space and time are transcendentally ideal, although they are also empirically real. Thus in the Transcendental Aesthetic Kant takes an important step in establishing the unknowability of things in themselves. These conclusions are based on profound arguments concerning the nature of space and time cognition. Although Kant does not identify his targets, thinkers such as Descartes, Locke, Berkeley, Newton, and Leibniz held opposing theories of both the ontological status of space and time, and our knowledge of them.

I. THE SENSIBILITY AND THE INTELLECT

Kant says at A22/B36 that the Transcendental Aesthetic will examine the sensibility, to determine whether it contributes *a priori* knowledge to experience. To accomplish this task, he must isolate the sensibility from the intellect, and then, within sensibility, separate *a posteriori* from *a priori* elements. Unfortunately this leaves the impression that Kant's arguments are based on premises concerning the *a priori* data of sensibility. But his theory of judgment prevents him from proceeding in this manner. In the Transcendental Analytic Kant will argue that all conscious representations, including sense perceptions, must have both sensible and intellectual aspects. (He obscures this point in the Aesthetic by speaking as though the sensibility alone could produce intuitions of objects.) But if all conscious representations incorporate concepts, humans cannot have access to the raw data received

The main question raised by the term "sensation" is whether it refers to a mental state or a state of the perceiver's body. There are texts supporting both readings. In some passages Kant appears, like Descartes, to take sensations as mental states representing qualities, such as colors, sounds, and hot and cold. On the traditional causal theory of perception, to which Kant evidently adheres, experiences of these qualities are caused by contact between a physical object and the perceiver's physical sense organs. The physiological processes this contact triggers in the nervous system result in a state of consciousness of some sensible quality. The question is whether Kant thinks of sensations as the physical changes in the perceiver's body or as the resulting mental states. At B44 he refers to "the sensations of colors, sounds, and warmth, which, however, since they are merely sensations and not intuitions, do not in themselves allow any object to be cognized." Here he appears to use "sensation" for the conscious experience. Other references to sensation could also be taken in this way. But there are strong reasons to think sensations are states of the body. Falkenstein makes a persuasive case for this reading, pointing out that Kant describes sensations as "ordered and placed" in space and time (A20/B34).[3] If sensations are ordered spatially, then they must have spatial location and characteristics, so they must be physical states. Since Kant holds that secondary qualities as we perceive them are not real physical properties of bodies, this is a good reason to think sensations are physical states of the perceiver rather than the qualities we consciously experience.[4] In any case, since the causal theory postulates a correspondence between the physical state of the perceiver and the experienced quality, our decision here will not affect our reading of Kant's arguments in the Aesthetic.

Finally we need to return to Kant's definition of "appearance" as whatever is given in sensible intuition. This could apply to conscious representation of the object, or to the intuited object itself. Kant uses it both ways in the *Critique*. The main use of "appearance" is in

[3] See Falkenstein, *Kant's Intuitionism*, chapter 3, 103–34, for a detailed argument for this interpretation.
[4] At A172/B214 Kant says, "every sense must have a determinate degree of receptivity for the sensations." Moreover, at A21/B35 he describes impenetrability, hardness, and color as "that which belongs to sensation" rather than sensations themselves.

contrast to "thing in itself," which clearly is an extra-mental thing. Because the ultimate thrust of the critical philosophy is to argue that knowledge is only of appearances and not things in themselves, it seems clear that appearances are fundamentally mental. At the same time, Kant will argue that appearances in general are not illusions, that they have objective features. So generally "appearance" means the empirical object we experience through the sensible data of intuition.

The last two sets of terms are less problematic. Kant's distinction between the matter and form of intuition is functional: the matter consists in the (intuited) elements, the form in the system for ordering and relating them. In the Aesthetic, Kant argues that space and time are merely the forms, systems of relations, lying "in the mind *a priori*" (A20/B34), in which we receive sensations, the data given through our contact with objects. In the Analytic, Kant will argue that humans also possess certain *a priori* forms of thought or conceptual schemes for ordering and relating the appearances given in sensibility. In general, a form of experience, whether supplied by the sensibility or the intellect, is a system for ordering and relating some content, which functions as the matter relative to that form.

Finally Kant distinguishes between inner and outer sense. As described at A22–3/B37, outer sense is our means of intuiting external objects, and inner sense is our means of intuiting our own mental states. Now in the definition, the phrase "objects as outside us" is ambiguous. It could mean either spatially external to or numerically distinct from the knowing subject. I take the latter meaning as primary: since inner sense is our means of intuiting our own mental states, outer sense must be our means of intuiting anything distinct from our own mental states. Moreover, if "outer" meant spatially external, then Kant's conclusion that space is the form of outer sense would be tautological. As for inner sense, Kant says by its means "the mind intuits itself, or its inner state," although it does not produce an intuition "of the soul itself, as an object." The function of inner sense is to provide a direct awareness of our own mental states, which is all we can intuit of the self as knowing subject. Inner sense is a kind of reflective awareness. Kant's theory that space is the form of outer sense and time is the form of inner sense means first, that everything that we intuit as distinct from our own mental states must be located in space; second, all mental states occur in time. Kant adds that "Time can no more be intuited externally than space can be intuited as something in us" (A23/B37). His point is that all representations are inherently temporal. Similarly, space is not "in us" as a formal feature of representing, as time is.

In this discussion Kant treats outer and inner sense as parallel and independent modes of awareness. This is misleading, however, since there are important differences between them. For one thing, Kant views time as more universal than space, since time is a condition for representing things outside the mind as well as our own mental states. Space, by contrast, is only the form of outer intuition (A34/B50). Another essential difference surfaces later in the section called the Refutation of Idealism, added in the B edition. Here, at B274–9, Kant argues that inner sense presupposes outer sense. Most commentators agree that Kant should have treated space and time together because of their interrelations. To understand the theory of the Aesthetic, however, we can consider outer and inner sense as parallel.

Before examining the arguments, let us review the definitions discussed so far:

An *intuition* is the kind of representation in which the knower immediately apprehends a "given" or existing state of affairs. More precisely, through intuition we are given a manifold (multiplicity) of sensible data for representing whatever exists.

Sensibility is our human capacity to intuit objects. Human sensibility has two modes: an *outer sense* consisting of our physical sense organs for intuiting things distinct from the mind, and a reflective *inner sense* for intuiting our own mental states. In both forms sensibility is passive or receptive rather than active.

The empirical data of intuition are originally given through *sensations*, which are modifications of the sense organs. These physical states result in representations of sensible qualities such as color, taste, and hot and cold. Both the sensations and their corresponding qualities are subjective effects in perceivers, since they depend on the perceiver and the conditions of perception as well as on objects. These empirical elements constitute the *matter* of experience: sensations are the *matter of intuition*; consciously represented qualities are the *matter of appearance*.

Finally, all intuitive representations of which we are conscious are *appearances*. The appearance is whatever is given to us through sensibility. Sometimes by "appearance" Kant just means the consciously represented intuitive data, both empirical and pure, and sometimes he means the object so represented.

2. THE PURE FORMS OF INTUITION AND SYNTHETIC *A PRIORI* KNOWLEDGE

At A21/B35 Kant says transcendental aesthetic is "a science of all principles of *a priori* sensibility." In this section he will argue that human sensibility contains two pure forms of intuition, space and time, which are the basis of the synthetic *a priori* cognitions expressed in mathematics and physics. Because these forms are contributed by the subject, Kant will argue that they can account for the necessity and universality characteristic of these sciences.

Before presenting his arguments, Kant sketches three possible theories of space and time. He first says space and time could be "actual entities." This refers to the absolute theory of space and time as propounded by Isaac Newton and followers such as Samuel Clarke, who defended it in the *Leibniz–Clarke Correspondence.*[5] The absolutists thought of space and time as real (although non-material) containers of all spatial and temporal objects. Because these "containers" are necessary conditions of the existence of spatiotemporal objects, they exist independently of the things occupying them. In this sense space and time are both *real* and *objective*. Moreover, they are *prior* to the objects they contain in two senses: first, objects must exist in space and time, although space and time could exist without them (God could have created empty space and time); and second, the spatial and temporal relations among objects are derived from the spatiotemporal positions these objects occupy. Absolute space and time are also *real* as opposed to *ideal*, since their existence does not depend on the experience of perceivers. Even if perceivers never existed, and even if material objects never existed, absolute space and time could exist.

---

[5] The classical texts are Newton's *Mathematical Principles of Natural Philosophy*, 1:6–10; and Leibniz, *The Leibniz–Clarke Correspondence*. I discuss these theories in *Space and Incongruence*, chapters 2 and 3.

As a second possibility, space and time could be "only determinations or relations of things, yet ones that would pertain to them even if they were not intuited." This refers to the major competitor to the absolute theory, the relational theory of space and time. It was championed by both rationalists and empiricists, including Leibniz and Berkeley.[6] In general, relationists believe that space and time are merely systems of relations whose existence depends on the prior existence of both perceivers and the objects or elements so related. Despite their epistemological differences, Leibniz and Berkeley both criticize the absolute theory as incoherent, since it entertains the existence of real entities that are not themselves substances. For relationists, spatial and temporal relations among things are constructed from the (non-spatiotemporal) properties and relations of metaphysical substances. Although Leibniz's monadic substances are not themselves spatiotemporal, our experience of space and time corresponds to their real properties. This is why Kant says relational space and time would belong to things "even if they were not intuited." The relationists held space and time to be *ideal* and *subjective*, since they are "constructed" through mental processes involved in representing existing things. Here the priority relations are reversed: empty space and time could not exist, since where there are no substances there could be no system of relations derived from them. And although spatiotemporal relations correspond to properties of monadic substances, their peculiar spatial and temporal character depends on the perceptual process.

The final possibility is Kant's own theory, that space and time are pure forms of human intuition. This theory denies both that they are absolute or real as things in themselves, and that they are derived from a prior experience of non-spatiotemporal things. Although Kant rejects both the absolute and relational theories, his position incorporates some features of each. He will agree with the Newtonians that space and time are logically independent of the objects they contain, but he will deny that they are completely independent of human perceivers. Kant will accept Leibniz's view that things in themselves are

---

[6] In addition to the *Leibniz–Clarke Correspondence*, Leibniz's position is spelled out in "First Truths," and the letter to Bayle of 1702, both in *Philosophical Papers and Letters*, 268–71 and 583. Berkeley's views appear in *De Motu* in *The Works of George Berkeley Bishop of Cloyne*, 4:1–52; and *A Treatise Concerning the Principles of Human Knowledge*, part I, articles 110–17.

not spatiotemporal, but he will reject the idea that space and time are constructed from relations or properties of experienced substances. We shall see how he argues for these views in the metaphysical exposition of space and time.

Kant's strategy in the Aesthetic is complex but methodical. First he divides the arguments or "expositions" into two kinds. The metaphysical exposition exhibits the concept *"as given a priori"* (A23/B38). Here Kant presents four arguments to establish that space and time are *a priori* forms of sensible intuition, without presupposing that we have synthetic *a priori* knowledge. The transcendental exposition, which was separated out in the B edition, begins with the premise that we have synthetic *a priori* knowledge, and argues that space and time must be pure forms of intuition to account for that knowledge.[7] On this reading, the two expositions draw the same conclusion, but differ in their starting points. The advantage of this strategy is to appeal to readers whatever their position on synthetic *a priori* knowledge.

Following his treatment of outer and inner sense, Kant separates the expositions of space and time. Although he intends the arguments to be parallel, his presentation is sloppy and the arguments are not properly arranged. First, whereas there are four arguments in the metaphysical exposition for space, there are five for time. This is because Kant mislocates the transcendental exposition in the third paragraph of the metaphysical exposition. In addition, although Kant is defending the same conclusions for space and time, we shall see that the proofs occasionally differ. For the most part, however, the thrust of the arguments is the same, so we shall generally treat them together.

The final preliminary remark concerns the fact that Kant subtitles these sections expositions of the *concepts* of space and time. Since he is arguing that space and time are pure forms of intuition, and since intuitions and concepts are distinct kinds of representations, this heading is cause for confusion. The explanation, however, involves Kant's blindness thesis, according to which we are not conscious of the intuitive data prior to any intellectual processing. Thus Kant

[7] In "Kant's 'Argument from Geometry'," Lisa Shabel argues, by contrast, that the transcendental exposition assumes the conclusion of the metaphysical exposition, and then shows how this analysis explains the synthetic *a priori* nature of geometry.

cannot begin with premises describing this data. Instead, he must analyze our conscious experiences of space and time, and then argue that these experiences could have the features they do if and only if space and time are forms of intuition. So the most straightforward solution is to take the term "concept" here to refer to a representation that has been intellectually processed, which includes perceptions of spatiotemporal objects. In the expositions, as we shall see, Kant returns to the standard use of "concept" for a general representation, as opposed to an intuition.

A. The metaphysical exposition

The metaphysical exposition argues that our original representations of space and time are *a priori* intuitions. The first two proofs conclude that these representations are known *a priori*, supplying necessary features of experience. The last two conclude that they originate in intuition as part of the manifold given in sensibility. Putting these two conclusions together yields the result that our original representations of space and time are *a priori* or pure forms of sensible intuition.

1. The first exposition: space and time are logically independent of the empirical data given in intuition

Here Kant argues that space and time are *a priori* in the weak sense that they are not derived from the empirical data given in experience. The premises refer to this empirical data as sensations, and, as we saw earlier, sensations are physical states of the perceiver. But because the sensible qualities we consciously represent correspond to these physical states, I shall refer to both sensations and sense qualities as the empirical data given in intuition. The main point here is that cognitions of space and time are not constructed from the empirical data, and hence are not known *a posteriori*. As Falkenstein explains, this argument is aimed against philosophers who held *sensationist, constructivist* theories of space and time cognition. This group would include relationists such as Leibniz and Berkeley, as well as Locke for his theory of time. Kant believes the empirical sensible data are *received* in spatiotemporal arrays. Here is the argument for space:

For in order for certain sensations to be related to something outside me (i.e., to something in another place in space from that in which I find myself), thus in order for me to represent them as outside one another, thus not merely as different but as in different places, the representation of space must already be their ground. (A23/B38)

This is the argument for time:

For simultaneity or succession would not themselves come into perception if the representation of time did not ground them *a priori*. Only under its presupposition can one represent that several things exist at one and the same time (simultaneously) or in different times (successively). (A30/B46)

The point is that any constructivist theory of space and time would actually have to presuppose spatial and temporal systems of relations. Now why does Kant think this?

One interpretation takes Kant's premises to be based on introspection: it just is apparent that the sensible data, whether pre-conscious sensations or qualities experienced consciously, are given in space and time. The color patches we see, for example, are spatially extended and related to each other. Correspondingly, the physical sensations causing these representations are located in our sense organs, and are brought about by contact with objects located in space. The same can be said for their temporal locations and relations. So it is an obvious fact that the intuitive data are given in space and time. While this version is plausible, it may not completely capture Kant's point. First, it does not explain why Kant thinks any constructivist account *must* presuppose space and time. One might object that for all we know, the pre-conscious data may not be ordered in space and time. In this case the spatial and temporal frameworks we consciously experience might arise through some constructive processes, as relationists maintain. To eliminate this possibility a stronger argument is needed, that a constructivist account is not a possible account of our experience.

Kant's premises suggest such an argument, in effect a dilemma for the constructivist, who thinks space and time are created from the relations of the sensible data given empirically. Now either these relations are themselves spatiotemporal or they are not. If they are spatiotemporal, then they presuppose the spatial-temporal frameworks encompassing such positions. So the constructivist cannot embrace the first horn of the dilemma without begging the question. On the other hand, if the relations among the sensible data are not spatial and temporal, then the constructivist must explain how spatial and temporal positions arise from these non-spatiotemporal features. This horn of the dilemma has two aspects to it, one general and one specific. The general problem is the one just stated, how one derives any spatiotemporal features out of non-spatiotemporal features. The specific problem is one Falkenstein calls the "localization" problem: if the sensible elements are not given in spatial and temporal arrays, then what could possibly determine the particular order or configurations in which they are experienced? Any answer to this question could only be pure speculation. More important, it is hard to see how the qualitative features of color patches could determine anything about the order in which they are experienced. The spatiotemporal positions and relations of the sensible data appear completely independent of the content of that data.

The problem for the second horn relates to another point implicit in the argument. Consider that for any theory that maintains that global space and time are constructed from relations among sensible elements, the elements must first be discriminated as numerically distinct. This requires identifying the individual relata independently of their spatiotemporal positions. Now the exposition for space implies that spatiotemporal position is both necessary and sufficient for discriminating distinct sensible elements. Kant says we represent the sensations "as outside and next to one another, thus not merely as different but as in different places" (A23/B39). Consider, for example, how we identify two qualitatively identical color patches as numerically distinct. It can only be because of their different spatiotemporal locations.

The first exposition argues that the original spatiotemporal manifolds are independent of the empirical data given in them, although they are given *with* that data. In other words, the sensible manifold has two aspects: the empirical data given *a posteriori*, and the spatiotemporal systems in which they are located. The logical independence of these systems establishes their *a priori* status in the weak sense that their content is not derived from the empirical data.

2. The second exposition: space and time are necessary conditions of experience

Here Kant argues that space and time are *a priori* in the strong sense that they are necessary features of experience. His strategy is to show that while it is possible for us to think of both space and time as empty of objects, we cannot represent the absence of space and time altogether. Here is the argument for space:

> One can never represent that there is no space, though one can very well think that there are no objects to be encountered in it. It is therefore to be regarded as the condition of the possibility of appearances, not as a determination dependent on them, and is an *a priori* representation that necessarily grounds outer appearances. (A24/B38–9)

The argument for time is virtually identical:

> In regard to appearances in general, one cannot remove time, though one can very well take the appearances away from time. Time is therefore given *a priori*. In it alone is all actuality of appearances possible. The latter could all disappear, but time itself (as the universal condition of their possibility) cannot be removed. (A31/B46)

The arguments differ only in the scope of their conclusions. Whereas space is the condition of outer intuition and the possibility of appearances, time is the condition of the actuality of all appearances. This refers to the different domains of outer and inner sense: by outer sense we represent things other than our representations; inner sense applies to all representations. When Kant says time is a condition of the "actuality" of appearance, he means that all appearances must exist in time. Otherwise the point is the same: space and time are both necessary features of appearances.

The problem here is how to interpret Kant's premises. The argument maintains that although one can *think* space and time as empty, one cannot *represent* the absence of space, or, as Kant says, "remove" time. The first part is fairly clear, since "think" means conceive of an empty space or time. As Falkenstein points out, this amounts to the claim that it is possible to conceive that some experience might be of a void space or time.[8] The problem is the sense in which one

---

[8] Kant does not believe, however, that any experience could prove that space and time are empty (A172/B214). Falkenstein discusses Kant's position on empty space and time in *Kant's Intuitionism*, 203–16.

cannot represent the absence of space or time. The solution, I think, depends on Kant's intention to show that space and time are conditions of appearances, and appearances are what is given in intuition. His point is that we cannot conceive ourselves intuiting things that are not located in space or time.

If this is correct, then the argument establishes that the original representations of space and time are *a priori* in the strong sense that they are necessary conditions of appearance. In other words, everything given in intuition must be located in space and time. Although Kant does not explain here what kind of necessity is involved, following the expositions he argues that space and time are necessary as epistemic conditions or conditions of human experience. Kant is not claiming that it is logically necessary that humans perceive things spatiotemporally. Neither is he claiming that space and time have an absolute metaphysical necessity. Rather, space and time are necessary relative to human intuition. We shall return to this point below.

The conclusion of the first two metaphysical expositions, that space and time are *a priori* representations, incorporates three theses:

1. The content of our spatial and temporal representations is logically independent of (not derivable from) the empirical data given in intuition (the first exposition);
2. Space and time are presupposed in the intuitions of objects (the second exposition);
3. We can conceive of space and time as empty, but we cannot conceive of anything appearing to us without space and time (the second exposition).

These arguments establish the first half of Kant's thesis – that the original representations of space and time are *a priori*. He next must show that they originate in the intuitive data rather than in concepts of the understanding.

3. The third exposition: space and time are intuitions because they are particular representations

In this argument (the fourth for time), Kant wants to prove that space and time are not discursive concepts of the understanding, but are supplied in the intuitive data given in sensibility. Here he clearly uses the term "concept" for a general representation of the understanding.

Kant offers three reasons to conclude that space and time originate in intuition. First, we can represent only one space/time; different spaces/times are parts of one unique space/time. Second, in contrast to the part–whole relation for concepts, the wholes of space/time are prior to their parts; the parts arise only by drawing boundaries in the whole. Finally, at A25/B39 and A32/B47, Kant mentions a point that belongs in the transcendental exposition, namely that synthetic *a priori* judgments concerning space and time are possible only if they are intuitions. Here I shall discuss the first two arguments and reserve the third for the discussion of the transcendental exposition.

(a) *Space and time are unique particulars.* Concerning space Kant says: "For, first, one can only represent a single space, and if one speaks of many spaces, one understands by that only parts of one and the same unique space" (A25/B39). Similarly, he says of time: "Different times are only parts of one and the same time. That representation, however, which can only be given through a single object, is an intuition" (A31–2/B47). The point is straightforward: global space and time are themselves complete particulars (although not empirical objects) rather than merely general or partial features of things. Their particularity is shown by the fact that any finite region is part of the larger encompassing space or time. Put another way, any two distinct spaces are themselves spatially related. Moreover, two qualitatively indistinguishable regions of space are numerically distinct only by virtue of being different regions of the same global space. The same is true of time.[9] Since concepts of the understanding are general rather than particular, they could not be the source of our representations of space and time.

(b) *For space and time, the whole is prior to the parts, unlike the part–whole relation for concepts.* Kant's second point reinforces the first by contrasting the part–whole structures of space and time with that of concepts. Of space he says:

these parts cannot as it were precede the single all-embracing space as its components (from which its composition would be possible), but rather are only thought *in it*. It is essentially single; the manifold in it, thus also the general concept of spaces in general, rests merely on limitations. (A25/B39)

---

[9] For this and the discussion that follows I am indebted to Melnick, *Kant's Analogies of Experience.* See especially 7–30.

The remark that follows, that "an *a priori* intuition (which is not empirical) grounds all concepts of it," is irrelevant to Kant's point, that the representation is intuitive rather than conceptual. It indicates, however, that we do have general concepts of space and time, for example, of spatial extensions and temporal durations. Nonetheless, Kant is claiming that these general representations are derived from our original intuitions of space and time as particulars.

The part–whole argument for time is, not surprisingly, mislocated in the fifth paragraph, in the middle of the fourth exposition. The portion relevant to the third exposition is this:

> But where the parts themselves and every magnitude of an object can be determinately represented only through limitation, there the entire representation cannot be given through concepts, (for they contain only partial representations), but immediate intuition must ground them. (A32/B48)

This argument makes an excursion into mereology, the science of part–whole relations. Kant is contrasting the part–whole relation for complex concepts with that for space and time. Recall that concepts are general representations of features of individuals rather than complete individuals. This is why Kant describes them as "partial representations." The generality of concepts entails that they can be logically arranged in species–genus relationships. The concept 'physical object,' for example, has among its subordinate concepts 'animal,' which similarly has the concept 'mammal' subordinate to it. The flip side of the coin is that any complex concept contains as its components other concepts. The concept 'mammal' contains (among others) the more general concept 'animal,' which similarly contains the more general concept 'physical object,' and so on. Now although the concept 'animal' is a component of the concept 'mammal,' the former concept can be apprehended independently of the latter. That is, we can think of animality in general without thinking of mammals or other types of animals. This is the sense in which the parts of complex concepts are *prior to* or logically independent of the whole. The content of any constituent concept is recognizable independently of its inclusion in another concept. Later in the *Critique* Kant will characterize wholes made up of independently existing parts as aggregates or composites.[10]

[10] See the Second Antinomy, A438/B466.

Space and time, by contrast, are wholes that are logically prior to their parts, which do not exist independently. For such wholes the parts are created by drawing boundaries or introducing "limitations" through the whole. Thus space and time are not composites of independently existing spatial and temporal regions; instead, we identify (finite) regions of space and time as we like, depending on how we draw the boundaries. For Kant, a point in space or time is not a part, but a limit whose "existence" depends on the previously given whole. The upshot, then, is that our representations of space and time are particulars, as shown by their part–whole structure, and thus they must originate in intuition rather than concepts of the understanding.

4. The fourth exposition: space and time are intuitions because they are given as infinite in magnitude

The fourth exposition uses the fact that space and time are "given as infinite" to prove that they originate in intuition. When Kant says they are infinite, he means primarily that they are unbounded, but he also believes they are infinitely divisible.[11] His various statements of the argument come at the point from several different angles. The earliest version, in the A edition for space, claims that "A general concept of space (which is common to a foot as well as an ell) can determine nothing in respect to magnitude" (A25). That is, the general concept of being extended spatially does not entail anything about the divisibility or size of a space, and thus could not be the source of our experience of space as infinitely divisible and unbounded.

In the B edition version for space, Kant emphasizes the difference between the ways concepts and intuitions can "contain" an infinity of representations:

Now one must, to be sure, think of every concept as a representation that is contained in an infinite set of different possible representations (as their common mark), which thus contains these **under itself**; but no concept, as such, can be thought as if it contained an infinite set of representations **within itself**. Nevertheless space is so thought (for all the parts of space, even to infinity, are simultaneous). (B39–40)

---

[11] For helpful discussions on the unbounded nature of space and time, see Falkenstein, *Kant's Intuitionism*, 232–2, and Parsons, "The Transcendental Aesthetic," 71.

As a general representation, a concept represents a characteristic that has a potential infinity of instances. Those to which the concept actually applies are its extension, and are said to fall *under* the concept. (The relation of a predicate to its extension is represented in set theory as the relation of a set to its members.) But considered in terms of its content or intension, no concept can be composed of an infinity of concepts, for such a concept would be unthinkably complex. Thus no concept could contain an infinity of parts *within* itself. Now as the third exposition has shown, space and time each contain a (potential) infinity of parts within the whole. In the fifth paragraph on time, Kant says this: "The infinitude of time signifies nothing more than that every determinate magnitude of time is only possible through limitations of a single time grounding it. The original representation *time* must therefore be given as unlimited" (A32/B47–8). Since spatial and temporal parts do not exist independently, the process of carving out finite spatiotemporal regions by drawing boundaries has no limit in principle. (The first edition refers to "boundlessness in the progression of intuition" at A25.)

Before going on to the transcendental exposition, it might be helpful to clarify Kant's view of space-time cognition. According to Melnick, when Kant says that space is given as an unlimited whole, he is not making "the (absurd) claim that I can only empirically perceive appearances occupying some part of space by perceiving the whole of space."[12] Kant holds that we perceive only finite spatiotemporal regions. His statements about the whole of space and time make claims about the form of every determinate representation in space and time. Melnick thinks Kant should say that through our finite perceptions, we have a "pre-intuition" of each finite region in space and time as embedded in a continuous, infinitely divisible, unbounded whole. On this theory, our intuitive capacities supply us, along with the empirical data, *a priori* manifolds of spatial and temporal data. All data given in intuition, both empirical and pure, are *determinable but indeterminate*. That means that they are not received as discriminated into determinate spatiotemporal regions. In the Transcendental Analytic, Kant will argue that such discrimination requires thinking the manifold by pure concepts of the understanding.

[12] *Kant's Analogies of Experience*, 8.

B. *The transcendental exposition*

Here Kant argues that space and time are pure intuitions based on synthetic *a priori* cognitions. As explained at B40, the transcendental exposition should show that the fact that space and time are pure intuitions is both necessary and sufficient to account for synthetic *a priori* judgments concerning space and time. These arguments are fairly straightforward.

The argument for space depends on the fact that we have synthetic *a priori* cognition of the nature of space, both directly and in geometry. In the Introduction Kant claimed that the judgment that a straight line is the shortest between two points is both synthetic and known to be necessarily true (B16). Here he makes the same point about our cognition of three-dimensional space. Recall that synthetic *a priori* judgments are both informative and yet thought with necessity. The transcendental exposition divides up these two characteristics neatly, attributing the synthetic nature of geometry to the intuitive character of space, and its *a priori* status to the *a priori* status of the spatial manifold. First, the fact that knowledge of space is synthetic shows that it cannot be originally derived from concepts of the understanding, for only analytic judgments can be obtained from concepts alone. But Kant believes there is no contradiction in the idea that space could have had fewer or more dimensions. So spatial cognition must be based in intuition. Furthermore, that intuition cannot be empirical, for then we could not account for the necessity and strict universality of geometry. By elimination, then, our original representation of space must be pure intuition. If one accepts Kant's premise that we have synthetic *a priori* knowledge of space, as well as his analysis of intuitions and concepts, this appears to be a sound argument.

The argument for time does not, as one might expect, depend similarly on the synthetic *a priori* status of arithmetic.[13] Instead, Kant's examples of synthetic *a priori* judgments in the third metaphysical exposition are, "It has only one dimension; different times are not simultaneous, but successive" (A31/B47). In the official transcendental exposition he connects time with the possibility of experiencing

---

[13] In the *Prolegomena* Kant does connect the pure intuition of time to arithmetic at section 10, 79.

changing states of things through the perception of motion, and consequently with the principles of mechanics. Only because time is an *a priori* intuition, he says, can we comprehend

> the possibility of an alteration, i.e., of a combination of contradictorily opposed predicates (e.g., a thing's being in a place and the not-being of the very same thing in the same place) in one and the same object. Only in time can both contradictorily opposed determinations in one thing be encountered, namely, **successively**. (B48–9)

In other words, whereas the principle of non-contradiction rules out the truth of a proposition and its negation, it is possible for an empirical proposition and its negation to be true at different times. The pure intuition of time, then, underlies "the general theory of motion," which includes synthetic *a priori* principles of mechanics. Kant does not specify any such principles here, but in the *Metaphysical Foundations of Natural Science* they include the laws that the quantity of matter is conserved in all changes, that all changes in matter have external causes, and that in all communication of motion, action and reaction are always equal.[14] Not until his discussion of mathematical construction in the Transcendental Dialectic does Kant explain the difference between arithmetic and geometry. Although we will examine those passages in more detail in chapter 11, for now let me indicate Kant's position briefly. The key idea is that arithmetic is not the "science" of time because time does not provide a model of pure arithmetic as space does of geometry. Although arithmetical operations involve temporal processes, Kant does not assume that the objects to which arithmetic and algebra apply must be temporal. Thus for him the "science" of time is mechanics or the doctrine of motion, that is, arithmetic as applied to spatial objects.

3. SPACE AND TIME AS TRANSCENDENTALLY IDEAL AND EMPIRICALLY REAL

In his concluding sections beginning at A26/B42 and A32/B39, Kant argues for the transcendental ideality and empirical reality of space

---

[14] *MFNS*, 541, 543, 544. The latter two are Kant's versions of Newton's first and third laws of motion.

and time. He actually foreshadows these conclusions in the transcendental exposition of space. There he claims that the only way we could have an outer intuition that precedes experience of objects and is determined *a priori* is if "it has its seat merely in the subject, as its formal constitution for being affected by objects and thereby acquiring **immediate representation**, i.e., **intuition**, of them, thus only as the form of outer **sense** in general" (B41). From the fact that space and time are pure intuitions, Kant concludes that they are merely forms of the subject's intuition. This is the basis of the transcendental ideality and empirical reality of space and time.

In the conclusions sections, Kant makes the essential argument in two paragraphs labeled (a) and (b). Paragraph (a) claims that space and time do not represent properties or relations of things in themselves, "For neither absolute nor relative determinations can be intuited prior to the existence of the things to which they pertain, thus be intuited *a priori*" (A26/B42). Clearly he agrees with Hume that, were our intuitive capacities to give us information about things as they exist independently of us, this knowledge could only be contingent. So the first step rules out the possibility that space and time provide information about properties or relations of things in themselves.

In paragraph (b) Kant takes the next step, arguing that space and time must therefore be subjective conditions of sensibility, or the forms of outer and inner sense. This follows by elimination, since if space and time are not "located" outside the subject, then the only alternative is to attribute them to the subject's cognitive capacities. As Kant notes, this conclusion is indirectly supported by the fact that it accounts for synthetic *a priori* spatial and temporal cognition, because the forms in which we are affected by objects can be logically independent of intuitions of the objects themselves.

In his conclusions on time, Kant adds a third paragraph labeled (c) to emphasize that time has a broader scope than space, since all appearances, both outer and inner, are subject to time. As the form of inner sense, all our representing occurs in time; so representations of outer or spatial things are also temporal. As Kant says at A34/B50–1, time is "the immediate condition of the inner intuition (of our souls), and thereby also the mediate condition of outer appearances."

In *Kant's Transcendental Idealism*, Henry Allison points out that Kant's notion of the form of intuition has several aspects to it.[15] From the subjective side, the forms of intuition are our particular modes of intuiting. Kant believes it is a fact about our human capacity to receive intuitive data that we intuit our mental states temporally, and things other than our mental states spatially. But this has implications for the objective side, since the forms of intuition are also forms of the objects intuited. As we saw at A20/B34, the form is the system that allows the matter (here the empirical data) to be organized and related. As forms of the subject's intuition, then, space and time provide the structure of the items intuited empirically. The spatial and temporal properties of appearances are due to their being given to perceivers with spatiotemporal forms of intuition.

From his conclusions in paragraphs (a) and (b), Kant develops his theory of the transcendental ideality and empirical reality of space and time. The thesis that space and time are transcendentally ideal means that they are nothing more than conditions of human sensibility. In reference to space Kant states the point as follows:

We can accordingly speak of space, extended things, and so on, only from the human standpoint. If we depart from the subjective condition under which alone we can acquire outer intuition, namely that through which we may be affected by objects, then the representation of space signifies nothing at all. This predicate is attributed to things only insofar as they appear to us, i.e., are objects of sensibility. (A26–7/B42–3)

He makes similar remarks about time at A34/B51. But if space and time are only subjective representations, then all spatiotemporal appearances are likewise subjective in the same sense. Kant spells out this consequence in his General Observations:

We have therefore wanted to say that all our intuition is nothing but the representation of appearance; that the things that we intuit are not in themselves what we intuit them to be, nor are their relations so constituted in themselves as they appear to us; and that if we remove our own subject or even only the subjective constitution of the senses in general, then all constitution, all relation of objects in space and time, indeed space and time themselves would disappear, and as appearances they cannot exist in themselves, but only in us. (A42/B59)

[15] Allison, *Kant's Transcendental Idealism*, 96–7.

The transcendental ideality of space and time means that were there no perceivers with these forms of intuition, space and time would not exist; neither, consequently, would the spatiotemporal properties of things. It follows that things in themselves, whatever they are, are non-spatial and non-temporal. This is one of the controversial implications of Kant's analysis, which we shall discuss below. Here Kant clearly rejects the theory of absolute space and time, according to which (in Kant's terms) space and time are transcendentally real, since they exist independently of perceivers.

Despite their ideality, however, Kant also maintains that space and time are empirically real. By this he means that they are not illusory, that the objects that appear to us really are given in space and time. Since, as Kant argued in the metaphysical exposition, space and time are necessary features of appearances, it follows that all objects of intuition are temporal, and all outer objects are spatial. Kant sometimes describes space and time as objectively valid, as in his conclusions on time: "Our assertions accordingly teach the *empirical reality* of time, i.e., objective validity in regard to all objects that may ever be given to our senses. And since our intuition is always sensible, no object can ever be given to us in experience that would not belong under the condition of time" (A35/B52). It is important to note the connection between objective validity and truth values. That space and time are objectively valid implies that we can make true or false judgments about them as well as about spatiotemporal objects. In connecting empirical reality with objective validity, Kant relativizes the notions of an object and objective truth. Empirical realism entails that what counts as an object *for us*, and therefore what counts as objective truth *for us*, is relative to our cognitive capacities. The Aesthetic establishes those conditions from the side of human sensibility. In the Transcendental Analytic Kant examines the contribution of the understanding to the objective conditions of cognition.

As a result of his "transcendental turn," in the rest of the *Critique* Kant generally uses the term "object" to refer to objects of knowledge or appearances, and he typically reserves the term "thing" for things in themselves. There are passages, of course, where Kant ignores this distinction, such as at A30/B45, where he says that "objects in themselves are not known to us at all." But generally he uses these terms in accordance with his conclusion that objects of experience are only appearances.

We can now appreciate the peculiar sense in which space and time are subjective, and the connection between transcendental subjectivity and the necessity of synthetic *a priori* judgments. At A28–9 and A28/B44, Kant contrasts the subjectivity of space and time with the subjectivity of secondary qualities, or experiences of color, sound, and hot and cold:

> Besides space, however, there is no other subjective representation related to something **external** that could be called *a priori* objective. For one cannot derive synthetic *a priori* propositions from any such representation, as one can from intuition in space (§3). Strictly speaking, therefore, ideality does not pertain to them, although they coincide with the representation of space in belonging only to the subjective constitution of the kind of sense, e.g., of sight, hearing, and feeling, through the sensations of colors, sounds, and warmth, which, however, since they are merely sensations and not intuitions, do not in themselves allow any object to be cognized, least of all *a priori*. (A28/B44; see also A28–9)

For scientific realists like Descartes and Locke, secondary qualities such as color, taste, heat, and so on are merely effects caused in perceivers by contact with the primary qualities of physical objects. Secondary qualities are subjective in the sense that they can vary from perceiver to perceiver, since they depend on the individual's sense organs as well as the conditions of perception. A color-blind person, for example, will not see the full range of colors seen by someone who is not color-blind. Now Kant assumes that all human perceivers share the same forms of intuition. Thus the subjectivity of space and time differs from the subjectivity of secondary qualities in two ways. First, space and time are universally or species-subjective, since they are forms of all human intuition. And this implies, second, that space and time are necessary rather than contingent features of experience. By contrast, secondary qualities are not necessary features of appearances, and so cannot provide a foundation for synthetic *a priori* cognition. In addition, these qualities do not yield direct cognition of objects, although scientific realists assume there are correlations between secondary qualities and the real properties causing the experiences. That space and time are pure forms of intuition, however,

can account for synthetic *a priori* knowledge of mathematics and mechanics. The transcendental subjectivity of space and time means that they are universal to humans and the ground of necessary features of appearance. This is not to be confused with the empirical subjectivity of contingent sensible qualities that vary from individual to individual.

This contrast between transcendental and empirical subjectivity is echoed in the distinction between transcendental and empirical notions of appearance at A45/B62–3. As Allison explains, the opposition between the subjective or ideal and the objective or real marks a division between what is in the mind and what is independent of the mind.[16] But this distinction can be drawn on both the transcendental and empirical levels. Considered transcendentally, "the mind" refers to all human subjects; empirically it designates only individual subjects. Accordingly, there are both transcendental and empirical versions of the distinction between appearances and things in themselves:

> We ordinarily distinguish quite well between that which is essentially attached to the intuition of appearances, and is valid for every human sense in general, and that which pertains to them only contingently because it is not valid for the relation of sensibility in general but only for a particular situation or organization of this or that sense. And thus one calls the first cognition one that represents the object in itself, but the second one only its appearance. This distinction, however, is only empirical. (A45/B62–3)

In other words, within experience we often call features such as colors and tastes, which depend on the individual perceiver, mere appearances. And we contrast those with the real physical properties of the object, which we consider the thing in itself. Kant uses the example of a rainbow: "we would certainly call a rainbow a mere appearance in a sun-shower, but would call this rain the thing in itself, and this is correct, as long as we understand the latter concept in a merely physical sense" (A45/B63). From the empirical standpoint, physical objects are real, and the secondary qualities they appear to have are ideal or mere appearances. At the empirical level the *real or objective* has universal validity for all humans, is publicly available, and expresses the relation between a perception and an object. The empirically

---

[16] *Kant's Transcendental Idealism*, 6–8.

ideal or subjective varies among humans, represents a private experience, and thus expresses a relation merely between perceptions. From the transcendental standpoint, however, empirically real objects are themselves mere appearances. On this level the *subjective or ideal* consists in necessary conditions of experience, which are valid for all human subjects. The transcendentally *real* are things in themselves, which Kant believes we cannot know. Later, in the deduction of the categories, Kant criticizes Hume for trying to account for transcendentally ideal features of experience in terms of the empirically ideal.

Kant's notion of transcendental subjectivity is the key to the necessity of synthetic *a priori* judgments. Earlier I called this an "epistemic" necessity, since it is grounded in human cognitive capacities. Kant reminds us repeatedly that it is logically possible for other subjects to have other forms of intuition. It is just a brute fact about humans that space and time are our forms of outer and inner sense. Although we cannot explain this fact, it does explain why human experience must have certain features. So space and time are necessary features of objects of experience, although the fact that they are our forms of intuition is not necessary. In the Transcendental Analytic Kant will give a similar analysis of pure concepts of the understanding, deriving their necessity from the logical forms by which humans judge. The epistemic necessity of synthetic *a priori* judgments, then, is weaker than either logical or absolute metaphysical necessity.

Before turning to some issues raised by the Aesthetic, we should note Kant's criticism of Leibniz's analysis of the sensibility at A43–4/B60–2. There Kant points out that Leibniz and his disciple Wolff analyzed sensory representations as confused intellectual representations. But the metaphysical exposition shows that space and time, and all the sensible data received in them, originate in the capacity for intuition, which is distinct from the understanding. As Kant says,

The Leibnizian-Wolffian philosophy has therefore directed all investigations of the nature and origin of our cognitions to an entirely unjust point of view in considering the difference between sensibility and the intellectual as merely logical, since it is obviously transcendental, and does not concern merely the form of distinctness or indistinctness, but its origin and content, so that through sensibility we do not cognize the constitution of things in themselves merely indistinctly, but rather not at all. (A44/B61–2)

Here Kant classifies the difference between clear and confused representation as "logical." As he says later at B415n, "a representation is clear if the consciousness in it is sufficient for **a consciousness of the difference** between it and others." Now degree of clarity is not what distinguishes sensory from intellectual representations. Instead they differ in kind – both in their relation to the object and their content as particular or general. In criticizing the Leibnizians, Kant carries out one prong of his attack on reductionistic theories of ideas. In the Transcendental Analytic, he will reject empiricism for an opposing error, claiming that all ideas originate in sensory impressions.

4. CRITICISMS OF KANT'S THEORY OF SPACE AND TIME

The most common objections against the theory of the Aesthetic are to the conclusions that things in themselves are non-spatial and non-temporal (henceforth NST), and that geometry and arithmetic are synthetic *a priori*. While this discussion will undoubtedly not settle any of these issues, I hope to identify the significant issues presented in the literature.

A. NST and the unknowability of things in themselves

From Kant's time up to the present, critics have made two charges against his conclusions on space and time. First, they have argued that he does not adequately support NST. And second, they have pointed out that both NST and the underlying presupposition that things in themselves exist are apparently incompatible with the unknowability thesis (UT). Here we will first examine whether NST is justified. In my concluding remarks at the end of this book I return to UT and the coherence of Kant's idealism.

The criticism typically raised against NST is called the "neglected alternative" view. This position was debated extensively by the nineteenth-century German commentators Adolf Trendelenburg and Kuno Fischer; the debates are discussed fully in Hans Vaihinger's *Commentar zu Kants Kritik der reinen Vernunft*.[17] Trendelenburg pointed out that even if one agrees that the space and time of our experience

---

[17] Vaihinger, *Commentar*, 1:134–50.

are subjective forms of intuition, it is still possible that things in themselves are also spatiotemporal, although their space-time would be numerically distinct from ours. Consequently, Kant's arguments do not preclude the possibility that appearances correspond to things in themselves, even if we could never know the nature of the correspondence.

In *Kant's Transcendental Idealism*, Allison defends NST. His first argument misses the mark, since it misconstrues the neglected alternative position, as maintaining that the numerically same spatiotemporal frameworks are both subjective forms of intuition and also systems relating things in themselves.[18] He then considers the relevant thesis, that there could be a correspondence between our forms of intuition and spatiotemporal relations among things in themselves. He argues that if this version avoids the charge of incoherence, "it does so only by virtue of its utter vacuity" (320). While he may be right, it does not explain why Kant thought he was justified in drawing the strong conclusion that things in themselves could not be spatiotemporal, rather than taking an agnostic stand on the question. As Paton remarks, it seems "we are entitled to say of things-in-themselves only that we do not and cannot know them to be in space and time. Since we do not know them at all, we cannot say what they are not."[19]

In *Space and Incongruence*, I defend NST based on the incongruent counterparts arguments, which Kant set out from 1768 up through the critical period. Although Kant uses the arguments to develop his distinction between the sensibility and the intellect, as well as his theory that space and time are pure forms of intuition, in his final versions in the *Prolegomena* of 1783 and the *Metaphysical Foundations of Natural Science* of 1786, he claims the phenomenon supports NST.[20] Although the arguments are too complex to explain here, by 1781 Kant took the existence of counterparts such as left and right hands to demonstrate that the kinds of relations exhibited in the space of our experience could not obtain among things in themselves. Although the argument itself does not appear in the *Critique*, the theory of relations on which NST is based does. One part of the

[18] See my *Space and Incongruence*, 93–9, for a discussion of Allison's views.
[19] Paton, *Kant's Metaphysics of Experience*, 1:180.
[20] See *Space and Incongruence*, chapters 3–5. A condensed version appears in Buroker, "The Role of Incongruent Counterparts in Kant's Transcendental Idealism."

theory is the metaphysical exposition views that space and time are wholes which are prior to their parts, as well as independent of the items located in them. The remainder occurs in the Transcendental Analytic section titled the Amphiboly of Concepts of Reflection. Here Kant agrees with Leibniz that, as understood by reason, a system of relations always presupposes independently existing relata. Kant expresses this in terms of the distinction between the "inner" or intrinsic determinations, and the "outer" or relational determinations of existing things: "Through mere concepts, of course, I cannot think of something external without anything inner, for the very reason that relational concepts absolutely presuppose given things and are not possible without these." He goes on to remark that the space of our intuition "consists of purely formal or also real relations," without presupposing something "absolutely inner" (A284/B340). When Kant refers to what is thought through "mere concepts" he means the logical conception of a relation. Here he agrees with Leibniz that relations among things in themselves logically presuppose independently existing relata. But our intuition of space is of a system of relations that is prior to and independent of the things occupying it. Accordingly, in *Space and Incongruence* I argue that the existence of incongruent counterparts convinced Kant that space and time are incompatible with the kinds of relations that could obtain among things in themselves, as represented by mere thought. This incompatibility licenses the strong conclusion that things in themselves could not be spatial or temporal.

This interpretation stimulated considerable discussion in the literature.[21] Recently Falkenstein has defended a "mitigated" version of NST based primarily on the arguments of the Aesthetic. With respect to the neglected alternative, his version maintains that if things in themselves stood in spatiotemporal relations, those relations could not correspond in any important way to our forms of intuition. Although Falkenstein does not characterize his interpretation this way, it seems to me an extension of my defense based on the theory of relations. But he delves more deeply into Kant's assumptions about orders and relations, as well as the various versions of NST. For these reasons his

---

[21] See Van Cleve and Frederick, eds., *The Philosophy of Right and Left*, for various viewpoints and a detailed bibliography.

account is the most thorough and charitable offered to date. Here I shall sketch its outlines.[22]

In considering the neglected alternative, Falkenstein divides the relevant possibilities into two: first, that space and time are themselves substances; and second, the relationist view that they are constructed from properties or relations of things in themselves. He finds Kant's argument against the substantival view in the proof of the thesis of the Second Antinomy, as the following *reductio ad absurdum*. If composite self-subsisting things were not made up of simple parts, and all composition were removed "in thought," no composite or simple part would remain. And therefore "no substance would be given." Thus self-substantial things must ultimately be composed of simple parts (A434/B462).[23] Now space and time are not composed of simple parts because they are infinitely divisible. Consequently they could not correspond to any conceivable substantival things in themselves. This explains Kant's remarks that were time self-subsistent, "it would be something that was actual yet without an actual object" (A32–3/B49), and that the absolute theorists have to admit "two eternal and infinite self-subsisting non-entities (space and time), which exist (yet without there being anything real)" (A39–40/B56). This disposes of the substantival version of the claim that things in themselves could be spatiotemporal.

Falkenstein thinks Kant's strongest defense against the relational version of the neglected alternative is based on an analysis of different types of orders. Recall the first metaphysical exposition assumption that the spatiotemporal positions of appearances are not determined by the empirical contents. It follows that the spatiotemporal order of appearances could not possibly be based on (intrinsic) properties of things in themselves. Falkenstein contrasts a "comparative order" of things based on their intrinsic qualities, with the "presentational" order of spatiotemporal locations: "In a comparative order, the locations of the ordered elements are determined by some scalable quality in the elements themselves. The order of colors in terms of their brightness, saturation, and hue, or of sounds in terms of pitch and volume is an example of a comparative order."[24] Thus we can

[22] The arguments outlined here are contained in chapter 9 of *Kant's Intuitionism*, 289–309.
[23] I discuss this argument in chapter 9, section 2.
[24] Falkenstein, *Kant's Intuitionism*, 184. See 183–5 for this analysis.

"locate" hues by their positions on a spectrum. But in this "color space" the positions of the hues are fixed: green will always appear between blue and yellow. The first metaphysical exposition shows, however, that the spatiotemporal positions of appearances are completely independent of their intrinsic (scalar) qualities: the fact that a color patch is green determines nothing about where or when it will appear. This provides the desired support for NST, for "even if there were a sense in which things in themselves might be in space or time, it would have to be a very different sense from that in which, according to the metaphysical expositions, the matters of appearance are in space and time" (303). The incompatibility allowing Kant to rule out a relationist alternative is that between the independent presentational order of our spatiotemporal experience, and a comparative order based on intrinsic features of things in themselves.

B. Is arithmetic analytic or synthetic?

Kant's view that mathematics is synthetic *a priori* has also been much debated by philosophers. The issues are complex, and are related to three important developments since Kant's time. These are, in chronological order, the development of non-Euclidean geometries in the nineteenth century, the failure of the Frege–Russell program to reduce mathematics to logic in the early twentieth century, and finally, the assumption in relativity theory that only empirical science can determine whether space is Euclidean or non-Euclidean. The first development apparently supports the synthetic nature of geometry, while the third poses a serious challenge to its *a priori* status. The failure of the reduction program has the more startling result of supporting Kant's view that arithmetic is synthetic. This section considers whether arithmetic propositions are synthetic, and the following section treats the synthetic *a priori* nature of geometry.

In claiming that arithmetic is synthetic *a priori*, Kant rejected Leibniz's view that arithmetic propositions are founded on the principle of contradiction. According to Leibniz, formulae such as "$2 + 2 = 4$" could be demonstrated from definitions of numbers and the analytic axiom "If equals be substituted for equals, the equality remains."[25]

---

[25] Leibniz, second letter to Clarke, *Leibniz–Clarke Correspondence*, 5. Also the *New Essays*, book IV, chapter 7, p. 413. My discussion here relies heavily on Brittan, *Kant's Theory of Science*, 43–67.

Leibniz thus held that mathematical truths could be reduced to logical truths and definitions. Early in the twentieth century both Gottlob Frege and Bertrand Russell actually attempted the reduction. Frege never doubted that geometry is synthetic, but he hoped to show that arithmetic could be reduced to general logical laws and definitions.[26] As Gordon Brittan explains in *Kant's Theory of Science*, the program would have two steps: the first would reduce different branches of mathematics to arithmetic, and the second would reduce arithmetic to logic. In their *Principia Mathematica*, Russell and Whitehead attempted the second step by giving logical definitions of the arithmetical terms appearing in the five Peano axioms at the basis of arithmetic, namely:

A.1: 0 is a number.
A.2: The successor of any number is a number.
A.3: No two numbers have the same successor.
A.4: 0 is not the successor of any number.
A.5: If P is a predicate true of 0, and whenever P is true of a number n, it is also true of the successor of n, then P is true of every number.[27]

The notions needing defining are "0," "is a number," and "is the successor of." If this could be done successfully in set-theoretic terms, then presumably all the properties of integers could be derived by logical proof. Since Frege defined analytic truths as those based on general laws of logic and definitions, a successful reduction would show arithmetic to be analytic in his sense.

Now the reduction failed because of Russell's famous discovery of the paradox of set theory. As Russell showed, a contradiction arises concerning the concept "is not a member of itself." If we have the class of all such things – classes that are not members of themselves – and we ask whether that class is or is not a member of itself, either way a contradiction arises. If the class is a member of itself, then it satisfies the condition of members, so it is not a member of itself. If it is not a member of itself, then it satisfies the condition, so it is a member of itself. Although Russell developed the theory of types to avoid the paradox, it led Frege to give up his view that

[26] See Frege, *The Foundations of Arithmetic*, 19–20.
[27] See Brittan, *Kant's Theory of Science*, 48.

arithmetic is analytic. Ultimately he came to the conclusion that the basis of all mathematics is geometry, which he believed to be synthetic.[28]

Independently of the logical paradox, however, the attempt to define arithmetical notions in set-theoretic terms would not have convinced Kant that arithmetic is analytic. This is because, as Brittan points out, the Zermelo–Fraenkel axiomatization of set theory includes two existential assumptions: the axiom that there exists a null set (null set axiom), and the axiom that there exists a set containing at least all natural numbers (axiom of infinity).[29] Absent these assumptions one cannot derive all of arithmetic. But for Kant all existential judgments must be synthetic. In criticizing the ontological argument he says, "in all fairness you must [concede], that every existential proposition is synthetic" (A598/B626). These considerations, then, lend support to Kant's view that arithmetic is synthetic in his sense.

C. Is geometry synthetic a priori?

Kant's view of geometry is less controversial than his view of arithmetic. From Euclid up to the nineteenth century, philosophers generally regarded Euclid's postulates as universally and necessarily true, but not based on laws of formal logic. With the development of non-Euclidean geometries in the nineteenth century by N. I. Lobachevsky and G. F. B. Riemann, it became apparent that the fifth postulate of Euclidean geometry is independent of the others, and thus can be denied without contradiction. In Lobachevsky's geometry, this entails that through a point not on a given line, more than one line can be drawn parallel to the given line, as well as that the sum of angles of a triangle is always less than two right angles. Riemann's geometry denied both Euclid's fifth postulate and the assumption that a straight line can be extended to any length. In this geometry space is finite; through a point not on a given straight line, no straight line can be drawn parallel to the given line, and the sum of angles of a triangle is greater than two right angles. When later developments proved that

[28] See Brittan, *Kant's Theory of Science*, n. 40, 59, for the source.
[29] Brittan, *Kant's Theory of Science*, 58–9.

both geometries are formally consistent, the question arose: which geometry is true of our space?

Although the development of non-Euclidean geometries supports the synthetic nature of geometry, following Hilbert, philosophers distinguished between pure and applied geometry. The uninterpreted formal system of pure geometry becomes applied when the non-logical terms are interpreted in terms of points, lines, and spaces. Based on this distinction, the logical positivists denied that either geometry is synthetic *a priori*. Pure mathematics could not be synthetic because its statements do not have truth values; applied geometry could not be *a priori* because only experience could determine which postulates were true of physical space. In fact, relativity theory favors Riemannian geometry, since it predicts that in a gravitational field the angles of a triangle composed of light rays will be greater than two right angles, and that between any two points light rays can travel along more than one "straight" path. Kant has commonly been charged with failing to distinguish pure from applied geometry. But Brittan points out that although Kant lacks a notion of an uninterpreted formal system, at B15 he distinguishes pure from applied mathematics, regarding the latter as empirical. Brittan defends Kant's view that pure geometry is synthetic given its "postulated" subject matter: unless one takes the basic terms to refer to points, lines, and planes, it is hard to see why a set-theoretical structure would count as geometry.[30]

5. SUMMARY

The Transcendental Aesthetic presents Kant's first arguments for synthetic *a priori* judgments, those contained in mathematics and mechanics. Kant traces this knowledge to the pure forms of intuition, space and time. After distinguishing between the sensibility and the understanding, he argues that our original representations of space and time are given *a priori* in sensible intuition. The metaphysical exposition contains two arguments that space and time are known *a priori*, and two arguments that they originate in intuition rather than the understanding. The transcendental exposition shows

---

[30] Brittan, *Kant's Theory of Science*, 81.

that this analysis can account for synthetic *a priori* judgments in mathematics and mechanics. These arguments show that space and time are pure forms of sensible intuition. Because they are *a priori* they are contributed by the subject. It follows that they are only forms under which objects appear to us, and not features of things in themselves. Thus Kant concludes that space and time are both transcendentally ideal and empirically real, since they are necessary conditions of objects of experience. By locating space and time in the subject, Kant can explain how it is possible to have knowledge that is both synthetic and *a priori*, at the cost of denying that we can know the nature of things in themselves.

CHAPTER 4

The Metaphysical Deduction: identifying categories

Kant's purpose in the Transcendental Analytic is to perform an analysis of the understanding parallel to that of sensible intuition in the Transcendental Aesthetic. There he showed that the sensibility contains pure forms, space and time, in which we receive the empirical data of intuition. In the Analytic, Kant wants to prove that the understanding similarly contributes pure concepts and principles to our knowledge of objects. Kant calls these pure concepts the categories; the heart of the Analytic is the Transcendental Deduction of the categories, where he justifies applying these concepts to objects given in intuition. But Kant's strategy is complex, and he carries it out in four stages. First, before justifying the use of categories in experience, he must prove that the understanding does in fact produce pure concepts. This is the task of the Metaphysical Deduction, where Kant derives the categories from the logical forms of judgment. The Transcendental Deduction of the categories then follows in chapter 2, in both A edition and B edition versions. Stage three is carried out in the Schematism, where Kant discusses the sensible conditions required to apply pure concepts to objects of intuition. Finally Kant offers detailed demonstrations of the pure principles of the understanding, the synthetic *a priori* judgments based on the categories. These principles constitute legitimate metaphysics. This chapter will focus on Kant's attempt to identify pure concepts of the understanding in the Metaphysical Deduction; the following chapters will examine subsequent sections of the Analytic. Before we look at the text, however, it will be helpful to discuss the philosophical issues connected with Kant's theory of categories.

Kant's theory of pure concepts intersects with several questions concerning the nature of knowledge. Here I shall focus on three issues debated by Kant's predecessors: the origin of ideas, the skeptical challenge to knowledge, and the notion of categorial concepts.

a. The origin of ideas

Since the ancient Greeks, philosophers disputed the origin of ideas. Plato and Aristotle established the debates between rationalists and empiricists. Plato believed that knowledge derives from innate ideas, which he thought were present at birth, unconsciously, in the soul. Reasoning consists in recollecting these ideas – bringing them to consciousness – and yields necessary knowledge of eternal Forms. Recollection could be aided by sense perception, although the content of innate knowledge is independent of sense experience. In the modern period, the rationalists Descartes, Spinoza, and Leibniz held versions of this theory.

Empiricists, following Aristotle, denied the existence of ideas not derivable from sense experience. Locke, for example, devoted book I of the *Essay Concerning Human Understanding* to refuting the theory of innate ideas. Hume codified the empiricist theory of ideas in his doctrine that all simple ideas are faint copies of simple impressions; he argued that complex ideas not based immediately on impressions were constructed from them by the imagination. Not only did empiricists reject innate ideas, some even denied that there are general ideas. Berkeley and Hume explicitly argued against ideas that are not particular sensible images. They admitted, however, that language contains general terms such as "human" and "gold," and they attempted to show how such terms function in the absence of general ideas.

In one respect Kant's categories resemble innate ideas, since their content is not derived from sense impressions. But Kant denies that the intellect has any ideas independent of its operations in experience.[1] Kant believes neither rationalism nor empiricism provides an adequate account of the relation between the intellect and the

---

[1] See chapter 5, section 4 for a discussion of this point.

senses. The rationalists treated the understanding as a kind of mystical instantaneous intuition; furthermore, they could not account for the application of innate ideas to the world without invoking divine benevolence. The empiricists not only failed to recognize the difference between general concepts and sense impressions, they analyzed thinking largely in terms of the associative functions of memory and imagination. In sensualizing thought, they completely overlooked the judgmental function of the intellect. Kant's critical theory offers a radically new analysis of the understanding, to remedy the defects of both traditions.

b. Skepticism and objective knowledge

The second significant issue is skepticism or the justification of knowledge. Greek philosophy included two schools of skeptics, the Academics and the Pyrrhonians. The Academics argued that although it was impossible to justify any claim to know conclusively, some beliefs were more likely to be true than others. By contrast, the Pyrrhonians argued that even claims to probable knowledge could not be justified, since attempts to establish a criterion of justification led to either circular reasoning or an infinite regress. Historically, skepticism has taken many forms. Greek skeptics such as Sextus Empiricus raised doubts about both sense perception and reason. In the modern period, the rationalists tended to mistrust the senses, but claimed a privileged status for knowledge derived from reason. Empiricists such as Locke and Hume recognized that sense experience could not justify claims to necessary knowledge of reality. In Hume's works these arguments turned into the most thorough and devastating attack on the certainty of scientific, metaphysical, and commonsense beliefs concerning mind-independent reality. Moreover, for Hume, knowledge of the self was just as unattainable as knowledge of the external world.

As one might expect, commentators disagree in interpreting Kant's response to skepticism. Because the Analytic contains several arguments for pure concepts and principles of the understanding, it is not always obvious what assumptions about knowledge Kant's arguments depend on.[2] Certain passages, however, are clearly aimed against some

---

[2] Guyer makes this point forcefully in *Kant and the Claims of Knowledge*, chapters 3–5.

forms of skepticism mentioned above. In the Analogies of Experience in the Analytic of Principles, Kant evidently intends to defend the metaphysical principles of substance and causality against Hume's attack. The Refutation of Idealism, added to the B edition Analytic of Principles, is explicitly directed against Descartes's view that self-knowledge is more certain than knowledge of the external world. In chapter 7 we shall assess Kant's response to the challenges posed by skepticism.

c. The notion of categorial concepts

There is no question that Kant intends his theory of pure concepts to replace Aristotle's theory of the categories. In his *Categories*, Aristotle identified ten classes as the fundamental ontological types under which all things fall: substance, quantity, quality, relation, place, time, posture, state, action, and passion. Although these are metaphysical classifications, the theory is based on semantics, since Aristotle derived these classes from types of predicates, and the distinction between essential and accidental predication. Every descriptive term denotes things falling under at least one of these ten classes. Nouns like "animal" and "plant" signify substances; adjectives such as "red" and "hot" signify qualities; others like "is next to" signify relations, and so on. Aristotle thought that things falling under all categories could be the subject of essential predications, but only substances could be the subject of accidental predications, since substances can retain their identity while undergoing change in time. In general, the categories express metaphysical principles that set limits on meaningful discourse. With the development of modern logic, Frege and Russell radically revised Aristotle's conceptual scheme, and twentieth-century philosophers debated whether there is any necessary conceptual scheme. Kant, however, remains squarely in the Aristotelian tradition in claiming that an exhaustive list of necessary ontological concepts can be derived from logical concepts. Let us now examine the first step in his argument for this position.

2. THE METAPHYSICAL DEDUCTION: DISCOVERING THE PURE CONCEPTS IN THE FORMS OF JUDGMENT

Kant's discussion falls into four parts. From A50 to A66/B74 to B79 he explains transcendental logic as a science of the pure understanding.

The second part contains the first step of the deduction at A66–9/B91–94, where Kant analyzes the logical use of the understanding. Following this passage is the third part, from A70 to A76/B95 to B101, which discusses the logical forms of judgment. The fourth part, where Kant argues that the concepts of these forms of judgment have a real use as categories, begins at A76/B102 and continues to the end of the chapter.

a. Introduction to transcendental logic (A50–66/B74–91)

Kant describes transcendental logic as the science of the rules of the pure understanding required for cognition. This conception presupposes two distinctions: first, between the understanding and the sensibility; and second, between the real as opposed to logical uses of the understanding. Kant first reminds us that understanding and sensibility play distinct roles in knowledge. Sensibility is a merely passive capacity for receiving impressions through the senses. The understanding, by contrast, is a spontaneous power to think of objects through concepts. Thus each capacity has a distinct function and produces a characteristic type of representation. Sensations given in intuition and the concepts that depend on them are empirical representations known *a posteriori*. The pure forms of intuition and the pure concepts arising solely from the activity of the understanding (if there are any) are *a priori* representations. Just as pure intuition represents only formal features of sensible objects, pure concepts would represent only the most general features thought in any idea of an object.

Kant next points out that these two capacities provide complementary and indispensable aspects of knowledge. At A51–2/B75–6 he sharply contrasts sensible affection with the power of thought. Human intuition is sensible and gives us access to existing states of affairs. But sensibility yields an undifferentiated manifold of data, which is only the *material* for representing objects. To take this data to represent objects requires classifying and organizing it in terms of some conceptual scheme. This is the role of the understanding. The senses do not think; the understanding does not sense: "Without sensibility no object would be given to us, and without understanding none would be thought. Thoughts without content are empty, intuitions without concepts are blind" (A51/B75).

This memorable passage expressing the "blindness thesis" neatly captures the essential contributions of sensing and thinking. When Kant says thoughts without content are empty, he means that thinking alone cannot give us access to existence. A mere concept neither informs us about what exists, nor guarantees its applicability to existing objects. Concepts are "empty" if they have no reference to the world, since we cannot know whether they are true or false of anything. On the other hand, until the data of intuition is thought, it is "blind." The sensory manifold as received is an undifferentiated array, not discriminated into particular objects or states of affairs. Now Kant argued in the Aesthetic that this manifold contains a pure part, the forms of space and time. It is important to understand, however, that the pure forms of intuition supply only one aspect of the undifferentiated manifold. They make object identification possible by providing the material for identifying spatial and temporal locations of objects. But no intuitive data, pure or empirical, is given as organized into recognizable patterns. Just as sense impressions must be bundled to relate to distinct objects, the spatiotemporal manifold must be conceived in certain ways to represent spatial and temporal locations. On Kant's view, the essential function of the understanding is to organize the sensible data, both pure and empirical, to make it intelligible, by thinking it in terms of some conceptual scheme.

Kant next distinguishes between general and transcendental logic. General logic is the science of the fundamental rules of all thought; Kant says it contains "the absolutely necessary rules of thinking, without which no use of the understanding takes place" (A52/B76). By general logic he means both the syntactic rules for forming judgments and the rules specifying valid inferences. This logic is "general" because it applies necessarily to any object, regardless of its nature. Any logic whose rules are restricted to a certain kind of object is a "special" logic.

At A53–5/B77–9 Kant remarks that the *Critique* concerns pure rather than applied logic. Pure logic is a formal science rather than a study of the way people in fact think. The latter is a branch of empirical psychology, which examines thinking processes "under the contingent conditions of the subject . . . which can all be given only empirically" (A54/B78–9). Thus it "can never yield a true and proven science" (A55/B79), which must begin with necessary principles. In his writings on logic Kant also characterizes pure logic as a prescriptive or normative science as opposed to the descriptive science of empirical psychology.[3]

Transcendental logic is a special logic falling under pure general logic, for it is the science of necessary rules of thought about objects given in space and time. Whereas general logic "abstracts from all content of cognition" (A55/B79), transcendental logic has a content, namely the pure forms of intuition identified in the Transcendental Aesthetic. It abstracts only from the empirical features of spatiotemporal objects. This is a logic of the real use of the understanding, and Kant will argue that its principles are synthetic *a priori* rather than analytic, as are the principles of general logic. Despite the fact that transcendental logic is restricted to objects given in intuition, its concepts and principles nevertheless originate in pure understanding. A science of these pure concepts would demonstrate their origin (in the Metaphysical Deduction), as well as their scope and objective validity (in the Transcendental Deduction). In other words, this science will identify and justify the privileged conceptual scheme by which the understanding organizes the data of intuition into representations of objects.

Before beginning the Metaphysical Deduction, Kant makes some general remarks about the nature of truth, and explains his division of Transcendental Logic into an Analytic and a Dialectic. At A58/B82 he offers a nominal definition of truth as "the agreement of cognition with its object." This definition is only nominal because it does not provide a criterion for recognizing cases. In fact, Kant argues, there can be no general criterion sufficient for all true judgments. A general criterion would apply without regard to differences in the objects, but the distinction between true and false judgments implies that objects differ. Thus Transcendental Logic can supply only a necessary condition for truth, "the *conditio sine qua non*, and thus the negative condition of all truth" (A59–60/B84). The Transcendental Analytic will argue that the pure concepts and principles of the understanding are necessarily true of objects of experience. Since there is no sufficient criterion of truth, however, it is possible to misuse these concepts and principles. The Transcendental Dialectic examines this

---

[3] See section II of the *Jäsche Logic, Lectures on Logic*, 531.

misuse of the understanding, showing that the traditional metaphysical debates result from applying the categories beyond the limits of experience.

b. Step one of the Metaphysical Deduction: the logical function of the understanding

At A64/B89 Kant states that a successful demonstration of categories must show that the concepts are pure rather than empirical, and that they originate in the understanding rather than the sensibility. This latter point separates categories from mathematical concepts which, although *a priori*, are derived from the forms of intuition. In addition, the list must include only fundamental concepts, and it must be systematic to ensure completeness. Kant believes it is possible to obtain a complete list because pure concepts express functions of the understanding, which is "a unity that subsists on its own" (A65/B89–90). Thus the key to a complete list is to assume that the understanding has one function.[4] This method is an improvement over Aristotle's, who merely conducted an empirical (Kant says "mechanical") survey of concepts, which can never guarantee the systematic completeness of the list. In the first stage of the Metaphysical Deduction, then, Kant analyzes this unified function of the understanding to identify a complete list of pure concepts.

At A68/B93 Kant remarks that up to now he has characterized the understanding by contrast with the sensibility, and he reiterates that cognition contains only two elemental representations, intuition and concept. Since the understanding does not yield intuitions, it must produce concepts, which Kant describes as "discursive" rather than intuitive. This is explained in a key passage: "All intuitions, as sensible, rest on affections, concepts therefore on functions. By a function I understand the unity of the action of ordering different representations under a common one" (A68/B93). There are several important points here. First, intuitions arise from the way the subject is passively affected by objects. Intuiting is not an activity, but a state the subject undergoes. (This is why Kant labels sensibility

---

[4] Bernd Dörflinger argues eloquently that Kant's table of categories is based on a teleological analysis, in "The Underlying Teleology of the First *Critique*."

a capacity rather than a faculty.) By contrast, the understanding is a spontaneous faculty that acts to perform a function. In describing these acts as "discursive," Kant recalls the Latin *discursus*, which means "running through." The understanding functions, he says, to unify different representations by bringing them under a general representation, namely a concept. Thus it operates by "running through" diverse representations and classifying them in terms of a concept. Consider the unifying role of the concept 'green.' When one classifies diverse objects (an apple, a leaf) as green, one unites them into the class of things falling under the concept. Now the German for "concept" is *Begriff*, which comes from the verb *begreifen*, meaning "to grasp." A concept, then, represents the unity grasped at once in the diverse things to which it applies. The function of concepts is to unify diverse representations by representing a characteristic common to them.

In the next step Kant identifies conceiving with judging: "Now the understanding can make no other use of these concepts than that of judging by means of them" (A68/B93). Here he departs from the classical view that conceiving is logically prior to judging. His point is that concepts have no use other than to think of something, an x, as a thing of a certain kind F. But this act of conceiving an x as an F is equivalent to thinking the proposition that x is F, which is an act of judging. (We shall see below in the discussion of modality that not all judgments make assertions; in a "problematic" judgment one may only consider the proposition that x is F.) The key to deriving a list of pure concepts, then, is the analysis of judgment.

Judgment, according to Kant, is "the mediate cognition of an object, hence the representation of a representation of it" (A68/B93). Considered most abstractly, a judgment is a way of representing an object or objective state of affairs. It yields knowledge indirectly, through its component concepts, which are also mediate representations of objects:

In every judgment there is a concept that holds of many, and that among this many also comprehends a given representation, which is then related immediately to the object. So in the judgment, e.g., **"All bodies are divisible,"** the concept of the divisible is related to various other concepts; among these, however, it is here particularly related to the concept of body, and this in turn is related to certain appearances that come before us. (A68–9/B93)

Here Kant points out that to predicate something of one or more objects requires a predicate-concept, which is by its nature general, and can apply to many things. But the objects of the predication must themselves be picked out or represented by the subject-term. In the sentence "All bodies are divisible," the subject-term is "bodies", also a general representation. Concepts can be applied to existing things only when connected to the data given in intuition. Thus both the subject-concept 'bodies' and the predicate-concept 'divisible' represent objects indirectly, through sensible intuition. The entire judgment, then, is a complex representation of objects by concepts. Kant regards judgments as syntactic structures that (in the simplest case) combine or unify subject- and predicate-concepts, which we shall call first-order concepts.

Kant next establishes the priority of judgment over concept by claiming that the only function of the understanding is to judge, and by analyzing concepts as predicates of possible judgment:

> We can, however, trace all actions of the understanding back to judgments, so that the **understanding** in general can be represented as a **faculty for judging**. For according to what has been said above, it is a faculty for thinking. Thinking is cognition through concepts. Concepts, however, as predicates of possible judgments, are related to some representation of a still undetermined object. (A69/B94)

If the only use of concepts is to judge, and if the understanding is essentially the power to think by means of concepts, it follows that the only function of the understanding is to judge. Now Kant does not deny that the mind produces concepts from other representations by comparison and abstraction. But on his view creating concepts in this way makes sense only because the concepts are used in judging. Moreover, he attributes concept formation to the faculty of judgment in its *reflective* mode, rather than the *determinative* mode involved in making cognitive claims. For Kant the primary activity of the understanding is to make determinative judgments concerning objective states of affairs; all other functions are derivative and presuppose this role.[5]

The second significant implication of this passage is to analyze both concept and object in terms of judgment. When Kant says a concept is a "predicate of a possible judgment," he means that the essential

---

[5] The only treatment of reflective judgment in the First *Critique* occurs in the Amphiboly of Concepts of Reflection. See chapter 8 below.

function of a concept is to serve as a predicate in judgment. As we saw above, concepts can also be used as subject-terms in judgments, but from the logical standpoint, what separates general from particular representations is that they signify predicates rather than the things of which they are predicated. Now by virtue of the fact that they are the means of judging objects, concepts are inherently *objective representations*. This distinguishes them from sensations, for example, which are merely subjective states. When Kant says concepts are "related to some representation of a still undetermined object," he means that as predicates, concepts are ways of classifying objects into kinds. The things being classified are the objects of judgment. A representation of an undetermined object would be some data given in intuition, which has not yet been classified as of a certain kind. The connection between concept, object, and judgment is only sketched here, but becomes central to the B edition Transcendental Deduction. For now we can say that in this analysis, Kant establishes that the notion of judgment is fundamental, and that the notions of concept and object are to be analyzed in terms of it.

In concluding this first half of the Metaphysical Deduction, Kant says, "The functions of the understanding can therefore all be found together if one can exhaustively exhibit the functions of unity in judgments" (A69/B94). In short, a complete list of pure concepts produced by the activity of the understanding can be derived from a list of the forms of judgment. What Kant does not say, which only becomes apparent in the next section, is that these are syntactic or second-order concepts expressing the logical properties of judgments. To see why this must be so, let us review his argument so far.

Kant's main premises are these:

1. All acts of the understanding are judgments.
2. Judgments are acts in which the understanding unifies diverse representations into a single, more complex, representation of an object.

What is needed here is an expansion on premise 2, concerning the nature of judgment. As we saw above, judgments are complex representations of objects by means of concepts. In the simplest case, a judgment has a subject-concept and a predicate-concept, which function as first-order concepts of objects. Now concepts are general representations that unify (other) diverse representations in a judgment. Since the first-order concepts are diverse representations, in order to combine them into a judgment, the understanding must employ second-order concepts. These higher-order concepts express the various ways to combine first-order concepts (and other representations, including judgments) to produce judgments of any form. Thus the pure concepts identified here are second-order concepts of the syntactical properties of judgments, which express the logical operations of the understanding. So to complete this part of the argument, we can add the following premise:

3. The function of a concept is to unify other representations in making judgments.
   From premises 1–3 Kant can draw the conclusion:
4. All judgments presuppose second-order, syntactical concepts expressing the forms for combining first-order concepts (or other representations) in judgment.
   From 4 and the following definition of a pure concept in 5:
5. Pure concepts express the logical operations of the understanding, Kant is then entitled to conclude:
6. Therefore, a complete list of forms for unifying representations in judgment will produce a complete list of pure concepts of the understanding.

Here Kant has argued that the understanding must produce a set of pure concepts from its own logical activities in judging. Clearly these concepts cannot be derived from experience, because they are presupposed in the act of recognizing objective states of affairs. At this point Kant has achieved his first goal in the Metaphysical Deduction, namely to demonstrate that there is a determinate set of pure concepts of the understanding, and that an exhaustive list is provided in the table of the forms of judgment. The method of derivation shows these concepts to be *a priori* in the weak sense that they are not derived from experience. In the next section Kant discusses these forms of judgment.

c. Interlude: the table of the forms of judgment (A70–1/B95–6)

Kant's table expresses his logical theory. As we saw, Kant's logic is an extension of Aristotelian syllogistic logic, which Kant thinks is complete and not capable of revision. We also noted that quantification theory, developed by Frege and Russell from the late nineteenth century, thoroughly revolutionized modern logic. This advance poses a problem for Kant, because he claims to derive a complete list of *a priori* concepts from judgment forms regarded today as hopelessly outdated. Even if one accepts the idea of a privileged set of categorial concepts, it seems likely that Kant has not identified the correct set. As one might expect, this is a standard verdict among commentators. Despite the shortcomings of Kant's logic, his assumption that the activity of judging presupposes a set of non-empirical concepts is plausible. Moreover, there are significant overlaps between Kant's logical forms and those recognized in contemporary theory. Here I shall present an overview of Kant's theory and its relation to contemporary logic.

At A70/B95 Kant notes that judgment forms are logical features that remain when one abstracts from the content (first-order concepts) of a judgment. Every judgment has four logical characteristics, which he calls "heads" (*Titel*): quantity, quality, relation, and modality. Under each head he identifies three "moments" which jointly express all possible forms under that head. The completeness of the table depends on this type of organization. In particular, the fact that there are three moments under each head indicates that the list is derived from a functional or teleological analysis of the understanding, rather than a purely mechanical procedure.[6] The organic nature of the table becomes apparent when one considers the interdependence of the three moments under each head.

As we shall see, Kant sets modality apart from quantity, quality, and relation, since only the latter three features concern the content (the logical syntax) of judgments. By modality Kant means the way in which the judgment is "held in the mind," that is, whether it is asserted or not. Today this aspect is called the *illocutionary force* of an utterance, and is classified under the pragmatics of judgment (or speech acts), rather than syntax. So Kant is on the right track in separating modality from the other three heads. The underlying flaw in the entire table is the view that quantity, quality, and relation are independent of one another. In modern logic all three aspects would

---

[6] See Dörflinger, "The Underlying Teleology of the First *Critique*," 820–2.

be subsumed under the heading of logical operators. Kant's table, then, reflects the classical tradition, which, as we shall see, did not have a sufficiently general theory of logical syntax.

Let us begin with quantity. Here Kant endorses the classical view that every judgment is either universal, particular, or singular, defined by the scope of the subject. The subjects of universal judgments are an entire class (e.g., "All humans are mortal"); subjects of particular judgments are part of a class (e.g., "Some philosophers are Greek"). Subjects of singular judgments such as "Socrates is Greek" are individuals, typically referred to by proper names or definite descriptions. On this view, the quantifiers "all" and "some" operate on the subject-concept, identifying the extension of the class to which the predicate applies. Kant also follows tradition in claiming that in inference, singular judgments can be treated like universals because "they have no domain at all" (A71/B96). They are similar to universal judgments inasmuch as the predicate is valid of the entire subject concept. Nevertheless, singular judgments are "essentially different" from universals as cognitions, since the singular stands to the universal "as unity to infinity"; that is, singular judgments ascribe a predicate to a distinct individual rather than to a set of individuals. Modern logic classifies singular judgments as *atomic*, and quantified judgments as *complex* because they include logical operators.

Although every judgment properly falls under one and only one moment, the moments are interdependent because the notions of class and individual are correlative or mutually imply one another. This is because a concept defining a class represents features of individuals, and individuals are recognizable in terms of their features. Hence if one can think of individuals as members of classes or sets, one can also subsume subsets under sets. In other words, the ability to judge by any one of these forms also entails the ability to judge by the others. This helps flesh out the idea that the understanding has a unified function, despite the variety of judgment forms.

Although he recognizes the distinction between quantified and unquantified judgments, Kant lacks our notion of a quantifier. Today, a singular sentence like "Socrates is Greek" is classified as an atomic sentence because it contains no logical operators, including quantifiers. It is expressed by a symbol such as 'Fa', where 'F' stands for the predicate "is Greek," and 'a' is an individual constant referring to Socrates. Universal sentences have a universal quantifier for the main logical operator and are symbolized as quantified conditionals. The judgment "All humans are mortal," for example, is symbolized $(\forall x)(Hx \supset Mx)$, read as "For everything, if it is human, then it is mortal." The particular judgment "Some philosophers are Greek" is today symbolized by a formula whose main operator is the existential quantifier: $(\exists x)(Px \ \& \ Gx)$, which is read as "There is something which is both a philosopher and Greek." One problem is that these three forms are not exhaustive. Kant overlooks unquantified complex judgments whose main operator is a truth-functional operator such as "if-then." For example, in the sentence "If Plato is a teacher, then Aristotle is a student," the main operator is the conditional. The sentence could be symbolized as follows: $Tp \supset Sa$. Although each component judgment is singular, the entire conditional does not fall under any of Kant's three moments of quantity. This illustrates one problem in Kant's treatment of quantity and relation as independent features.

The second head classifies judgments under quality into affirmative, negative, and infinite. Most commentators view Kant's notion of infinite judgments as rather tortured, and more for the sake of symmetry than any logical reason. The real focus of this heading is the theory of negation, where we see the same lack of generality as above, despite a clear advance over the classical view. In classical accounts, the negative particle "not" was viewed as attached to the copula "is" connecting the subject and predicate, and thus as extending to the entire judgment. But many thinkers treated negative judgments as denials, or actions opposed to affirmations. Since in affirming one unites the predicate and the subject, in denying one must "separate" the subject from the predicate.[7] Accordingly, negation characterizes the action rather than the content being judged. Since denying means separating the component concepts, however, there is no unity to the judgment, which is required for it to have a truth value. A more general problem is that it is not always clear how to classify judgments as affirmative or negative. Since the propositions "God is just" and "God is not unjust" are logically equivalent, it seems pointless to classify the first as affirmative and the second as negative. Although Kant takes

---

[7] This is true of the *Port-Royal Logic*. See Arnauld and Nicole, *Logic or the Art of Thinking*, part II, chapter 3.

the classical position in separating negation from the other logical operators, he rejects the view of negation as denial, placing it in the content of the judgment.

The moments under quality are affirmative, negative, and infinite. Examples of each are "The soul is mortal," "The soul is not mortal," and "The soul is non-mortal." Now Kant admits that the infinite judgment is an affirmation in logical form. The negation in the infinite form falls on the predicate ("non-mortal") rather than on the copula "is." From the standpoint of general logic there are really only two qualitative modes, affirmative and negative. Kant thinks the infinite form must be recognized, however, because transcendental logic "also considers the value or content of the logical affirmation made in a judgment by means of a merely negative predicate" (A72/B97). And he goes on to state that infinite judgments are "merely limiting," which will be significant in terms of the *a priori* knowledge provided in transcendental logic. If Kant's identification of infinite judgments as a distinct moment depends on transcendental logic, then this looks like the tail wagging the dog. In any case, two aspects stand out from the logical point of view. First, in spite of Kant's three moments, logically speaking the only distinction is between judgments in which negation is the main operator and those in which it is not. Second, and more important, Kant correctly locates negation in the content of the proposition rather than the action of judging. We shall return to this point in discussing modality.

The remainder of Kant's analysis of content falls under relation, where he explicitly indicates the forms of simple and complex judgments. The three forms are subject-predicate, hypothetical (or conditional), and disjunctive judgments. Subject-predicate judgments are the simplest or atomic form, since they have no judgment as a part. Hypotheticals and disjunctions are complex forms, which express different ways of relating judgments. Today we are struck by the absence of conjunction, so in this respect Kant's table seems incomplete. This threefold division of relational forms stems from Kant's view that there are only three ways in which two concepts can relate to one another. The first, found in the categorical form, is the inherence of a predicate in a subject. The second is the relation of ground to consequent as expressed in hypothetical judgments. And finally, disjunctive judgments express the relation of opposition among the members of a division. Let me comment briefly on each of these forms.

It was traditional to analyze simple judgments as composed of a subject, a predicate, and a copula connecting the two. Some logicians recognized that subjects and predicates could themselves contain embedded judgments, as in the sentence "God who is invisible made the world which is visible."[8] But given the overall subject-predicate structure, all embedded judgments had to be located in the subject or the predicate. There were many difficulties with this theory. For one thing, the grammatical subject of a sentence was not always the logical subject, and it was often not obvious how to distinguish the subject from the predicate of a sentence. This analysis also could not account for immediate inferences, such as from "All horses are animals" to "All heads of horses are heads of animals." Frege replaced the subject-copula-predicate analysis with the distinction between singular terms (constants and variables) and functions, including predicates and logical operators (truth-functional connectives and quantifiers). He eliminated the copula by analyzing predicates as incomplete expressions naming functions (e.g., "is Greek") and singular terms as complete expressions naming objects (e.g., "Socrates"). Thus the unity of the proposition was achieved by the fit between incomplete and complete expressions. Although Kant accepts the subject-copula-predicate analysis for atomic judgments, he did not force complex judgments into the subject-predicate mold.

The two logical operators under relation are the conditional (if-then) and disjunction (either-or). Kant's views of both are traditional, differing from the truth-functional treatment today. At A73/B98–9 Kant says:

The hypothetical proposition, "If there is perfect justice, then obstinate evil will be punished" really contains the relation of two propositions, "There is a perfect justice" and "Obstinate evil is punished." Whether both of these propositions in themselves are true, remains unsettled here. It is only the implication that is thought by means of this judgment.

---

[8] This example is from the *Port-Royal Logic*. Arnauld and Nicole's analysis of restrictive and non-restrictive subordinate clauses made an important contribution to semantics. See *Logic or the Art of Thinking*, part I, chapter 8, and part II, chapter 6.

Here Kant recognizes that asserting a conditional does not commit one to asserting either the antecedent or the consequent, but only a relation between them. In characterizing this relation as implication, however, Kant takes the conditional as non-material rather than the weaker material conditional of truth-functional logic.[9] In the material conditional the "if-then" expresses the weak truth-functional relation that whenever the antecedent is true, the consequent is true. This interpretation does not capture stronger relations such as logical and causal relations between the antecedent and consequent. Kant's view of the conditional as non-material was actually standard for his time.

The noteworthy feature of Kant's view of disjunctive judgments is his exclusive interpretation. This is clear from A73/B98–9:

the disjunctive judgment contains the relations of two or more propositions to one another, though not the relation of sequence, but rather that of logical opposition, insofar as the sphere of one judgment excludes that of the other, yet at the same time the relation of community, insofar as the judgments together exhaust the sphere of cognition proper.

After stating his example, "The world exists either through blind chance, or through inner necessity, or through an external cause," he says, "To remove the cognition from one of these spheres means to place it in one of the others," and vice versa, since the alternatives "mutually exclude each other, yet thereby determine the true cognition *in its entirety*" (A74/B99). In other words, for Kant disjunctions express a (potentially) complete inventory of mutually exclusive alternatives. In contemporary logic this is called an exclusive interpretation, in which the entire disjunction is true just in case exactly one disjunct is true. Typically, however, the wedge '∨' is used today to symbolize 'or' in the weaker, inclusive sense, in which the disjunction is true if at least one disjunct, and possibly both, are true.

Kant's treatment of modality is undoubtedly the most interesting part of his theory of judgment, for he is the first philosopher to separate entirely the content of the proposition from the act of asserting it. Descartes came close to this view when he distinguished perceptions of the understanding, which included propositional thoughts, from the act of the will involved in judging. It was essential to Descartes's

---

[9] Melnick makes this point in *Kant's Analogies of Experience*, 52–6.

perceptions of particular objects, from which we abstract concepts, which we then combine in judgments. Kant's point is this: in order to produce empirical concepts by comparing and analyzing our intuitions of distinct objects, we first must discriminate those individual objects. In the Aesthetic, Kant showed not only that existing particulars are intuited in space and time, but that their spatial-temporal locations are necessary conditions for identifying and individuating them. So a prerequisite for individuating objects of experience is to identify their spatiotemporal locations. Carving out locations and regions from the undifferentiated manifold given in pure intuition just is the pure aspect of synthesis.

At A78/B104 Kant uses the example of counting to illustrate this act. In counting (or measuring) one arrives at a number, which represents some plurality of units. The sum arrived at is thought as a totality made up of the units. The implicit connection here is between delineating spatiotemporal regions and the mathematical procedures involved in measurement. For example, to recognize a table as a distinct object occupying a particular place at a certain time, one must conceive the place and time as measurable regions of global space and time. In their real use pure concepts enable us to think of the pure manifold of space and time in terms of measurable locations and regions that can be occupied by objects of experience. Since this is a conceptual act, and the only use of concepts is to judge, it is thereby an act of judging. Hence pure concepts function both syntactically – to combine first-order concepts (or other representations) in judgment – and semantically – to synthesize the pure manifold of spatial-temporal data given in the forms of intuition. In the latter role, pure concepts function as categorial concepts insofar as they provide ways of conceiving necessary spatiotemporal features of objects.

At A80/B106 Kant presents the table of categories, the semantic versions of the logical forms of judgment. He says very little about them here, reserving details for the arguments in the Analytic of Principles. At B110, however, he divides the four headings of categories into two groups: he calls quantity and quality *mathematical* categories, and relation and modality *dynamical* categories. Mathematical categories are the pure concepts required merely to think an object of intuition. As we shall see, these categories are used to identify individuals and the properties we predicate of them. Dynamical categories enable us to think of relations among objects. The relational categories are concepts of temporal relations and properties of objects; the modal categories express the ways we relate objects to the understanding. This will become clearer as we look more closely at the categories in later chapters. Here I plan merely to focus on their relation to the forms of judgment, to give a sense of the plausibility of Kant's theory.[14]

The three categories under quantity are unity, plurality, and totality. According to the deduction, to make judgments of universal, particular, or singular forms, we must conceive of the objects we are judging in quantifiable terms, as individual members of sets and subsets. Many commentators have noticed that Kant correlates the concept of unity (an individual) with the universal judgment, and totality with the singular judgment, although it seems more logical to reverse the pairings. Despite this oddity, Kant is certainly correct that in order to judge by quantified forms, we must identify a domain of objects that can be individuated and divided into classes. This makes it possible to judge about one, all, or some members of a class. As indicated above, the conceptual scheme we use in experience typically identifies individuals in terms of spatial-temporal locations and properties. We can easily recognize these features in our commonsense ideas that every existing (physical) object must occupy some place at any given time, and that numerically distinct objects cannot occupy the same place at the same time. Similarly, we assume that when an object changes its spatial location, it must traverse a continuous path from one place to the other, and so on. Put semantically, the primary function of the quantitative categories is to allow us to identify the individuals to which singular terms refer.

The categorial concepts listed under quality are presupposed in ascribing predicates to individuals in affirmative and negative judgments. Our basis for recognizing predicates is the empirical data given in sensation, which we represent as sensory qualities located in space and time. In order to formulate empirical predicates we must be able to differentiate qualities, which means we must conceive of the sensory

---

[14] My account follows the discussions in Melnick's *Kant's Analogies of Experience*, 37–42, Allison's *Kant's Transcendental Idealism*, chapter 6, and Falkenstein's *Kant's Intuitionism*, 241–4.

data in terms of reality and negation.[15] The presence of a quality corresponds to the reality of some property, which we can predicate of objects. Conversely, the absence of a quality corresponds to the negation of a property, which can be expressed in a negative judgment. Kant says the third moment, limitation, "is reality combined with negation" (B111). This is spelled out later, in the Anticipations of Perception in the Analytic of Principles, where Kant analyzes the nature of sensation. There he argues that we can know *a priori* that every sensation must have some intensive magnitude or degree. Examples of intensive qualities are the brightness of colors, sensations of hot and cold, and the loudness of sounds. Kant believes that in order to recognize a particular degree of intensity, we must think of the given degree as representing a limit on the reality being sensed. Like the quantitative categories, the qualitative categories are interdependent, with all three required to recognize the presence or absence of a sensory quality having some degree of intensity.

The relational categories corresponding to simple and complex judgment forms are the controversial metaphysical concepts of substance–accident, cause–effect, and mutual causal interaction. Kant himself admits at B111–12 that the correlations in the first two cases are more obvious than in the third. The concepts of substance and accident are real correlates of the logical notions of subject and predicate. In a typical categorical judgment, the predicate signifies a property, and the logical subject signifies a bearer of properties. When these notions are interpreted temporally, they become the notions of substance and accident. Substances are things persisting through time (Kant will argue that they must be permanent), and accidents are their transitory states. Now Kant is not claiming that all categorical judgments in fact ascribe accidents to permanent substances. For example, in the judgment "Red is a color," the logical subject 'red' does not designate a substance, and being a color would not be a temporary state. What Kant is claiming, however, is that to judge existing states of affairs by the categorical form requires us to distinguish between transitory states and the permanent bearers of those states.

---

[15] Kant's claim is not that the real property is identical to the quality, but rather that the quality provides evidence of the property. We do not literally sense gravitational or magnetic forces, for example, but take them to be causes of the weight and motions of bodies. See A226/B273.

Similarly, the concepts of cause and effect are temporalized versions of the logical notions of ground and consequent expressed in hypothetical judgments. As we saw earlier, Kant thinks of the conditional as expressing a necessary connection between the antecedent and consequent. When this notion is applied to events in time, it becomes the idea of a state that follows necessarily from another state according to a rule. In the case of real relations among states, the rules are causal laws. As with categorical judgments, Kant is not claiming that all hypothetical judgments are used to make causal claims. Rather, his point is that whenever we apply the notion of ground and consequent to existing states of affairs, we must conceive of the two states as related by causal laws.[16]

Finally, Kant correlates the category of causal interaction with disjunctive judgments. He thinks the concept of a system of substances that mutually determine each others' states is the real version of the logical idea of a systematic totality of alternatives. As I remarked above, he himself admits this is obscure. Again, we examine this view more closely in the Analogies of Experience. Kant's proofs of the principles corresponding to the categories in that section demonstrate how these categories function to order states of affairs in time.

The categories under modality are the three pairs of concepts possibility–impossibility, existence–nonexistence, and necessity–contingency. Since Kant says almost nothing about them here, I shall briefly sketch his views. Just as the modal forms of judgment are not part of the content of judgment, the modal categories do not add content to our concepts of objects, but only concern the ways the understanding thinks the states of affairs about which we judge. Since the modal categories are semantic rather than syntactic concepts, they are concepts of real (rather than logical) possibility, actuality, and necessity. Here is what Kant has in mind. In order to formulate a proposition that is assertible, that is, to judge problematically, one has to think the objects being judged in terms of whether they are really possible. Really possible objects are those that agree with the formal conditions of experience, namely the pure

---

[16] Commentators who discuss the correlation between conditionals and causal claims include Broad, *Kant*, 100, Paton, *Kant's Metaphysic of Experience*, 1:299, Bird, *Kant's Theory of Knowledge*, 105–7, Melnick, *Kant's Analogies of Experience*, 55–6, and Allison, *Kant's Transcendental Idealism*, 120–2.

forms of intuition and the categories of quantity, quality, and relation. For example, whereas a three-dimensional spatial object would be a really possible object of experience for us, a four-dimensional spatial object would not. Corresponding to the assertoric mode of judging are the concepts of real existence (or actuality) and nonexistence. Thus, asserting that some state of affairs does or does not obtain presupposes that we can recognize whether the objects of judgment do or do not actually exist. We do this by means of empirical intuition. Finally, our ability to draw conclusions according to rules of inference implies that we can discriminate between states of affairs that do and do not follow necessarily from other states according to causal laws.

This discussion gives us some idea of how Kant conceives the relation between the categories and the forms of judgment. We have seen that the concepts of the forms of judgment are logical or syntactic concepts, whereas the categories are real or first-order concepts of objects. One question commentators have raised concerns how many sets of concepts there are: are these two distinct sets, or is there one set of concepts with two different uses? As Allison points out, Kant says explicitly at B143: "the *categories* are nothing other than these very functions for judging, insofar as the manifold of a given intuition is determined with regard to them."[17] This implies that there is one set of concepts with two uses, logical and real. Strictly speaking, the categories are pure concepts of the understanding in their real use. The meaning of each category thus has two components, one logical and one sensible. As we saw above, for example, the concepts of substance and accident interpret the logical notions of subject and predicate temporally as permanent bearers of transitory states. Similarly, the concepts of cause and effect interpret the logical notions of ground and consequent as a necessary succession of states in time. Kant calls the sensible component the *schema* of the category. In the Analytic of Principles, in the chapter on the Schematism, Kant explains why a schema is necessary and what it consists in. From a semantic point of view, the schema provides a criterion for applying the pure concept to the data of intuition.

---

[17] Allison, *Kant's Transcendental Idealism*, 126–7. Other passages where Kant makes the same point are the *Prolegomena*, section 39, and the *MFNS*, *Theoretical Philosophy after 1781*, 189.

Before we leave this exposition of the Metaphysical Deduction, there is a last point to make about Kant's theory of the forms of judgment and the categories. Kant believes that it is simply a brute fact about humans that we judge by these logical forms. At B145–6 he says this about the unity of apperception or self-consciousness, which is the starting point for the B edition Transcendental Deduction of the categories:

> But for the peculiarity of our understanding, that it is able to bring about the unity of apperception *a priori* only by means of the categories and only through precisely this kind and number of them, a further ground may be offered just as little as one can be offered for why we have precisely these and no other functions for judgment or for why space and time are the sole forms of our possible intuition.

Just as we cannot explain why we intuit objects in three-dimensional Euclidean space and one-dimensional time, so we cannot explain why our judging has exactly these logical characteristics. There is no absolute necessity attaching to either the pure forms of intuition or the forms of judgment: there could be beings whose forms of intuition and judgment are different from ours. Clearly a being who did not intuit objects temporally could not think according to the categories of substance and cause as explained above. Such an experience would be so removed from ours that we could not fathom it. Like the judgments of mathematics, the synthetic *a priori* cognitions of the understanding are necessary only in a relative sense, for perceivers with our forms of sensibility and understanding. Why we have these forms of intuition and thought is beyond explanation.

3. CONCEPTS AND SINGULAR JUDGMENTS

The last point concerns how to reconcile Kant's notion of singular judgments with the view that concepts are general representations. One question is whether Kant's theory of representation allows for the notion of a singular term. As we saw above, all simple judgments are composed of a subject and a predicate, united by the copula. In singular judgments, the subject represents an individual rather than a class. But this apparently contradicts Kant's view that all concepts are general. If there are no singular concepts, then we must ask how he would analyze singular terms such as proper names and definite descriptions. Jaakko Hintikka argues that "Kant's notion of intuition is not very far from what we would call a singular term."[18] In response, Manley Thompson claims that Kant's doctrine precludes taking intuitions "as the subjects and as being represented by either proper names or demonstrative pronouns."[19] Despite lacking a theory of language, Kant makes some remarks about linguistic meaning in his lectures on logic. These suggest an account of singular terms that tends to support Thompson's view.

First, despite some sloppy terminology, Kant consistently maintains that concepts are general representations. These remarks from the *Jäsche Logic* are characteristic:

A concept is opposed to intuition, for it is a universal representation . . . It is a mere tautology to speak of universal or common concepts – a mistake that is grounded in an incorrect division of concepts into *universal, particular,* and *singular.* Concepts themselves cannot be so divided, but only *their use.*[20]

Hintikka is right that Kant frequently misrepresents this position in his writings. For example, in section 21 of the *Jäsche Logic* he says "in a singular judgment . . . a concept that has no sphere at all is enclosed, merely as part then, under the sphere of another."[21] Despite this misstatement, he more consistently maintains that although concepts are general, they can have singular *linguistic uses.* In the *Vienna Logic* he illustrates universal, particular, and singular uses of the concept 'house': "If I say of all houses, now, that they must have a roof, then this is the *usus universalis* . . . But a particular use is concerned only with many. E.g., some houses must have a gate. Or I use the concept only for an individual thing. E.g., this house is plastered in this way or that."[22] And in the *Dohna-Wundlacken Logic* he says this about language: "As soon as I make use of words, the representation [Socrates] is an individual concept."[23] These passages show Kant distinguishing between representations and their linguistic expressions. Following Thompson, we can make sense of his view.

---

[18] Hintikka, "On Kant's Notion of Intuition," 43.
[19] Thompson, "Singular Terms and Intuitions in Kant's Epistemology," 329.
[20] *Jäsche Logic, Lectures on Logic,* 589. See also the *Blomberg Logic,* 201, and the *Vienna Logic,* 349.
[21] *Lectures on Logic,* 598.   [22] *Lectures on Logic,* 352.   [23] *Lectures on Logic,* 487.

Kant recognizes that both the name "Socrates" and the demonstrative term "this house" are used to refer to individuals, even though the latter expression contains the general term "house." Now reference to individuals presupposes the ability to individuate objects in experience. And according to Kant's theory of synthesis, individuating objects requires synthesis of intuition by concepts. As Thompson points out, language is by its nature discursive and rule-governed.[24] It is a mistake to try to correlate linguistic expressions or their uses with either concepts or intuitions. So rather than speaking of subject-concepts in the case of singular judgments, Kant should have spoken of subject-terms or (as we would today) referring expressions. Once we distinguish between concepts and their linguistic expressions, there is no difficulty reconciling the generality of concepts with the fact that subject-terms in judgments may be singular linguistic expressions.

4. SUMMARY

The Metaphysical Deduction is the first stage in Kant's argument for the categories, in which he identifies the pure concepts of the understanding. The argument has two parts. First Kant establishes that the understanding has one function, which is to judge. He then identifies the pure concepts based on the forms of judgment, all the possible ways in which one can judge. The concepts of these judgment forms represent logical or syntactic features of judgment, such as subject and predicate. Thus a list of the forms of judgment yields a complete system of pure concepts in their logical use. In the second part Kant argues that these pure logical concepts also have a real use, as first-order or semantic concepts of the objects about which one judges. This follows from his analysis of judgment as synthesis, and the claim that the same synthetic operations that produce judgments also produce unified representations of space and time from the manifold of pure intuition. Thus Kant concludes that the pure concepts expressing logical features of judgment can represent categorial features of the objects being judged. This is the first step in arguing for synthetic *a priori* knowledge of the understanding.

---

[24] Thompson, "Singular Terms and Intuitions in Kant's Epistemology," 333–5.

CHAPTER 5

The Transcendental Deduction of the categories

The Transcendental Deduction of the categories is the heart of the *Critique of Pure Reason*. Here Kant argues that we are justified in applying pure concepts of the understanding to objects of experience. His strategy is to show that the categories are necessary conditions for experiencing objects given in intuition. Kant completely revised this section in the B edition; here we shall examine both the A and B edition versions, to understand what was lacking in the 1781 version. As many readers are disappointed to discover, both deductions treat the categories as a group. Not until the Principles of Pure Understanding does Kant defend individual categories.

In the A edition Preface to the *Critique*, Kant says the deduction of the categories "has two sides," one objective, the other subjective. The objective side must "demonstrate and make comprehensible the objective validity of its concepts *a priori*" and thus is essential to his project. The subjective side is less essential and concerns "the powers of cognition on which [the understanding] rests" (Axvi–xvii). Many commentators have assumed that Kant is referring to two distinct proofs, one concerning conditions for experiencing objects, the other the subjective sources of experience. As we shall see, there is reason to reject this reading.

This chapter proceeds as follows. Section 1 treats the introduction, common to both editions, and then considers the question of the objective and subjective deductions. The A edition argument and its weaknesses are the subject of section 2. Section 3 then discusses the complex B edition argument. Finally, in section 4 I highlight the revolutionary nature of Kant's theory of judgment.

The introduction is undoubtedly the most comprehensible part of the Transcendental Deduction. The first paragraph explains that a transcendental deduction is a normative argument justifying the use of a concept, as opposed to a factual argument concerning its actual use. Empirical concepts do not require such a deduction because experience can "prove their objective reality" (A84/B116–17), or their application to objects of experience. There are also "usurpatory concepts," such as fortune and fate, whose validity is subject to question. But the deduction concerns the pure concepts of the understanding, which are not derived from experience, and therefore require a special proof to justify their use in experience.

Kant next explains the particular difficulty in justifying these concepts. First, transcendental deductions differ from empirical deductions, which can show only how a concept is acquired through experience, and thus cannot justify *a priori* concepts. There are actually two types of *a priori* concepts: those originating in the forms of sensibility, space and time, and those originating in the understanding (A85/B118). His reference to "concepts" of space and time is not accidental; all mathematical concepts as well as concepts of spatial and temporal features are also pure despite their basis in the forms of intuition. From A88 to A90/B120 to B122 Kant explains why it is more difficult to justify pure concepts produced by the understanding. First, despite their *a priori* origin, mathematical concepts (e.g., a triangular shape) can be displayed in intuition, but this is not true of concepts such as substance–accident and cause–effect. Second, Kant believes the Aesthetic proofs that space and time are forms of intuition establish the validity of spatiotemporal and mathematical concepts for objects given to the senses. By contrast, pure concepts of the understanding have no original connection to the sensibility, and so their application to appearances demands an additional argument. As he says at A90/B122–3, objects given in intuition must accord with the pure forms of sensibility since "otherwise they would not be objects for us"; but that they must also accord with the conditions of thought "is a conclusion that is not so easily seen." And just below: "Appearances would nonetheless offer objects to our intuition, for intuition by no means requires the functions of thinking" (A90–1/B123).

Now it is important not to misunderstand this point. Kant will in fact argue that for any intuition to represent an object, it must be subject to the categories. All he is claiming here is that the independence of the sensibility from the intellect entails the logical possibility that we receive sensory data to which pure concepts do not apply. For example, appearances might be so haphazard that no causal connections can be discerned. The problem is precisely how subjective forms of thought can apply necessarily to the data given through the senses.

At section 14 Kant details his strategy. He reiterates the alternatives previously outlined: either the object makes the representation possible, or the representation makes the object possible. In the first case, the representation depends on the nature of the object, and so only *a posteriori* representations can arise. By implication, the only way a representation can apply necessarily to an object is if it makes the object possible. Kant is careful to specify at A92/B125, however, that only the nature and not the existence of the object depends on the representation. Thus by "making the object possible" Kant means the representation *presents as an object* whatever is given to us as existing. Clearly he rejects the phenomenalist view that particular acts of representing bring objects into existence.

Following this analysis, the issue is whether pure concepts are necessary conditions under which anything can be "thought as object in general" (A93/B125–6). If so, then these concepts are presupposed in all experience of objects. The Transcendental Deduction must show that pure concepts of the understanding relate "*a priori* to objects of experience, since only by means of them can any object of experience be thought at all" (A93/B126). In closing the A edition Introduction, Kant lists the three subjective sources of experience: sense, imagination, and apperception or self-consciousness, which is the ultimate basis of the understanding. He also remarks that each of these capacities has both empirical and transcendental functions. By contrast, the B edition emphasizes the failures of the empiricists to account for such concepts as substance and causality. Unlike Locke, Hume recognized the impossibility of a straightforward empirical deduction. But since he did not think the mind could produce ideas independent of impressions, Hume traced metaphysical concepts to the psychological process of association, thus offering an indirect empirical deduction.

As Kant sees it, Hume mistakes the objective necessity of pure concepts for a merely subjective necessity based on experience.

Before proceeding, let us return to Kant's distinction between an objective and a subjective deduction. Taken literally, the objective proof should proceed without any reference to subjective capacities. But since this is not possible, commentators have gone to interesting lengths to identify the two sides.[1] In *Kant and the Mind*, however, Andrew Brook sensibly remarks that both editions base the objective validity of the categories on the theory of synthesis, an account of the subjective sources of experience. Thus the distinction cannot mark out two different proofs.[2] In fact, Kant makes the same point at A97. Since the objective validity of the categories depends on their necessity for thinking of objects, "we must first assess not the empirical but the transcendental constitution of the subjective sources that comprise the *a priori* foundations for the possibility of experience" (A96–7). Clearly the distinction between "objective" and "subjective" sides of the deduction marks two aspects of one argument. In fact, Kant drops the distinction in the B edition, where the argument is clearly continuous.

2. THE A EDITION DEDUCTION

Everyone agrees that the 1781 proof fails miserably. Nevertheless, the argument introduces the key notions of the synthesis of imagination, the transcendental unity of apperception, and the correlation between objectivity and subjectivity. Moreover, independently of Kant's larger project, it soundly refutes the empiricist doctrine that all ideas are derived from experience. Finally, the contrast between the A and B edition deductions brings into relief the key elements of the more successful proof. Thus there are good reasons to examine the first edition proof.

Kant begins by claiming that it is impossible for an *a priori* concept to represent an object independently of intuition, for only intuition can give objective reality or content to the concept. Otherwise it

[1] Whereas Kemp Smith claims the B edition ignores the subjective side, Paton thinks both sides appear in both editions. See Kemp Smith, *Commentary*, xliv, 235–48 *passim*; and Paton, *Kant's Metaphysic of Experience*, 1:350–3, 499ff, 526ff.
[2] Brook, *Kant and the Mind*, 120.

would "be only the logical form for a concept," and not a concept through which one thinks an object. Since the "objective reality" of a concept is its application to whatever exists, his point is that the content of any meaningful concept must relate in some way to spatiotemporal appearances. If it failed to do so, the concept might have the logical form of a predicate, namely generality, but would lack any feature allowing us to recognize instances in experience. At A96 Kant says establishing the validity of pure concepts requires demonstrating their necessity for experience of objects.

Kant next makes a point essential to the deduction, that to qualify as a cognition, a representation must be inherently complex. Perhaps because of its intuitive plausibility, he offers no support for it here, remarking only that cognition "is a whole of compared and connected representations" (A97). At A99 he implicitly links this claim to the fact that all representations occur in one time. According to this view, a simple, unanalyzable impression could not by itself represent an object. In the B edition Kant justifies the complexity of cognition more systematically.

Although most commentators take the four numbered sections detailing the threefold synthesis to constitute the A edition deduction, the Preliminary Remark claims that this discussion is only preparatory to the systematic exposition, located in section 3. In fact, that later discussion contains many points that assume prominence in the B edition deduction. Despite Kant's description of that exposition as systematic, his failure to present a unified argument clearly necessitated the complete reworking of the deduction.

To understand the A edition strategy we need to recognize his peculiar treatment of the threefold synthesis. As Paton points out, the three "parts" are not separate stages but different ways of describing the same process. The parts are related in Chinese box fashion, so that each subsequently described synthesis is contained in the stage previously described.[3] Thus the first description, of the synthesis of apprehension in intuition, gives the most general characterization. Kant then argues that that process must include the second "part," the synthesis of reproduction in the imagination. The third step similarly argues that the synthesis of reproduction presupposes the synthesis

[3] See Paton, *Kant's Metaphysic of Experience*, 1:354–5.

of recognition in the concept. Finally Kant introduces the ultimate necessary condition of the entire complex process, the transcendental unity of apperception or "I think."

Kant begins the three-step argument by claiming that all representations are subject to time, and therefore bear temporal relations to every other representation (A98–9). Consequently "they must all be ordered, connected, and brought into relations" in time. He next returns to his characterization of cognition as complex, pointing out that as a cognition of an object, every intuition contains a manifold. In order to recognize this complexity, we must apprehend the parts successively, at distinct times. The process of unifying the successively apprehended parts into one representation is the synthesis of apprehension in intuition. Kant says that although the intuition provides a manifold, it cannot be "contained *in one representation*, without the occurrence of such a synthesis" (A99). Not until the next step does he attribute this activity to the imagination.

This first step assumes that we in fact have empirical intuitions that we recognize as complex. A complex representation is a representation of a single, unified thing made up of parts. Recognizing the complexity means being aware of both the parts and their unity. To intuit an apple, for example, as red, hard, juicy, in a certain space, and existing through a certain time, means representing it as one object having these diverse characteristics. Now because the sensibility passively receives the intuitive data, our recognition of both complexity and unity requires us actively to discriminate the parts before unifying them. As Kant says, "for **as contained in one moment** no representation can ever be anything other than absolute unity" (A99). In other words, any data apprehended only instantaneously or nonsuccessively cannot be recognized as having parts. Now this view has an interesting implication, namely that the manifold of intuition is not composed of absolute or "simple" parts. Because space and time are infinitely divisible, any intuited manifold can be discriminated into parts of any degree of complexity (e.g., spatial and temporal parts). In consequence, the degree of complexity is relative, depending on the fineness with which one discriminates parts. Kant's point is that producing a unified complex representation presupposes two distinct capacities: apprehending the parts successively and unifying them into a whole.

At A99–100 Kant remarks in passing that synthesis must also be performed on the *a priori* manifold given in intuition. Space and time, too, are represented as wholes divisible into parts. Just as sense impressions must be connected to represent unified objects, so the spatial and temporal data must be connected to represent one space and one time. This hints at the dual role of pure intuition: as forms of sensibility, space and time provide frameworks for receiving the empirical data; as pure manifolds, they provide a content for pure concepts of the understanding. The A edition focus on empirical intuition obscures the crucial second role, a defect remedied in 1787. Here Kant merely asserts that there is a pure as well as an empirical synthesis of apprehension. He should say, of course, that the synthesis of apprehension has both pure and empirical aspects.

The next step argues that for the synthesis of apprehension to occur, the imagination must reproduce representations. Unfortunately the order of presentation muddles the argument, which has two steps. The main point, located in the second half of the second paragraph, is that apprehending identifiable objects requires reproducing in imagination the previously apprehended parts. Kant then argues that this process is a transcendental act of the imagination, presupposed in all empirical association. The entire argument assumes that when we have a single complex representation, we are aware of both the discriminated parts and the unity binding them into a whole. Now previously Kant stated that the parts must be discriminated in successive moments. So to end up with a unified representation, the imagination must reproduce the parts previously apprehended. Consider the example of counting. The resulting number is a complex whole composed of units. Kant points out that if one did not reproduce the previously apprehended units as one progresses, "no whole representation . . . could ever arise" (A102). When counting to two, for example, one must think of the second unit as distinct from the first unit. Otherwise one would merely apprehend one unit twice. But in order to represent this relation between the two units, the imagination must actually reproduce the thought of the first unit. The same is true in drawing a line or thinking of some period of time. Each succeeding part must be thought in its relation to the already apprehended parts to represent the entire line or time period. As Michael Young points out, this does not mean "reliving" the experience, but rather incorporating the thought of the previous parts into the thought of each successively represented part.[4] These examples are noteworthy because they involve the synthesis of parts of space and time: even our *a priori* intuitions provide cognition only on the condition that they contain a thoroughgoing synthesis of reproduction. Consequently the synthesis of imagination is grounded "on *a priori* principles, and one must assume a pure transcendental synthesis of this power, which grounds even the possibility of all experience" (A101).

Kant reinforces this conclusion at A100–1, by criticizing attempts to derive ideas of objects from associations based on experience. Here he argues that the psychological process of association presupposes the *a priori* synthesis of the manifolds of space and time. Suppose, for example, that smelling a certain odor evokes a certain childhood memory. In this empirical association, the imagination must connect not only the qualitative aspects but also the times and places of the two experiences. But the ground that permits identifying times and spaces cannot be derived from the association, since spatiotemporal regions are presupposed in discriminating experiences. Thus Kant concludes that the imagination must perform a transcendental function, presupposed by experience, enabling us to "call up" the previously apprehended parts of the manifold. Reproducibility is a necessary condition for representing not only empirical objects but also space and time themselves as complex wholes.

The third section is the most complex, for here Kant introduces both the relation between concepts and the transcendental unity of apperception, and the correlation between objectivity and subjectivity. In this way he relates pure concepts to both the necessity of self-consciousness and the idea of objectivity. Unfortunately, the argument is completely done in by its unsystematic presentation. Kant first argues that the synthesis of reproduction requires the synthesis of recognition in a concept: "Without consciousness that that which we think is the very same as what we thought a moment before, all reproduction in the series of representations would be in vain" (A103). This requires the use of concepts because recognizing something as the same thing previously apprehended requires conceiving that thing under some predicate F. In counting, for example, one can reproduce

---

[4] Young, "Kant's View of Imagination," especially 147ff.

previously apprehended units only if one recognizes the reproduced parts as the same units previously apprehended. Ultimately, to represent the resulting integer, we must conceive the units as parts related by the addition operation: Kant says the concept of number "consists solely in the consciousness of this unity of the synthesis" (A103). In other words, to generate representations of unified things composed of parts, we must employ concepts of both the whole towards which one is progressing, as well as the parts composing it. Although Kant has not yet connected these concepts to the categories, he has shown that a system for conceiving part–whole relations is presupposed in experience of complex particulars.

The remainder of this passage links pure concepts to the experience of objectivity and the necessity of self-consciousness. Kant's presentation is so badly organized, however, that it is not easy to see the connections between these ideas. From A103 to A111 he appears to make this argument:

1. Consciousness of conceptual unity presupposes a unitary consciousness. (A103–4)
2. The notion of an object of representation includes the idea of a necessary unity. (A104–6; A108–9)
3. Consciousness of objective unity requires a transcendental self-consciousness (as opposed to an empirical self-consciousness). Awareness of this identical self makes possible the notion of a transcendental object. (A106–7; A108)
4. A transcendental self-consciousness is consciousness of unity of synthesis by means of pure concepts. (A107–8)
5. Thus the pure concepts are presupposed in all objective awareness. (A109–11)

One can see from this summary why the A edition deduction is deemed a failure. Nevertheless, let us examine the main points, to prepare for the B edition proof.

At A103–4 Kant connects the unity thought through concepts with a unitary consciousness. We saw that in counting, the concept of the number represents the whole resulting from a successive addition of units. Like the concept of number, all concepts represent the unity of a manifold, insofar as they are ways of thinking part–whole relations. Now Kant argues that consciousness of conceptual unity presupposes a unitary consciousness. To end up with a single complex representation, the manifold being unified must be united in a single consciousness. William James revisited this point in the nineteenth century by arguing that giving each of twelve persons one word of a twelve-word sentence does not result in any consciousness of the entire sentence.[5] Despite its necessity, however, Kant says we may not always be aware of this unity of consciousness:

> This consciousness may often only be weak, so that we connect it with the generation of the representation only in the effect, but not in the act itself, i.e., immediately; but regardless of these differences one consciousness must always be found, even if it lacks conspicuous clarity, and without that concepts, and with them cognition of objects, would be entirely impossible. (A103–4)

Although it is not apparent, Kant is getting at more than the point that "it takes one to know one," as Allison puts it.[6] For from A107 on, Kant wants to connect concepts not just to numerically identical consciousness, but to *awareness* of the identity of consciousness, that is, identical *self*-consciousness. His term for this self-consciousness is the *transcendental unity of apperception* (henceforth t.u.a.). This slide from a unitary consciousness to a necessary self-consciousness is one weakness in the A edition argument.

Kant actually introduces the necessity of self-consciousness through an analysis of objectivity, which he then connects to pure concepts. At A104–5 he notes that the object of a representation is thought of as something "corresponding to and therefore also distinct from the cognition." That is, in taking a mental state to represent an object, I at least implicitly distinguish the object from my awareness of it. Although I may think that my awareness corresponds to the object, I must also recognize that the object is independent of it. This leads to the second aspect, the necessity implied by objectivity. Kant says the object is that which prevents "cognitions being determined at pleasure or arbitrarily rather than being determined *a priori*, since insofar as they are to relate to an object our cognitions must also necessarily agree with each other in relation to it" (A104). Representations of an object must conform to the rules governing it, and hence they must possess a necessary unity. At A109 Kant labels the object of

---

[5] Cited by Kemp Smith, *Commentary*, 459.
[6] Allison, *Kant's Transcendental Idealism*, 139.

a representation the "transcendental object = X." This notion of the transcendental object is merely formal and has no particular content; it is common to every representation of an objective state of affairs. Kant says it "cannot contain any determinate intuition at all," and thus represents only the unity of a "manifold of cognition insofar as it stands in relation to an object" (A109).

The next stage connects the necessary unity of the transcendental object to the t.u.a. Recall that the Aesthetic argues that we are directly acquainted only with appearances, which, from the transcendental standpoint, are our own representations. Whatever the appearances stand for – the thing in itself – is a cipher (X) to us. Since we cannot get "behind" the appearance, our awareness of unity cannot be derived from the thing itself. By elimination, the only source of this necessary unity is the subject, the unity of consciousness: "the unity that the object makes necessary can be nothing other than the formal unity of the consciousness in the synthesis of the manifold of representations" (A105). In short, the data of intuition acquires its representative relation to an object only when it is brought to the t.u.a. The thought that what appears in intuition is an object existing independently of one's awareness of it, is produced in the process of uniting the manifold in an identical consciousness. At A108 Kant reiterates that pure apperception is simply consciousness of the act of synthesis: for the mind could not think its own identity *a priori* in the manifold of representations "if it did not have before its eyes the identity of its action, which subjects all synthesis of apprehension (which is empirical) to a transcendental unity." As we saw above, this entails only the *possibility* of recognizing the identity of self-consciousness, rather than its *actual* recognition.

Kant next distinguishes this transcendental self-consciousness from empirical self-consciousness. He agrees with Hume that consciousness of the self given in intuition is empirical and constantly changing: "it can provide no standing or abiding self in this stream of inner appearances . . . That which should *necessarily* be represented as numerically identical cannot be thought of as such through empirical data" (A107). Empirical apperception is awareness of oneself as a particular subject. As Hume puts it, it is awareness of one's own "bundle of perceptions," which has a constantly changing content. In representing our empirical selves, we take ourselves as objects of experience, distinct from other objects, including other subjects. Thus the concept of the empirical self differs for each consciousness. By contrast, the t.u.a. is a merely formal consciousness, and not the awareness of an object. It is simply the thought of the numerically identical subject of any mental state. Because it does not pick out a particular subject, it is the same thought for each thinker. Kant agrees with Hume that a flux of perceptions cannot provide the notion of a numerically identical consciousness. Hume failed to see, however, that such a consciousness is required to represent the necessary unity of any object, including oneself as an empirical consciousness. This is why Kant describes the t.u.a. as original:

> This pure, original unchanging consciousness I will now name *transcendental apperception* . . . even the purest objective unity, namely that of the *a priori* concepts (space and time) is possible only through relation of the intuitions to it. The numerical unity of this apperception therefore grounds all concepts *a priori*. (A107)

The t.u.a. is a primitive fact of our mental life, and cannot be derived from any other features of consciousness. On the contrary, all unified representations, pure or empirical, of physical or mental objects, presuppose it.

Kant's theory that the objectivity of representation originates in synthesis has a second important implication, namely that the ideas of the transcendental object and of the necessary unity of apperception are correlates. At A123 Kant says, "For the standing and lasting I (of pure apperception) constitutes the correlate of all our representations so far as it is merely possible to become conscious of them" as representations. To say they are correlates means that the ideas mutually imply one another: to be aware of an object of my representation is (at least implicitly) to distinguish objective from subjective states, and vice versa. This point becomes prominent in the B edition deduction.

The final step of the argument identifies the synthetic functions required to produce the idea of objectivity with pure concepts. The necessary unity essential to the idea of objectivity "is impossible if the intuition could not have been produced through a function of synthesis in accordance with a rule that makes the reproduction of the manifold necessary *a priori*" (A105). That is, the rules governing the synthetic operations that produce the idea of an object in general are contained in the categories. When we represent a triangle, for example, the relations among the sides of the triangle must conform to certain rules (e.g., that they enclose angles totaling 180°). These rules governing the ways the manifold is connected – the functions of synthesis – are contained in the concept of the triangle. Not until A110–11 does Kant argue explicitly that these concepts must be pure or *a priori*. Merely empirical concepts could not represent the necessity and universality required for objectivity. Thus Kant concludes that the categories "are fundamental concepts for thinking objects in general for the appearances, and they therefore have *a priori* objective validity" (A111). In sum, the categories contain the rules required to think the data given in intuition as representing objects or objective states of affairs. Consequently they apply necessarily to anything represented as an object.

In section 3, from A115 to A119, Kant presents the same ideas again, in an order closer to that of the B edition deduction. At A120 he then states that he will demonstrate the relation between the categories and appearances by starting from the opposite point, namely from the empirical data. In what follows he rehearses the argument concerning the threefold synthesis, from empirical unity to transcendental unity. It is understandable if the reader feels that Kant is rehashing the same material, without a clear sense of progress.

Although it foreshadows many of the ideas of the B edition deduction, the A edition version has several crucial defects. First, Kant fails to establish the necessity of transcendental self-consciousness for all thinking. Although awareness of objects requires a numerically identical consciousness, Kant does not explain the connection to *self*-consciousness. Second, Kant does not support his claim that this self-consciousness can occur only through synthetic acts. Finally, the notion of judgment is completely lacking in the A edition discussion. This is especially egregious, since Kant derived the pure concepts in the Metaphysical Deduction from the forms of judgment, and also claimed that the only function of the understanding is to judge. We shall see how his strategy in the B edition addresses these problems.

3. THE B EDITION DEDUCTION

a. Preliminary remarks

Commentators generally agree that the B edition proof divides into two parts, the first located in sections 15–20, and the second in sections 21–6. As stated in the title of section 20, the first part concludes that "All sensible intuitions stand under the categories, as conditions under which alone their manifold can come together in one consciousness" (B143). Kant's final conclusion, located at the end of section 26, is this: "all synthesis, through which even perception itself becomes possible, stands under the categories, and since experience is cognition through connected perceptions, the categories are conditions of the possibility of experience, and are thus valid *a priori* of all objects of experience" (B161). The difficulty is explaining the relation of the two parts.

Dieter Henrich made the first plausible argument that the two proofs are separate, yet both required to show that the categories are necessary conditions for experience of objects given in intuition. In the first step Kant assumes that the intuitions already "contain" unity, and he argues that wherever there is unity, it must be thought by means of the categories. But this does not yet guarantee that whatever we intuit will be subject to the categories. Kant needs the second argument to bring spatiotemporal intuitions under the range of intuitions containing unity, to prove that whatever we intuit spatially and temporally must thereby be thought by the categories.[7]

Henry Allison agrees that the two arguments are two steps in a single proof, but disagrees about the relation between them.[8] He maintains that the two steps use different notions of an object, drawing different conclusions about the categories. In the first step, Kant argues that the categories necessarily apply to any object of judgment for a discursive intelligence, one that thinks about objects given independently in an "intuition in general."[9] The notion of the object here

---

[7] Henrich, "The Proof-Structure of Kant's Transcendental Deduction," 642.

[8] See chapter 7 of *Kant's Transcendental Idealism*, 133–72. Allison criticizes Henrich's interpretation at 35in6.

[9] Kant classifies intelligences into intuitive and discursive. An intuitive intellect can, through the mere act of thinking, provide its own data for judgment (B135). Human intellect is discursive, since the sensibility provides our data for thought. The term "intuition in general" refers to any data given to a discursive intellect, regardless of its form.

is the object of thought, denoted by the German *Object*. This step attempts to demonstrate the *objective validity* of the categories, to show that they are required for thinking about objects. The second step argues that the categories apply necessarily to objects of experience, and thus have *objective reality*. The German word for object here is *Gegenstand*, which denotes the object given in intuition. Only in the second stage does Kant connect the categories to our form of spatiotemporal intuition. In this discussion I shall follow Allison's interpretation, since it provides a more coherent reading of the text.

b. Stage one: sections 15–20

Section 15: general characterization of synthesis

Section 15 establishes a claim crucial to Kant's theory of cognition, that for a discursive intellect, the manifold of intuition is not given as unified. Instead, (complex) representations are unified by means of thinking. This act of combining is a spontaneous act of the understanding (B130). Kant calls it *synthesis*,

> to draw attention to the fact that we can represent nothing as combined in the object without having previously combined it ourselves, and that among all representations *combination* is the only one that is not given through objects but can be executed only by the subject itself, since it is an act of its self-activity. (B130)

This is an important corrective to theories that overlook the role of the understanding in unifying sense impressions. Because sensibility is passive, it cannot combine the data given in intuition. Furthermore, even sense impressions given as spatially or temporally contiguous are not thereby unified into impressions of an object. Kant's point is that any combination recognized in a unified representation must be a *thought* combination. This is true even of the pure forms of space and time, which provide only *a priori* manifolds. This data can represent one space and time only insofar as we think of it as belonging to one space and time. At the end of this first paragraph Kant points out that such combinatory synthetic acts are always presupposed by analysis, acts which divide representations into parts. In order for us to separate out the parts of a complex representation, they must first have been combined. He will say more about this in section 16.

The final point of section 15 concerns the unity of consciousness required for synthetic acts of the understanding. Unified representations are those in which one is conscious both of the manifold parts and also of the their interconnection. In such a combination, the unity is *thought* by means of a concept. (This is important since there are forms of connection, such as association, which do not arise by means of concepts.) At B131 Kant points out that conceptual unity cannot result from the act of combining, since the former makes the combinatory act possible. Moreover, the fundamental unity of consciousness precedes even the category of unity correlated with the quantitative form of judgment, since all use of concepts in judgment presupposes unity of thought. Kant says this unity must be sought "someplace higher, namely in that which itself contains the ground of the unity of different concepts in judgments, and hence of the possibility of the understanding, even in its logical use" (B131). This is Kant's beginning point for his deduction in section 16.

Section 16: the original synthetic unity of apperception

The deduction officially begins here, where the first sentence states the first premise: "The *I think* must *be able* to accompany all my representations; for otherwise something would be represented in me that could not be thought at all, which is as much as to say that the representation would either be impossible or else at least would be nothing for me" (B131–2). This sentence includes several claims. First, it is necessarily true of me, as a discursive intellect, that I *can* attach the "I think" to any state that represents something to me. Kant is not saying that in fact I always do this, only that it must be possible for me. If I could not, he says, the representation would be "nothing for me." This means that states that represent something to me have two features: first, I can recognize them as my own states; and second, they have an intentional object of which I can be conscious. In other words, states that are representations for me have both subjective and objective aspects, which I can distinguish.[10]

Now the act of attaching the "I think" is the act of apperception or *self-consciousness*. Insofar as I recognize a representation as mine, I

---

[10] Allison says that the claim that such representations would be "nothing for me" does not imply that they would not exist, but rather that I would not be conscious of them as my representations. He believes Kant thinks we could have unconscious representations. See *Kant's Transcendental Idealism*, 137 and 353n18.

ascribe it to myself, and thus must be conscious of myself as the subject of the state. As in the A edition, Kant calls this self-consciousness the *transcendental unity of apperception* (t.u.a.), and he distinguishes it from empirical self-consciousness. The t.u.a. is original because it is not derived from any other representation, but is a primitive fact of consciousness. It is pure rather than empirical because it has no distinguishing content of its own. Kant says it is in all consciousness "one and the same, [and] cannot be accompanied by any further representation" (B132). Recall that empirical self-consciousness is awareness of oneself as a particular subject. In addition to the "I think" it includes the specific content of inner sense. By contrast, "through the I, as a simple representation, nothing manifold is given" (B135). In a later section in the Dialectic, Kant calls the I of apperception "a *single thing* that cannot be resolved into a plurality of subjects, and hence a logically simple subject" (B407). Thus the t.u.a. is the bare thought of the *numerical identity* of the self as the thinking subject.

In several passages Kant says this first premise is analytic: "this principle of the necessary unity of apperception is, to be sure, itself identical, thus an analytic proposition" (B135; also B138 and B407). Now it is important to understand exactly what claim is analytic, since from this premise Kant wants to derive the synthetic conclusion that the categories apply necessarily to any object of thought. The key is the scope of the statement, "The *I think* must be able to accompany all my representations." Kant is claiming not that this statement is analytically true of all conscious beings, but rather that it is analytically true for any consciousness that can recognize its own representations. There are two relevant contrasts here. At B138–9 Kant distinguishes human consciousness from an intuitive intellect which generates its own manifold through its thinking. For such an intellect, there is no distinction between subjective and objective states, and so such an intellect would not be capable of this original self-consciousness. The second contrast is with animal perceivers, which lack intellectual capacities altogether and thus cannot recognize their representations as such. They might have a unified consciousness, but they would lack a unified *self-consciousness*. In other words, it is a brute fact (and therefore a synthetic truth) that human perceivers are discursive intellects who can recognize their own representations. But it is an analytic truth that any consciousness that can recognize its own representations can attach the "I think" to any of them.

The second premise occurs at B133: "this thoroughgoing identity of the apperception of a manifold given in intuition contains a synthesis of the representations, and is possible only through the consciousness of this synthesis." To say that the t.u.a. "contains" a synthesis means that in order to think the identity of the "I" one must connect a manifold of representations in thought. To recognize that it is the same "I" in "I think a" and in "I think b" one must connect the thoughts so that one thinks "I think a + b." Kant's strong claim here is that performing such a synthesis is a necessary condition for recognizing the identity of self-consciousness. In thinking one's self-identity by ascribing representations to oneself, one both connects the representations and (at least implicitly) recognizes this connection. At B133–4 Kant repeats his A edition claim that consciousness of one's numerical identity cannot be derived from empirical self-consciousness. Instead, to recognize the empirical self requires one to unite the empirical manifold in a numerically identical consciousness. Thus empirical self-consciousness presupposes the t.u.a.

The final point in section 16 concerns Kant's claim at B133–4 that the apperception, like concepts, has both an analytical and a synthetic unity. This is easier to grasp if we begin with his discussion of concepts in the footnote. Here Kant argues that although both kinds of unity are essential to general representations, the synthetic unity provided by concepts is more fundamental than their analytical unity. The analytical unity of a concept is the unity it provides as a common characteristic of things. In thinking the concept "solidity," we recognize it as a feature that belongs to potentially many things. In representing a feature common to its instances, the concept provides analytic unity. But these instances are complex things, which have many different properties. For example, they must also be spatially extended and have other physical properties. Kant says the objects analytically united under the concept "also have something *different* in themselves" (B134). And he concludes: "therefore only by means of an antecedently conceived possible synthetic unity can I represent to myself the analytical unity." That is, to represent the objects that possess common characteristics, one must first represent the unity of the complex object. In its synthetic function, a concept unifies diverse features of the object. For example, the concept "chair" unifies the diverse properties such as shape, size, weight, and location that belong to a chair. Kant's point is that although concepts contain both kinds of unity, synthetic unity is more fundamental because it is presupposed by analytical unity.

At B133–4 he makes the same claim about the t.u.a.: "the *analytical* unity of apperception is only possible under the presupposition of some *synthetic* one." In other words, the "I think" as attached to each representation functions on one hand as a common characteristic. Abstracted from all content of representation, it has an analytic unity. But since this identical self-consciousness requires a synthesis of representations, the "I think" also produces a synthetic unity. In this respect it functions as the form of any thought in which one unifies different representations. For this reason Kant calls it "the highest point to which one must affix all use of the understanding ... indeed this faculty is the understanding itself" (B134n). In short, the t.u.a. is the very basis, and thus the form, of all thinking.

Section 17: the relation between the t.u.a. and the notion of an object

In section 17 Kant establishes what Allison calls the "reciprocity thesis," namely that the t.u.a. is both necessary and sufficient for representing objects.[11] This is equivalent to showing both that whenever one performs the "I think" one thereby represents an object (or objective state of affairs), and that whenever one represents an object one thereby connects representations in the synthetic unity of apperception. It does not become clear until section 19 that this act is judgment. Once we put these points together we can get a better idea of what Kant means by the *objective validity* of representation.

Kant's entire argument in section 17 is contained in the second paragraph:

> *Understanding* is, generally speaking, the faculty of *cognitions*. These consist in the determinate relation of given representations to an object. An *object*, however, is that in the concept of which the manifold of a given intuition is *united*. Now, however, all unification of representations requires unity of consciousness in the synthesis of them. Consequently the unity of consciousness is that which alone constitutes the relation of representations to an object, thus their objective validity, and consequently is that which makes them into cognitions and on which even the possibility of the understanding rests. (B137)

Let us take this argument point by point.

---

[11] See *Kant's Transcendental Idealism*, 144–8.

First Kant describes the understanding as the faculty of cognition, which implies that the mere data given in intuition are not in themselves cognitions. Next he defines a cognition as a "determinate relation of given representation to an object," which simply means a representation of a determinate object. His point is that the function of the understanding is to know objects. Implicit is the idea that at the first order, the representations are those given in the manifold of intuition. Next comes the key to this section, Kant's definition of an object as "that in the concept of which the manifold of a given intuition is *united*." This tortured sentence in effect defines an object as whatever is thought as a unified manifold by means of a concept. The object here is the object of thought; the definition establishes that it must be a complex whose parts (the manifold) are unified by a concept. Drawing on section 15, the next sentence states that all unified representations contain consciousness of unity. From section 16 we know that consciousness of unity is based on the t.u.a. Thus, Kant concludes, it is the t.u.a. that confers objective validity on representations. That is, the act of bringing representations to the "I think" is necessary and sufficient for making them into representations of an object. Put less technically, Kant has argued that when one unifies some manifold by means of a concept, one thereby renders the manifold *thinkable* as an object or gives it objective validity.

At B137–8 Kant emphasizes that the mere manifold given in intuition does not by itself represent an object, but provides only the data for cognition: "the mere form of outer sensible intuition, space, is not yet cognition at all; it only gives the manifold of intuition *a priori* for a possible cognition." To cognize some spatial region requires connecting the spatial manifold in some determinate way by means of a concept. Thus to represent a line in space one must delineate the part of space making up the line by means of the concept of a line. Kant concludes that this consciousness of synthetic unity is required of all cognitions, and thus applies to any manifold given in intuition "*in order to become an object for me.*" It is important to notice the subtle shift in this last sentence, which claims that the object *is* the (manifold of) intuition itself. In other words, this analysis has taken place on the second-order level, where the objects (of thought) are one's representations (the manifold given to one in intuition). At the end of this chapter we shall see the significance of this aspect for Kant's response to skepticism.

For now, let us summarize the steps of the argument in sections 16 and 17:

1. It is necessarily true of humans as discursive intellects that they can attach the "I think" to any of their representations, and, by doing so, express the numerical identity of self-consciousness.
2. Attaching the "I think" is possible only insofar as one connects one's self-ascribed representations by means of synthetic acts.
3. Any synthetic unity of representations requires unification under a concept.
4. Any manifold unified under a concept counts as a thought of an object.
5. Therefore, thinking of an object is necessary for the t.u.a.
6. Therefore, the t.u.a. is a sufficient condition for representing an object.

Section 18: objective vs. subjective unity

Here Kant distinguishes an objectively valid unity of representations from a unity that has only subjective validity, as a way to introduce the notion of judgment in section 19. The first kind is the unity contained in the thought of an object; the second kind is characteristic of a mere association of representations. Unfortunately Kant confuses two different notions of subjective validity. He begins section 18 by contrasting the *objective unity* of the t.u.a. with "the *subjective unity* of consciousness, which is a *determination of inner sense*" (B139). By the latter he means a mere association of representations in consciousness: "One person combines the representation of a certain word with one thing, another with something else; and the unity of consciousness in that which is empirical is not, with regard to that which is given, necessarily and universally valid" (B140).[12] The point is that although a mere association of representations has a kind of unity in consciousness, it is not a thought unity. Association occurs

---

[12] The process of association has historical significance because Hume took it to be the source of all metaphysical concepts, including personal identity. But Kant takes association as the paradigm example of a subjective unity since it connects representations in time without thereby representing an object.

when one representation immediately triggers another in time. It depends on memory and psychological processes arising from what Hume called the "customary conjunction" of representations. For this reason Kant assigns it to the reproductive imagination at B141. To say that an association is only subjectively valid means that it does not produce a representation of an object. (It is also subjective in the secondary sense that the association of representations depends on contingent facts about the subject.) When Kant calls this type of connection "a *determination of inner sense*" he means that it represents a temporal ordering of the actual contents of consciousness. But the connection is not conceptual; a mere association does not represent an object, and hence lacks objective validity. Associated perceptions are united temporally in consciousness, but do not produce a unity of self-consciousness. Now one can of course take an association as an object of thought by reflecting on it. In recognizing the sequence as one in which one representation triggers another, one thereby confers objective unity on it. This is equivalent to taking a unity *in* consciousness as a unity *for* consciousness. Clearly, however, the ability to associate representations does not entail the ability to represent the association as such. Kant thinks that animals possess the former ability but lack the intellectual capacities for the latter.

Unfortunately, in this passage Kant confuses the subjectivity of an association of perceptions with that of the empirical unity of apperception. The latter, as we have seen, is awareness of oneself as a particular subject. Empirical self-consciousness includes the content of inner sense, but is not a mere association of perceptions, since it represents the self as an object. Although empirical apperception varies in content by subject, and thus is subjective in the secondary sense, it nevertheless contains an objective unity of representations. Thus Kant is mistaken to use empirical apperception to exemplify a non-objective unity, which is the kind of subjectivity relevant to the deduction here.

Section 19: objective unity and judgment

In section 19 Kant argues that representing an object is equivalent to judging. He begins by complaining that the standard definition of a judgment as a relation between two concepts fails to specify the nature of the relation. At B141–2 he says that in judgment one brings a manifold to the objective unity of consciousness. In the simplest case of a categorical judgment, this objective relation is represented by the copula "is" connecting the subject- and predicate-concepts.[13] Now to say that judgment possesses a necessary unity is not to deny that there are empirical or contingent judgments. The objective unity of the judgment, even if empirical, resides in the fact that judgments represent assertible thoughts about objects or objective states of affairs. Even if it is only a contingent truth that my cat is orange, the judgment "Buroker's cat is orange" unifies diverse representations to produce an assertible claim about an object. Unfortunately Kant's examples at the end of the section obscure this point, since he tries to express an association of perceptions by the conditional judgment "If I carry a body, I feel a pressure of weight." By his own argument, however, once one judges an association, one has thereby unified the representations in the objective unity of apperception.[14] As Allison points out, Kant's theory of synthesis entails that all judgments confer objective validity on representations, even if the objects of judgment are "subjective" states.

This step clarifies the notion of objective validity, for unlike associations of representations, judgments are true or false. For a representation to have objective validity is for it to be capable of having a truth value. What Kant has shown, then, is that subjects who can recognize their own representations must be able to ascribe them to themselves by the "I think." This act is synthesis, which connects a given manifold of representations in the (objective) unity of self-consciousness. But synthesis is equivalent to judging; in judging one conceives a manifold as related in a way that can be asserted to obtain. Since assertions are true or false, Kant has argued that the t.u.a. is both necessary and sufficient for producing representations that have *objective validity*, that are assertible. The objects here are objects of

[13] For hypothetical and disjunctive judgments the objective unity of two judgments is effected by the logical operators "if-then" and "or."
[14] This is reminiscent of Kant's discussion of judgments of perception and judgments of experience in the *Prolegomena*. The former merely report perceptions, whereas the latter make objective claims. Kant's examples of the first are "The room is warm, sugar sweet, wormwood nasty" (see section 19). In this case he claims two sensations are referred to the same subject, but not to an object. Only when a judgment makes a claim about an object does it have objective validity. This view apparently contradicts Kant's position in the *Critique* that every judgment contains objective unity. Allison explains this and other difficulties with the *Prolegomena* account in *Kant's Transcendental Idealism*, 149–52. I am also indebted to his discussion at 152–8.

judgment or thought. There is as yet no reference to spatiotemporal objects of human intuition.

Section 20: the categories necessarily apply to all objects of judgment

The final step of this first stage relates judgment to the categories. Kant does this in the last three sentences of section 20:

> Therefore all manifold, insofar as it is given in **one** empirical intuition, is **determined** in regard to one of the logical functions for judgment, by means of which, namely, it is brought to a consciousness in general. But now the **categories** are nothing other than these very functions for judging, insofar as the manifold of a given intuition is determined with regard to them (§13). Thus the manifold in a given intuition also necessarily stands under categories. (B143)

Section 19 shows that insofar as a manifold is ascribed to oneself in the t.u.a., it must be judged. To judge a manifold is to think it as an object under the logical forms of judgment. As the Metaphysical Deduction shows, the logical forms of judgment are "functions of synthesis," or the particular ways one connects the representations making up a judgment in consciousness. Here Kant points out that the categories are these same logical functions in their real use. They are the pure concepts of the understanding as applied to whatever objects one judges.

To make the point clearer, consider that whenever I take several representations to be my representations, I judge that they belong to me. In so judging them I make them objects of thought. To judge them to belong to me requires conceiving of them in ways suitable for judging under the logical forms of judgment. For example, to judge them under the quantificational forms presupposes that I am able to identify and individuate them. This requires conceiving them under the concepts of unity, plurality, and totality. Thus I can make judgments about one representation, some representations, and all my representations. The same would presumably be true for the categories correlated with the logical forms of quality, relation, and modality.

There are two further points to mention here. First, Kant's reference to empirical intuition implies only that the manifold is given independently of the understanding, regardless of the forms of intuition. When the objects of thought just are one's representations, of course, the manifold is that given in inner sense. The second point concerns Kant's statement that the manifold must be determined by *one* of the logical functions for judgment. This is a clear mistake. First, Kant wants to argue that all the categories are necessary for judging objects. Moreover, as I argued in chapter 4, the three forms under each heading are interdependent. What Kant should say is that *all* the categories apply necessarily to the objects of judgment.

c. Stage two: sections 21–6

Sections 21–3: preliminary remarks to the second stage

At B144 Kant summarizes the argument so far, pointing out that it abstracts "from the way in which the manifold for an empirical intuition is given," attending only to the unity produced in intuition by means of the category. The second paragraph specifies that the argument assumes only that the manifold of intuition is given independently of the understanding. Thus the first part of the deduction establishes that any discursive intelligence, regardless of its particular mode of intuition, must employ categories to think about objects. The second stage of the deduction, by contrast, concerns the necessity of the categories for experiencing objects given in our spatiotemporal forms of intuition. Thus it attempts to show that the categories apply necessarily to all objects of human sensibility. To do this Kant will have to show that the same functions of synthesis employed in thinking about objects are also required to perceive objects in space and time. He makes this point at the beginning of section 26:

> Now the possibility of cognizing *a priori through categories* whatever objects *may come before our senses* . . . is to be explained. For if the categories did not serve in this way, it would not become clear why everything that may ever come before our senses must stand under the laws that arise *a priori* from the understanding alone. (B159–60)

Proving the necessity of the categories for cognition of objective states of affairs in our space and time involves demonstrating their *objective reality*.

Sections 22 and 23 merely reiterate these points, emphasizing the role of intuition in distinguishing between a thought and a cognition of an object. A concept to which no corresponding intuition could be given "would be a thought as far as its form is concerned," but without an object (*Gegenstand*), could not serve as a cognition (B146). Kant repeats the point at B150–1 in section 24. Only when given reference to intuition do the categories "acquire objective reality, i.e., application to objects that can be given to us in intuition" (B150–1). The second stage of the deduction, then, has to show that objects experienced in space and time must be thought by means of the categories.

Section 24: the transcendental synthesis of imagination

This section contains the first part of the second stage; section 26 completes the proof. Here Kant argues that the categories are required to represent one time in intuition, thus linking the categories to the perception of time. (Although Kant does not emphasize it here, the same process is required to represent one space.) The second step then links the categories to empirical intuition. The argument in section 24 is hard to make out, however, because it is embedded in a discussion of the "paradox" of self-representation, which is actually irrelevant to the deduction. I shall discuss first the argument proper and then the paradox as explained in sections 24 and 25.

The significance of time becomes clear if we see this stage as a continuation of the first stage. There Kant argued that the categories necessarily apply to objects of thought, which objects were in fact one's own representations. For humans, the form by which we intuit our own representations in inner sense is time. From the Aesthetic we know that there is only one time, and that all our representations occupy determinate positions in this unified time. Thus Kant will show in section 24 that the synthetic processes by which we locate our representations in one time are governed by the categories.

Kant assigns the transcendental synthesis of the *a priori* spatiotemporal manifold, called the figurative synthesis, to the productive imagination. At B151 he defines the imagination as "the faculty for representing an object even **without its presence** in intuition." We usually think of the imagination as the source of sensory images of objects that are not present or are even nonexistent. Here, however, Kant points out that the imagination plays a more basic role in experience, namely unifying the pure manifold into a representation of one global time. This act is transcendental because it is a necessary condition for representing anything as existing in time. Now although we do not perceive global time in its entirety, in perceiving determinate times, we think of each duration as bounded by past and future times, and thus as a finite portion of infinite time. These past and future times are of course not actually present in the perception; our awareness of them is a construction of the imagination. Similarly, our perceptions of finite regions of space include the recognition that these regions are embedded in an infinite space.

At B152 Kant attributes this figurative synthesis to the *productive* rather than to the *reproductive* imagination. Whereas the latter merely "calls up" (and associates) previously apprehended representations, the former produces a new representation. The figurative synthesis differs from the purely intellectual synthesis discussed in the first stage because it issues in an intuition. Intuitions of determinate positions and regions of one unified time require that the form of inner sense be linked to the t.u.a. and the categories. So there must be a faculty that mediates between the sensibility and the understanding. Now Kant's own descriptions of the imagination are fairly confusing. At B151 he says the imagination belongs to sensibility; but at B152 and B153 he says that its synthesis is an effect of the understanding on sensibility. For several reasons it is most consistent with his theory of faculties to treat the imagination as a separate power, mediating between the understanding and the sensibility. At B154–5 Kant uses examples of drawing figures in space to illustrate the transcendental synthesis of imagination. This is appropriate for two reasons: first, we can produce an image of time only through spatial representation; and second, the same imaginative processes are required to represent determinate spatial regions.

In effect Kant uses the theory that time is the form of inner sense to link the forms of intuition to the t.u.a. From the first stage of the deduction we know that any manifold brought to the t.u.a. must conform to the categories. Section 24 establishes that the *a priori* manifold given in inner sense is unified by the transcendental synthesis of the imagination. Thus the imaginative synthesis of the temporal manifold is also subject to the rules expressed in the categories. Alternatively, from the standpoint of judgment, to recognize each finite region of time is to judge that it is part of the all-encompassing time. Thus the temporal manifold must be thought by means of the categories. In this way the pure manifold is "objectified," or made a (formal) object of thought.

Section 26: link between categories and empirical intuition

In the final step, Kant needs to demonstrate the necessity of the categories for "whatever objects **may come before our senses**, not as far as the form of their intuition but rather as far as the laws of their combination are concerned" (B159–60). In other words, he must demonstrate that anything given through sensation "must stand under the laws that arise *a priori* from the understanding alone" (B160). His strategy is to link the categories to the synthetic processes required to unify the empirical manifold, that is, the sensible qualities constituting the matter of appearance. Kant calls this the synthesis of apprehension, which results in "the composition of the manifold in an empirical intuition, through which perception, i.e., empirical consciousness of it (as appearance), becomes possible" (B160). In Hume's terms these are the processes by which one "bundles" sense impressions. This was the primary focus of Kant's analysis in the A edition.

The key premise is that the synthetic operations performed on the empirical manifold must conform to the operations unifying the *a priori* manifold in the figurative synthesis discussed in section 24. There Kant argued that "space and time are represented *a priori* not merely as **forms** of sensible intuition, but also as **intuitions** themselves (which contain a manifold), and thus with the determination of the **unity** of this manifold in them" (B160–1). In a footnote he distinguishes the form of intuition, the uncombined manifold given *a priori*, from the formal intuition, the manifold unified by the transcendental synthesis of imagination. The second half of this footnote appears to contradict itself by attributing the unity of space and time both to sensibility and to the understanding. Kant's point, however, is that the manifold as given in sensibility makes it possible to experience one space and one time; synthesis by the understanding is required to experience a unified space and time. Thus everything appearing in intuition is subject to the synthetic functions that produce unity in our experiences of space and time, namely the categories:

Consequently all synthesis, through which even perception itself becomes possible, stands under the categories, and since experience is cognition through connected perceptions, the categories are conditions of the possibility of experience, and are thus also valid *a priori* of all objects of experience. (B161)

In other words, the three types of synthesis Kant discusses in the Transcendental Deduction are different aspects of the synthesis required to perceive objects of spatiotemporal intuition. What Kant has shown at each step is that only the categories can provide rules for unifying representations brought to the t.u.a. His deduction proceeds from the unity involved in the thought of an object (the intellectual synthesis), to the unity experienced in the formal intuitions of space and time (the figurative synthesis), and finally to the unity experienced in objects perceived in space and time (the synthesis of apprehension). It is important to recognize that these three syntheses are really three aspects of one process that takes place in sense perception.

This is the point of Kant's examples of perceiving a house and the freezing of water at B162–3. When I perceive a house, my perception of it as a determinate (measurable) object is constrained by the rules governing the processes by which I "carve out" the region of space it occupies. Similarly, my perception of the freezing of water as the fluid state followed by the solid state must also conform to the rules by which successive times are determined. Kant details these arguments in the Axioms of Intuition and the Analogies of Experience, in justifying the pure principles corresponding to the categories. These two examples capture the two aspects of Kant's conclusion, namely that the categories provide rules for unifying the manifold into perceptions of objects, as well as for connecting these perceptions in experience of an objective order of events.

Sections 24–5: the paradox of self-knowledge

To complete this discussion, let us look at Kant's view of self-knowledge in sections 24 and 25. At B152–3 he describes the "paradox" of self-knowledge as following from the Aesthetic doctrine that in inner sense we are presented to ourselves "only as we appear to ourselves, not as we are in ourselves, since we intuit ourselves only as we are internally **affected**, which seems to be contradictory, since we would have to relate to ourselves passively." The paradox follows from transcendental idealism. Because space and time are merely subjective forms of sensibility, all objects intuited in space and time are only appearances, and not things in themselves. This applies equally to the empirical self, given in inner sense. Accordingly, we can no more intuit the self in itself than we do physical objects in themselves. In the Analytic, however, Kant has shown that the "I" that thinks is active and spontaneous. Judging is an activity consisting of synthetic operations the "I" performs on the manifold given in intuition. So it seems paradoxical to claim both that the "I" must be active and that it can know itself only as it passively appears to itself.

Kant's solution is to deny both that the "I think" is a cognition of the self, and that we can cognize the thinking self. In transcendental self-consciousness, Kant says, "I am conscious of myself not as I appear to myself, nor *as* I am in myself, but only *that* I am. This *representation* is a *thinking*, not an *intuiting*" (B157). Self-awareness in the t.u.a. is not a cognition of the self as an object, but a merely formal representation of one's existence as thinking. (This is why Kant disagrees with Descartes's view that the "I" of the *cogito* must be a mental substance.) This self-awareness is devoid of the intuition required to distinguish oneself from other objects and thus to represent oneself as a particular object. In his footnote at B157 Kant says, "The **I think** expresses the act of determining my existence. The existence is thereby already given, but the way in which I am to determine it, i.e., the manifold that I am to posit in myself as belonging to it, is not yet thereby given." And at B158n he denies that we can intuit the activity of thinking: "Now I do not have yet another self-intuition, which would give the **determining** in me, of the spontaneity of which alone I am conscious . . . thus I cannot determine my existence as that of a self-active being, rather I merely represent the spontaneity of my thought." Thus Kant dispels the paradox by denying that the t.u.a. is a cognition of the thinking self. It is only a formal awareness of the activity of thinking, identical for all discursive intelligences. Since the sensibility yields only appearances, we can know ourselves only as we appear to ourselves, not as things in themselves. Although this too seems paradoxical, the "I" of "I think" is neither an appearance nor a thing in itself, but a condition of all thought.[15]

4. KANT AND INNATE IDEAS: A NEW MODEL OF THE UNDERSTANDING

When we compare Kant's account of categories to previous theories, it is tempting to classify his view as a theory of innate ideas.

---

[15] See chapter 12 of Allison, *Kant's Transcendental Idealism* for a discussion of difficulties in the notions of inner sense and apperception.

After all, Kant agrees with the rationalists that the mind produces representations whose content is not derived from sense experience. Moreover, just as they believed that innate principles represented necessary truths, Kant argues that the necessity of metaphysical and mathematical knowledge can be traced to *a priori* concepts and intuitions. So readers are often surprised to find Kant explicitly rejecting innate ideas in favor of a theory of "original acquisition" in his later works. One famous passage occurs in the 1790 essay *On a Discovery whereby Any New Critique of Pure Reason Is To Be Made Superfluous by an Older One*:

> The *Critique* admits absolutely no implanted or innate *representations*. One and all, whether they belong to intuition or to concepts of the understanding, it considers them as *acquired*. But there is also an original acquisition . . . According to the *Critique*, these are, *in the first place*, the form of things in space and time, *second*, the synthetic unity of the manifold in concepts; for neither of these does our cognitive faculty get from the objects as given therein in-themselves, rather it brings them about, *a priori*, out of itself. There must indeed be a ground for it in the subject, however, which makes it possible that these representations can arise in this and no other manner, and be related to objects which are not yet given, and this ground at least is *innate*.[16]

To understand Kant's position, we should begin with the claims characteristic of innate or nativist theories of knowledge. As Falkenstein points out, nativist theories deny one or both of two views maintained by empiricists: first, that all the original input to the mind is derived from experience, and second, that the processes performed on the original input result from past experience.[17] Innate ideas philosophers maintain that the mind contains original input and thus deny the first view. Innate mechanisms philosophers claim that the mind contains certain inborn processing mechanisms. The theory of innate ideas typically includes these four claims:

1. The mind is the source of "innate" original input.
2. This original input can be recognized independently of sense experience.
3. The original input is the source of (innate) principles, which are necessarily true.
4. These principles give us knowledge of things in themselves.

---

[16] *Theoretical Philosophy after 1781*, 312.　　[17] See *Kant's Intuitionism*, 6–12, 91–6.

Specifying these four theses allows us to contrast Kant's theory with the theory of innate ideas. Regarding both pure intuition and the categories, Kant accepts 1 and 3, and rejects 2 and 4. As for 1, Kant believes the mind "contains" innate input in the sense that the innate capacities of sensing and thinking are the source of original representations. His view that no representations occur prior to experience, however, commits him to rejecting 2. Kant also accepts 3, since one criterion of *a priori* cognitions is their necessity. But his transcendental idealism contradicts 4.

Falkenstein argues that the pure forms of intuition are neither innate ideas nor innate mechanisms, but a pure manifold given with the empirical manifold in experience. The innate ideas version – that independently of experience we have two pure forms "lying ready in the mind" – violates the axiom that no representations occur prior to experience. The pure forms are "original acquisitions" because we "acquire" these representations only through the processed output, namely experience. By contrast, pure concepts and principles originate in innate thinking mechanisms, the logical forms of judgment. In terms of the input-processing-output model, they are operations for processing the manifold of intuition. The categories express rules governing these innate operations. But as with pure intuition, we "acquire" our representations of these rules only through the resulting experience.[18] Although the categories are "present" before experience, the subject can represent them only by reflecting on the process.[19]

Kant rejects the term "innate ideas" for *a priori* representations, then, primarily because the mind can represent nothing before processing the empirical data of intuition. Although the content of *a priori* representation is not derived from empirical data, all representation acquires its significance through its relation to empirical intuition. In fact, this is an advantage of Kant's theory over theories of innate ideas. For the view that the mind has a storehouse of innate knowledge that can be called up by reason fails utterly to connect such knowledge to experience.

---

[18] In *Metaphysik Vigilantius* of 1794–5, Kant says, "All concepts are acquired, and there cannot be any innate idea <*idea connata*>. For concepts presuppose a thinking, are made or thought through a comprehension of features." *Lectures on Metaphysics*, 423.

[19] Kant attributes our possession of the pure concepts to reflection in the *Metaphysik Mrongovius* of 1782–3. *Lectures on Metaphysics*, 123–4.

Kant's theory of cognition differs radically from both rationalism and empiricism. First, he rejects the rationalist doctrine of intellectual intuition. It follows that the human intellect is discursive and can operate only on data given independently. Moreover, the Analytic shows that all complex representations must be combined through acts of thought. Thus rationalists are mistaken in thinking that humans can instantaneously "intuit" complex cognitions of reality. Second, Kant rejects the view that sense perception is independent of judging. Unlike sensations, sense perceptions are objective representations, produced by judging the manifold of intuition. Perceptions, then, incorporate judgments, and perceiving cannot be a passive process. Now although many empiricists believe complex impressions are constructed, none of them identifies these constructive acts with judgment. In fact, in analyzing beliefs as complex ideas, Hume overlooks entirely the logical features of judgment.

5. SUMMARY

The Transcendental Deduction contains Kant's central justification for applying the categories to objects of experience. The A edition version argues that apprehending the data of intuition successively requires the imagination to reproduce previously apprehended representations, which presupposes concepts of the understanding. Although this version introduces Kant's theory of synthesis and the t.u.a., it does not link the categories to judgment. The significantly revised B edition version corrects this defect, arguing that the categories are required to represent objects of both thought and perception. By analyzing the notion of an object in terms of judgment, Kant links the categories to the logical forms of judgment identified earlier. Thus he defends the application of pure concepts expressed in synthetic *a priori* principles to the objects of experience. Because these metaphysical concepts and principles have their seat in the subject, they apply only to appearances and not to things in themselves. But because they are necessary for experiencing objects, they represent real features of appearances, and thus ground empirical knowledge. Like the forms of intuition, they represent transcendentally ideal but empirically real features of experience.

CHAPTER 6

The Schematism and the Analytic of Principles I

The final stage in justifying the categories consists in Kant's arguments for the synthetic *a priori* principles correlated with them. In the Analytic of Principles, Kant defends these metaphysical principles, including those of substance and causality that Hume attacked. As mentioned earlier, he also added to the B edition the argument titled the Refutation of Idealism, aimed at Descartes's view that knowledge of physical reality is less certain than self-knowledge. Thus it is here rather than in the Transcendental Deduction that Kant responds directly to the skeptical challenge.

The first chapter of this section, the Schematism, forms a bridge between the Transcendental Deduction and the arguments for the principles. It explains how pure concepts of the understanding, which have no original connection to sensibility, can apply to objects of intuition. The schema of each category is the condition relating the pure concept to spatiotemporal objects. It provides the empirical content that turns the syntactic concept into a real concept of an object. Contrary to the view of many commentators, this chapter is not incidental to Kant's argument. As Allison points out, the Transcendental Deduction shows only that the categories apply necessarily to objects given in time. But from that argument no particular metaphysical propositions can be derived. The Schematism specifies the particular temporal condition connected with each category.[1] In particular, it describes how the productive imagination mediates between the understanding and the sensibility. Despite its importance, the discussion raises two serious questions. First, does Kant need to "deduce" the schema of each category? And second, are any concepts identical

---

[1] Allison, *Kant's Transcendental Idealism*, 175–6.

with their schemata? After examining the text of the Schematism, I shall return to these points.

This chapter then examines the introduction to the Principles and Kant's arguments for the principles of quantity and quality. The latter justify applying mathematics to the spatiotemporal and qualitative features of objects given in intuition. Chapter 7 treats the remaining arguments for the principles of relation and modality, including the Refutation of Idealism.

I. THE SCHEMATISM

The Schematism begins by distinguishing the power of judgment from both the understanding and reason, where reason is the higher-order intellectual faculty that produces judgments by inference from other judgments. Here he wishes to elucidate the transcendental function of the power of judgment. At A131/B170, for the first time in the *Critique*, he separates this power from the understanding as a faculty of concepts. This distinction is required not only to set off theoretical judgment from practical and aesthetic judgment – neither moral judgments nor judgments of beauty are governed by concepts of the understanding – but also to highlight the problem of applying pure concepts in experience. Kant characterizes the pure principles as rules for directing the power of judgment.

At A132/B171 Kant describes judgment as the faculty "of determining whether something stands under a given rule." This activity is a natural talent, a product of "mother-wit" (A133/B172), and cannot be taught, since all learning requires one to apply rules to cases. Unlike general logic, transcendental logic supplies rules directing the power of judgment. These principles specify not only the rule (the pure concept), but also the *a priori* condition for applying the rule to an instance. This condition is the transcendental schema. Without this condition, the pure concepts would be "without all content, and thus would be mere logical forms" (A136/B175).

As the Transcendental Deduction shows, this condition must link the category to time. Thus the schema represents the temporal element giving the pure concept significance as a first-order concept of objects. For example, the logical relation between ground and consequent in hypothetical judgment becomes the objective concept of the relation of cause and effect when interpreted as a necessary succession of states in time. The Schematism chapter lists the schema for each category or moment. The Principles chapter then offers transcendental deductions for the synthetic *a priori* judgments asserting the necessity of each schema for experiencing spatiotemporal objects.

The problem of the schematism goes back to Plato's "third man" dilemma: how does a general concept apply to a particular instance? It cannot be by means of another concept, on pain of infinite regress. Similarly, no particular representation can mediate the relation without begging the question. Kant's theory of the schematic function of the imagination offers a third alternative. First, the instance must be "homogeneous" with the concept; that is, the concept must contain a "mark" of some feature of the object. Although the "third man" problem also arises for empirical and mathematical concepts, it is particularly acute for pure concepts of the understanding, because they have no original connection to intuition.[2] As Kant remarks at A137/B176, they "can never be encountered in any intuition"; we cannot intuit the substantiality or causal efficacy of objects, although we can think of these features.[3]

By contrast, both empirical and mathematical concepts contain intuitable marks of objects. Unfortunately, Kant obscures this point with his example of the plate: "Thus the empirical concept of a **plate** has homogeneity with the pure geometrical concept of a **circle**, for the roundness that is thought in the former can be intuited in the latter" (A137/B176). Although we would expect him to claim homogeneity between the concept of a plate and the plate, Kant locates the homogeneity between the empirical concept and the pure concept of a circle. His real point is that the pure concept "circle" can be exhibited in intuition. Thus we can apply the concept "plate" to an object because the concept incorporates the intuitable roundness derived from a pure sensible concept. Homogeneity ultimately has to obtain between concepts and their instances. Because pure concepts

---

[2] In *Kant and the Claims of Knowledge*, Paul Guyer denies that Kant is concerned generally with concept application, since he thinks empirical and mathematical concepts include their own rule of application. See 158–9. I discuss this point below.

[3] Although we intuit spatiotemporal patterns and the intensities of sensations, Kant's point is that the quantitative and qualitative pure concepts apply in experience only insofar as we conceive of appearances under the numerical systems required for extensive and intensive measurement.

of the understanding do not represent intuitable features, they are "heterogeneous" with their instances.

Heterogenity concerns two distinctions: first, between concept and instance, and second, between intellectual and sensible representations. The transcendental schema which "mediates" between the concept and the appearance must somehow represent all four aspects. Kant says it "must be pure (without anything empirical), and yet **intellectual** on the one hand and **sensible** on the other" (A138/B177). The latter implies that it has both general and particular features. Kant's solution identifies the transcendental schema of the category with a rule that produces a "transcendental determination of time."

Kant introduces this notion by distinguishing between a schema and an image. Because both empirical and pure sensible concepts represent intuitable features, they also have images. For example, we can recognize images of dogs as well as of circles and triangles. Images are produced by "the empirical faculty of productive imagination" (A141/B181). But because they are particular, images are never adequate to their concepts, never fully exhausting their content. So the schema that connects the concept to the image must itself be general. For concepts having images, the schema is a "representation of a general procedure of the imagination for providing a concept with its image" (A140/B179–80). This procedure, Kant says, can exist only in thought, and "signifies a rule of the synthesis of the imagination" (A141/B180). For mathematical concepts, the schema yields a procedure guiding the imagination in constructing an *a priori* spatial intuition. An example would be representing a plane triangle in Euclidean space, by beginning with a point from which one draws a continuous straight line to a second point, and from there to a third point, and back to the original point. For the empirical concept "dog," the schema is a rule specifying the shape of a four-footed animal, "without being restricted to any single particular shape that experience offers me" (A141/B180). For concepts having images, the schema represents a *procedure* by which the productive imagination creates an image for a general concept, thereby exhibiting a universal in intuition.

Although the categories apply to individuals given in intuition, they lack images. There is no image of totality or reality or cause as there is of a dog and a triangle. Consequently, the connection between the schema and image does not apply to transcendental schemata. What does apply is the notion of *a procedure for exhibiting a universal in intuition*. Whereas schemata of empirical and mathematical concepts are procedures for constructing images, transcendental schemata are procedures for constructing intuitions of objects in time. Thus we arrive at the idea that the schema is a transcendental determination of time.

In the Transcendental Deduction Kant defended the objective reality of the categories by demonstrating their necessity for intuiting objects in global time. At A138/B177 he reminds us that to apply to objective states of affairs, the categories must relate to the pure synthesis of the temporal manifold. Allison identifies the transcendental schema with the pure (formal) intuition of time, constructed by conceiving of time in terms of a pure concept.[4] This appears reasonable, given Kant's claim that "The schemata are therefore nothing but *a priori* **time-determinations** in accordance with rules," namely the categories (A145/B184). More recently, however, Sarah Gibbons has argued that Allison's interpretation begs the question of how pure concepts apply to the data of intuition. For identifying the schema with the formal intuition merely presupposes that categories do apply to the pure manifold. She thinks Kant identifies the schema with the *procedure* for constructing the formal intuition of time.[5] This reading both avoids begging the question, and unifies the doctrine of the schematism with Kant's theory of mathematical construction. In both cases the productive imagination constructs a determinate representation of time or space, which is a pure formal intuition exhibiting a universal rule. Gibbons argues that schemata are not rules in the same sense as the categories. Rather they represent the *procedure* "which makes possible the instantiation of the concept and constitutes the pure formal intuition".[6] By means of this constructive act, the productive imagination mediates between the understanding and the sensibility. The result, as Allison explains, is to objectify time by representing "a temporal order as an intersubjectively valid order of events or states of affairs." Since we cannot perceive time itself, the

[4] Allison, *Kant's Transcendental Idealism*, 61–79.
[5] Gibbons, *Kant's Theory of Imagination*, 56–7.   [6] *Kant's Theory of Imagination*, 74.

resulting time-determination is a "necessary characteristic of things in time."[7] Time-determinations, then, are ways of conceiving of objective temporal properties and relations of objects.

The best way to grasp this idea is by examples. Here we shall just focus on the correlations between schema and concept, since the Principles arguments present a more detailed view. First, Kant correlates each of the four headings with a temporal aspect of experience. Kant links the categories under quantity (unity, plurality, totality) with the generation of time itself as a unified (formal) intuition. The quantitative concepts are necessary for extensive measurement; their schema is number, which represents "the successive addition of one (homogeneous) unit to another" (A142/B182). In other words, to judge via the quantitative forms, one must identify the objects being judged as distinct individuals occupying determinate locations in time (and space). Thus we must be able to construct measurable extents of time (and space), by conceiving them in terms of a plurality of units.

The qualitative categories (reality, negation, limitation) are ways of conceiving what exists in time. A being is something that fills time; nonexistence is represented by an empty time. In appearances, the data of intuition that represent real things are sensations. Thus being and non-being correspond to the presence and absence of sensation. The schemata of the categories of quality are, therefore, procedures for measuring the intensity of sensations.

The relational categories are ways of conceiving real relations between existing states of affairs in time. Their schemata express the three temporal features of states: duration, succession, and coexistence. The schema of substance–accident is duration or permanence, which is presupposed in distinguishing enduring things from their temporary states. The category of cause–effect is correlated with the existence of a necessary succession of states in time. And the category of reciprocal causal interaction is expressed through the representation of coexisting states.

Finally, the modality of a judgment concerns how we judge objective states in relation to the whole of time. Really possible existence is the existence of a thing at some time or another. Actual existence is existence at some determinate time. And necessary existence is

---

[7] *Kant's Theory of Imagination*, 183.

existence at all times.[8] Although these characterizations are sketchy, the Principles arguments spell out the relation between categories and schemata in more detail.

In mediating between the pure logical concepts and the data of intuition, the schemata perform a double-edged function: they both permit us to apply the categories to appearances and restrict their meaning. For example, the logical concepts of subject and predicate have no real use until they are interpreted temporally as enduring things and their changing states. Similarly, the logical notion of a ground and its consequent acquires objective significance only when applied to a causally governed succession of states. Thus Kant's theory of schematism solves the "third man" problem for pure concepts by appealing to procedures in the imagination for constructing temporal features of appearances required to judge them as objective states of affairs.

Before turning to the Principles, let us return to the two issues raised earlier: first, whether Kant needs to "deduce" the schema correlated with each category, and second, whether he identifies any of the three types of concepts with their schemata. Regarding the first, I think Allison and Gibbons are correct that the "deduction" of the schema is reserved for the Principles arguments. Kant's purpose here is to identify the schema for each category. In the Principles he presents transcendental deductions for the categories as applied *under their corresponding temporal condition.* Thus he does not need separate arguments for the correlations between category and schema.

The second issue is more complex, and commentators disagree over whether Kant identifies concept with schema in any case. Guyer thinks Kant correctly identifies them for both empirical and mathematical concepts. Lauchlan Chipman believes Kant identifies them only for empirical concepts, but does so in error.[9] On my reading, Kant distinguishes schema from concept in all three cases. Recall that schemata are procedures for applying concepts to their instances. For empirical and mathematical concepts, this involves providing an image for the concept. Now in the first place, Kant attributes the

---

[8] As Allison points out, since a causally necessitated state need not exist at all times, we should take the schema of necessity to be existence of a state produced causally in relation to the whole of time. See *Kant's Transcendental Idealism,* 192.

[9] Chipman, "Kant's Categories and their Schematism," 107–9.

schema in all cases to the imagination: "The schema is in itself always only a product of the imagination" (A140/B179). This immediately distinguishes the schema from concepts, which Kant attributes to the understanding.[10] Second, Kant repeatedly describes the schema as mediating between the concept and the image. For example, he says the schema of sensible concepts is a product of the pure imagination, which makes images possible. But these images "must be connected with the concept, to which they are in themselves never fully congruent, always only by means of the schema that they designate" (A141–2/B181). Now if schemata were identical with either empirical or mathematical concepts, there would be no point in describing them as mediating between the concept and the image.[11]

Clearly several elements stand or fall together. If, following Gibbons, we take the schema to be a procedure for constructing either images or pure intuitions of spatiotemporal features, then Kant does respond to Plato's dilemma. Moreover, in emphasizing the necessity of imaginative procedures for exhibiting universals in intuition, the Schematism doctrine is of a piece with Kant's theory of mathematical construction. Now let us turn to Kant's arguments for the principles.

2. THE ANALYTIC OF PRINCIPLES: INTRODUCTION

The task of the Principles is to defend the judgments that result when the schematized categories are applied to objects of intuition. These judgments will be synthetic *a priori*, since they represent necessary presuppositions of experience. The proofs offer transcendental deductions, arguments that each principle is necessary to experience states of affairs having objective temporal features. Kant remarks that these arguments do not address the truth of mathematical principles, since he believes that was established in the Transcendental Aesthetic. Instead, arguments for the principles of quantity and quality justify applying mathematical principles to objects given in intuition.

[10] Kant defines the understanding as the faculty of concepts at A51/B75, A68/B92–3, A78/B103, and A126.
[11] Chipman argues that Kant should not identify empirical concepts with their schemata, since one can possess a concept (e.g., 'tadpole' and 'bone marrow') without being able to recognize instances. See "Kant's Categories and their Schematism," 109–11.

Kant next contrasts the supreme principles of analytic judgments and synthetic judgments. By a "supreme principle" he means a necessary condition for such judgments to be meaningful. The principle of contradiction, "the proposition that no predicate pertains to a thing that contradicts it" (A151/B190), serves for all judgments as a negative criterion, that is, a necessary but not sufficient condition of truth. For analytic judgments, it is also a positive criterion since it is sufficient for determining their truth value. Kant also criticizes the common expression of the principle as "It is impossible for the same thing to be [F] and not be [F] at the same time" (A152–3/B191–2). This version is mistaken since it illegitimately imports the sensible condition of time into a purely logical principle.

Unlike analytic judgments, the truth value of synthetic *a priori* judgments cannot be determined by the principle of contradiction alone, since the latter are ampliative. Consequently "a third thing is necessary in which alone the synthesis of two concepts can originate" (A155/B194). This "third thing" can only be the "possibility of experience," since the objects of synthetic cognition can only be given in intuition. But experience takes place in time, and requires a synthesis by the imagination in accord with the t.u.a. In other words, we can make objectively valid synthetic judgments only by representing objective states of affairs in one time. The pure principles are thus rules governing the synthesis of the empirical manifold in time.

Kant begins the third section by attributing the lawlikeness of experience to these principles. The understanding is the faculty of concepts, and concepts are rules describing the nature of objects. Even empirical laws of nature, although discovered *a posteriori*, express necessary connections between features of objects. This necessity must be grounded in principles governing the synthesis of all data given in intuition. Thus pure principles are higher-order principles that govern the application of specific empirical concepts and laws to objects of experience.

Following his distinction between mathematical and dynamical categories in the Metaphysical Deduction, Kant distinguishes mathematical from dynamical principles. As we saw in chapter 4, at B110 Kant labels the categories of quantity and quality *mathematical* because they govern the operations that identify individual objects and their properties in the data of intuition. The relational and modal categories are *dynamical* because they govern the relations of objects to one another and to the subject. Kant now applies this distinction to the principles. At A160/B199 he explains that mathematical principles pertain "merely to the **intuition**" of objects, whereas dynamical principles pertain "to the **existence** of an appearance in general." At A178/B221 Kant also labels these constitutive vs. regulative principles.

In consequence, mathematical and dynamical principles differ in their manner of evidence. The former are "unconditionally necessary" and allow of intuitive certainty. By contrast, dynamical principles are necessary "only under the condition of empirical thinking in an experience." Therefore they lack "the immediate evidence that is characteristic of the former" (A160/B199–200). As the Schematism points out, the quantitative and qualitative features of objects governed by the mathematical principles are exhibited in intuition. This is required to intuit spatiotemporal objects at all. But the objective temporal relations between states of affairs, and their relations to thinkers, are merely thought. At A178–9/B221–2 Kant connects this point with the fact that only the intuitions of objects, and not their existence, can be constructed. That is, in intuition we are given a spatiotemporal array to be discriminated into individual states of affairs, but we are not given objective temporal positions and relations. Moreover, having intuited an event, we can infer that it follows necessarily from some prior state, but we cannot identify that state *a priori*. Now we turn to the arguments for the mathematical principles in the Axioms of Intuition and the Anticipations of Perception.

3. THE AXIOMS OF INTUITION

The synthetic *a priori* principles of quantity and quality govern the mere intuition of objective states of affairs. The Axioms of Intuition concern the synthesis of formal (spatiotemporal) properties; they specify that to experience determinate objects, they must have extensively measurable properties. The Anticipations of Perception apply to the synthesis of the matter of intuition, the sensations correlated with real properties of objects. They state that both sensations and the properties corresponding to them must have some degree of intensity. Although Kant refers to Axioms and Anticipations in the plural, in fact there is only one principle for each heading. This is because the notions of extensive and intensive measurement each incorporate all three categories under their respective headings.

Kant expresses the principle of the Axioms differently in the A and B editions, but the point is the same.[12] The A edition says, "All appearances are, as regards their intuition, **extensive magnitudes**" (A161). The B edition reads, "**All intuitions are extensive magnitudes**" (B201). Kant's point is that appearances must have extensively measurable spatiotemporal properties to be perceived as individual objects or states of affairs. Thus the Axioms (and the Anticipations) attempt to justify the application of pure mathematics to empirical objects. In the paragraph preceding the Axioms he explains that these pure principles are not themselves mathematical principles, but only principles "through which the former principles all acquire their possibility" (A162/B202). This also explains the title "Axioms of Intuition." For although the Axioms are not themselves mathematical axioms, they establish the validity of mathematical axioms for empirical objects.[13]

The B edition contains a new argument in the first paragraph; the A edition argument then follows in the second paragraph. Only the B edition version refers to the schema of number, while the earlier version focuses instead on the concept of extensive measurement. In both cases, however, Kant argues that since the synthesis of space and time underlies the synthesis of intuitions of objects in space and time, the mathematical procedures governing the former must also apply to the latter. The B edition argument explains that the synthetic processes for representing determinate spaces and times require us to combine the homogeneous spatiotemporal manifold into unified wholes. The concepts governing this synthesis are the arithmetical concepts of number. In other words, to perceive distinct empirical objects occupying determinate spatiotemporal positions, the intuitions of these objects must be extensively measurable. At B203 Kant concludes: "appearances are all magnitudes, and indeed **extensive magnitudes**, since as intuitions in space or time they must be represented through

---

[12] I am indebted to Paton's discussion, *Kant's Metaphysic of Experience*, at 2:111–33.
[13] Kant gives as axioms of geometry "space has only three dimensions" (B41), and "between two points only one straight line is possible; two straight lines do not enclose a space, etc" (A163/B204). For time: "It has only one dimension; different times are not simultaneous, but successive" (B47).

the same synthesis as that through which space and time in general are determined." As H. J. Paton points out, this implies that intuitions are measurable as extensive quantities only insofar as they are intuitions of objects. Dream objects and other "pseudo-objects of our imagination" cannot be measured since they do not occupy determinate locations in objective space-time.[14]

The earlier version analyzes the notion of extensive measurement and shows how it applies to space and time. Kant begins by defining an extensive magnitude as one in which the representation of the parts precedes and makes possible the representation of the whole. The key to the notion of extensive measurement is the *successive addition of parts* to generate a whole. When one draws a line, for example, one begins at some point in space and then generates its parts successively. Similarly, in thinking of determinate (measurable) times, one thinks "the successive progress from one moment to another," whose addition produces a determinate duration (A163/B203). Extensive magnitudes are those produced by combining or adding previously delineated parts. In a long footnote at B202, Kant labels a whole of extensive parts an aggregate, and a whole of intensive parts a coalition. The feature essential to extensive measurement is the addition process; as we shall see below, degrees of intensity are not constructed in the same way.

This helps clarify Kant's conception of the connection between the pure concepts of quantity and the schema of number. Recall from chapter 4 that the quantitative logical concepts express the forms of universal, particular, and singular judgments. The three categories that result from schematizing these concepts are (respectively) unity, plurality, and totality. When applied to objects, these categories make it possible to measure spaces and times. For example, to measure the length of an object or a time period, one must first select a unit of measurement (e.g., a foot, a minute). Then one applies it repeatedly as required to obtain the resulting magnitude, which is a totality composed of a plurality of units. Extensive measurement consists in adding the independently defined units successively to arrive at the resulting sum. This is the sense in which the representation of the parts precedes the representation of the whole. Kant correlates the category

standpoint the argument parallels the Axioms argument, that the procedures of extensive measurement are necessary to confer objective reference on the spatiotemporal features of appearances.

As with the Axioms, Kant revises the principle in the second edition, and adds a new proof at the beginning of the section. The A edition principle states, "In all appearances the sensation, and the **real**, which corresponds to it in the object (*realitas phaenomenon*), has an **intensive magnitude**, i.e., a degree." The B edition version reads: "**In all appearances the real, which is an object of the sensation, has intensive magnitude**, i.e., a degree" (A166/B207). Whereas the A version claims that both sensations and real properties of objects must have intensive magnitude, the B version appears to concern only the objects of sensation. As suggested above, however, the point should be that sensations must have a degree of intensity corresponding to an intensive magnitude in the real properties of the object being sensed. Thus the A edition version of the principle appears more precise.

Kant recognizes the paradox of an *a priori* principle "anticipating" the nature of perception: "it seems strange to anticipate experience precisely in what concerns its matter," since this is given *a posteriori* (A166–7). He does not directly answer the point until A175–6/B217–18, where he distinguishes the quality of a sensation from its degree of intensity. It is true that we cannot know *a priori* what qualities we will sense; knowledge of sense qualities is contingent on the actual experiences. What we can know *a priori*, however, is the "form" of any sensation, namely that it must have a degree of intensity in order to fill space-time. As Paton puts it, the principle of the Anticipations deals with the "form of the matter of appearance."[20]

Before we examine the proofs we need to review some key terms, previously discussed in chapter 3. *Sensations* are defined in the Aesthetic as "the effect of an object on the capacity for representation, insofar as we are affected by it" (A19–20/B34). In chapter 3 we accepted Falkenstein's view that sensations are modifications of the sense organs, and thus physical states. What Kant calls *real of sensation* is the consciously represented *sense quality*, that which fills space and time. Color, sound, taste, odor, and warmth are examples of sense qualities. Because qualities are the way we apprehend sensations,

---

[20] See *Kant's Metaphysic of Experience*, 2:134–5n5.

there is a correspondence between the quality and the sensation. For this reason Kant slides easily from talk about sensation to talk about the quality of sensation, as at A175–6/B217–18.

Recall that *appearance* is the "undetermined object (*Gegenstand*) of an empirical intuition" (A20/B34), where *Gegenstand* refers to an existing thing. Thus appearances are whatever is given in intuition. Now the term the *real in appearance* is ambiguous: it could refer either to the represented quality or to the properties of objects. In the Principles, Kant characterizes the real in appearance as that "which corresponds to [the sensation] in the object" (A edition) and that "which is an object of the sensation" (B edition). I agree with Paton that for Kant the real in appearance are the properties of matter as determined by empirical science.[21] Twice Kant gives as an example of a degree of reality the moment of gravity, certainly a scientific notion (A168–9/B210–11). These properties may or may not resemble the consciously represented sense qualities.[22]

The A edition proof from A167–9/B209–10 proceeds as follows:

1. Apprehension by means of sensation is instantaneous, i.e., it does not take time.
2. Therefore, apprehension in sensation is not a successive synthesis proceeding from the parts to the whole.
3. Therefore, the thing apprehended in sensation does not have extensive magnitude.
4. That in empirical intuition which corresponds to sensation is reality; that which corresponds to its absence is negation.
5. Every sensation is capable of diminishing gradually until it disappears.
6. Therefore, between reality in appearance and negation there is a continuum of sensations, such that between any two sensations there is always a sensation; there is no smallest possible sensation.
7. Thus the real in appearance always has a magnitude which is not extensive.

---

[21] See *Kant's Metaphysic of Experience*, 2:137–8. I disagree, however, with Paton's identification of sensation with "the sensum considered as modification of the mind."

[22] Given the primary–secondary quality distinction, Kant believes that sense qualities do not resemble the real properties in objects causing them. Moreover, *MFNS* presents a dynamical theory of matter in which the ultimately real properties are fundamental forces of repulsion and attraction.

8. A magnitude which can only be apprehended as a unity, and in which multiplicity can only be represented through approximation to zero, is an intensive magnitude.

9. Therefore, every reality in appearance has intensive magnitude, i.e., a degree.

This version begins with the premise that apprehension in sensation is instantaneous. Although Kant does not defend it, it is plausible as an account of the perception of something occupying space-time. Either the senses are affected or they are not. In apprehension the understanding "takes up" this sensory material into consciousness and presents it as a sense quality. Thus it would seem to be an all-or-nothing affair. Conclusions 2 and 3 follow from this and the Axioms view that the synthesis required to represent extensive magnitudes takes time because the whole is generated from the parts. Therefore the instantaneous apprehension of sensation cannot take place by means of such a synthesis. In consequence what is apprehended in sensation cannot have extensive magnitude.

Premise 4 introduces the concepts of reality and negation by establishing the "fact" on which the Transcendental Deduction depends, namely that we take sensations to represent real properties of objects given in intuition. Reality is that in the object which corresponds to the sensation; negation represents its correlate, the absence of a property. The key to the argument is premise 5, the controversial claim that every sensation can diminish gradually until it disappears. Unfortunately Kant offers no support, and it is not obvious how to defend it. Some commentators see it as based on Kant's physics, which explains the impenetrability of matter by intensive forces of repulsion and attraction. This reading reverses the order of argument, however, since the Principles provide necessary conditions for experience and consequently are presupposed by empirical laws and theories. Kant says this explicitly in both the *MFNS* and in a discussion of the possibility of empty space and time near the end of the Anticipations. (We will look at this passage below.)

An alternative reading bases premise 5 on the phenomenology of sensation and the notion of something filling time. It is a fact that at least some aspects of sense qualities can diminish gradually. The brightness of light and the loudness of sound are two such aspects. Premise 5 makes only the weak claim that it is possible for sensations to diminish gradually until they disappear. Admitting the slide from sense qualities to sensations, this could be justified as a brute fact about sensory consciousness. Based on these examples, one might argue that the notion of something filling time entails the possibility in principle that it can diminish gradually to nothing. A problem with this defense concerns a scope ambiguity. One reading would take the "possibility" in a weak sense, so that it is possible for every sensation to diminish gradually, although perhaps some in fact do not. Kant's conclusion, however, apparently requires the strong sense that every sensation is such that it can diminish gradually. We shall return to this point below. In any case, the phenomenological approach has the advantage of not basing Kant's view of sensation on a particular physical theory. As we shall see, the B edition version supports this reading.

The rest of the proof follows from the analysis of intensive magnitude. Statements 6 and 7 are conclusions from premise 5. In line 6 Kant states that both sensations and the "real in appearance" have a magnitude such that they can diminish continually to nothing. He then concludes in line 7 that the real in appearance has a non-extensive magnitude. Premise 8 defines intensive magnitudes as those apprehended only as unities, and in which the parts can be represented only "through approximation to negation." Kant then concludes that every reality in appearance has some degree of intensity.

The gist of the argument is this: in order to represent objects filling time (and space), we must conceive of sensations and the real properties of objects as having some degree of intensity. This presupposes a conceptual scheme that permits us to take sensations to correspond to real properties of objects. On Kant's view this is the function of the schema of intensive measurement. It is the correspondence in intensity that makes it possible for sensations to represent empirically real objects.

The argument in the B edition is essentially the same, although Kant uses the technical vocabulary of matter and form, and emphasizes the synthesis of the understanding in relating sensations to objects. The proof is this:

1. Perception is empirical consciousness in which there is sensation.
2. As objects (*Gegenstände*) of perception, appearances are not pure intuitions like space and time, but contain the matter for an object in general.

3. Through this matter something is represented as existing in space and time.
4. This matter is the real of sensation, which is a merely subjective representation by which one is aware of being affected.
5. This matter is related to an object in general (by a synthesis of the understanding).
6. From empirical consciousness to pure consciousness a gradation is possible in which the real disappears and a merely formal consciousness of the spatiotemporal manifold remains.
7. Thus there is also possible a synthesis in representing the magnitude of sensation from 0 to any arbitrary magnitude.
8. Sensation is not in itself an objective representation, since neither space nor time is found in it.
9. Therefore, it has no extensive magnitude.
10. But it does have a magnitude (such that through its apprehension, empirical consciousness can grow in a certain time from 0 to a given measure).
11. Therefore, it has an intensive magnitude.
12. Corresponding to this all objects of perception, insofar as *it* contains sensation, must be ascribed an intensive magnitude, i.e., a degree of influence on sense (emphasis added).[23]

This version begins with the analysis of empirical consciousness. Premises 1–4 are based on the Aesthetic and so should not be controversial. Here Kant emphasizes that perceiving objects involves sensing something filling space-time, which he calls the matter of appearance. This matter, which we consciously apprehend as sense qualities (the real of sensation), makes possible our awareness of things existing in space and time. Premise 5 restates this as the transcendental "fact" that we relate this matter to an object in general. Since an object in general is the judgmental notion of an object, Kant is here reminding us that the understanding refers the matter to an object by means of pure concepts.

At line 6 Kant introduces the notion of the gradual diminution in the degree of reality through an analysis of empirical consciousness.

---

[23] I emphasize "it" to indicate that I have altered Guyer and Wood's translation. They take the pronoun *diese* to refer to objects of perception rather than perception. But the verb for "contain" is in the singular – *enthält* – rather than the plural; moreover, it makes no sense to say that objects contain sensation.

Here the point is explicitly phenomenological: it is always possible for the real of empirical consciousness to disappear gradually until nothing remains but consciousness of the spatiotemporal manifold. We can conceive of a sensation of color, for example, as fading until the color disappears. From this Kant concludes at line 7 that it must be possible for the understanding to perform a synthesis which produces the magnitude of the sensation.

The remainder of the argument presents a revised version of the first edition proof. Here Kant argues that sensations lack extensive magnitude because of their subjective nature, which he bases on the view that sensations are inherently aspatial and atemporal. The latter claim would follow from Kant's distinction in the Aesthetic between the form and the matter of intuition. In line 10 Kant claims that sensation has some magnitude; he then concludes that its magnitude must be intensive, and accordingly the real properties represented through sensation must have intensive magnitude.

Another passage in the 1787 edition of the *Critique* yields additional evidence that Kant bases his view of sensation on a general theory of consciousness. In the Paralogisms of Pure Reason in the Dialectic, where Kant criticizes Mendelssohn's proof that the soul is immortal, he says this at B414–15: "For even consciousness always has a degree, which can always be diminished;* consequently, so does the faculty of being conscious of oneself, and likewise with all the other faculties."[24] In the footnote indicated by the asterisk, he relates the degree of consciousness to the degree of clarity and distinctness in a representation:

Clarity is not, as the logicians say, the consciousness of a representation; for a certain degree of consciousness . . . must be met with even in some obscure representations . . . Rather a representation is clear if the consciousness in it is sufficient for **a consciousness of the difference** between it and others. To be sure, if this consciousness suffices for a distinction, but not for a consciousness of the difference, then the representation must still be called obscure. So there are infinitely many degrees of consciousness down to its vanishing.

Here the degree of consciousness is related to the degree to which one can discriminate a representation from others. Since identity is

---

[24] I thank Falkenstein for drawing my attention to this passage.

a feature of all representation, this account is independent of any particular physical theory. Unfortunately even this view may not be sufficient to secure Kant's claim that all sensations must be subject to a continuum of degrees of intensity. To see why, let us look at the notion of intensive magnitude.

We can understand the concept of intensive magnitude by comparing measuring procedures for intensive properties such as temperature with those for extensive properties such as length or mass.[25] We shall see that extensive and intensive properties differ in two related ways. First, they are subject to different types of empirical measuring procedures. Second, as a result, their magnitudes are represented on scales having different mathematical structures. Let us first examine the procedures for measuring length, an extensive property.

Although there are various ways to interpret the notion of an extensive magnitude, as we saw above Kant takes additivity to be essential. In measuring length, some unit measure is applied successively to the object; the resulting magnitude is the product of the unit and the number of times it is applied. Thus a key characteristic of extensive magnitudes is that they are *additive*. Combining a length x with a length y produces a length z where "x + y = z" is a valid arithmetical formula. In terms of measurement theory, extensive properties are those measured on *ratio scales*. For ratio scales the choice of unit is arbitrary, but the origin or zero point is fixed. So zero feet is always equivalent to zero meters, or zero length expressed in any unit. Ratio scales are related by a transformation function known as a *similarity* transformation, or multiplication by a positive constant. Thus we can convert a length given in meters into a length given in feet by multiplying by 3.28 (1 meter = 39.37 inches). It is characteristic of ratio scales that the empirical measuring operations determine *equality of ratios*. So the ratio of two lengths l_1/l_2 is invariant regardless of the unit being used: let $l_1 = 1$ meter and $l_2 = 2$ meters; the ratio 1/2 is preserved in the equivalent measurement in feet, where $l_1 = 3.28$ feet and $l_2 = 6.56$ feet.

By contrast, intensive magnitudes are measured differently, because they are not additive. Consider that combining a quart of water at

[25] This discussion is taken from my article, "Descartes on Sensible Qualities," 593–7. There I argue that Descartes rejects sensible qualities as real physical properties precisely because they are intensive magnitudes.

72° F with another quart of water at 72° F does not produce two quarts of water at 144° F. Intensive properties like temperature are measured on *interval scales* rather than ratio scales. The Fahrenheit and Celsius scales for temperature are constructed by selecting two fixed points, and dividing the range between them into a certain number of intervals, which is also arbitrarily selected. Both Fahrenheit and Celsius scales use the ice point of water and the temperature of steam over boiling water as fixed points, but they assign them different values: the Fahrenheit values are 32° and 212°, the Celsius values 0° and 100°. Consequently they divide the range between these points into different numbers of intervals. Thus interval scales have both an arbitrary zero point and choice of unit, although the units are uniform as they are for ratio scales. But measurements on such scales are not additive because there is no empirical procedure for combining the properties these scales measure. Moreover, although *ratios* of temperatures are not invariant, the *ratios of intervals or differences* of temperatures are invariant. Consider the following assignments:

Fahrenheit temperatures			*Celsius temperatures*	
F_1	50	=	C_1	10
F_2	68	=	C_2	20
F_3	86	=	C_3	30

Notice that while the *ratio* F_1/F_2 is not preserved by C_1/C_2, since $50/68 \neq 10/20$, the *ratio of intervals* $F_1 - F_2/F_2 - F_3$ is preserved by the ratio $C_1 - C_2/C_2 - C_3$ since

$$\frac{50 - 68}{68 - 86} = \frac{10 - 20}{20 - 30}$$

$$\frac{-18}{-18} = \frac{-10}{-10}$$

$$1 = 1$$

Interval scales are related by a transformation function ϕ, known as a *linear transformation*, so that to convert a reading from one scale to another, one uses an equation of the form $\phi(x) = ax + b$, with $a > 0$. To convert a reading in degrees Fahrenheit (x) to degrees Celsius [$\phi(x)$], we use the transformation: $C = 5/9F - 160/9$. To sum up, then, here are the salient differences between ratio and interval scales:

Scale type	Basic empirical operations	Mathematical group structure
Interval	Determination of equality of intervals or differences	Linear or affine group: $\phi(x) = ax + b, a > 0$. Zero point and unit arbitrary; no addition operation.
Ratio	Determination of equality of ratios	Similarity group: $\phi(x) = ax, a > 0$. Zero point fixed; unit arbitrary; addition operation.

Although Kant was probably unaware of the mathematical group structures of these scales as represented here, he certainly was aware that intensive magnitudes are not additive. He also recognizes that measuring procedures for such properties involve comparison. Now as we can see, this is a fair description of the process of measurement using an interval scale, since degrees of intensity are constructed by making relative comparisons from one or more fixed points. One difference between Kant's conception and the example of temperature concerns the zero point. Clearly Kant assumes that there is a non-arbitrary zero point for intensive magnitudes, namely the absence of the property or the sensation. In fact the notion of an absolute zero for temperature in terms of the minimum volume of a gas was developed during the eighteenth century, although the current value (-273.15 $\pm.02°$ C) was not established until the middle of the nineteenth century.[26]

This analysis clarifies the relation between the pure concepts of quality and their schemata. Recall that the logical concepts express the forms of affirmative, negative, and "infinite" judgments. As applied to objects, affirmation corresponds to reality understood as the presence of some property represented in sensation (the "real" expressed by a predicate). Negation then corresponds to the absence of a property, and infinite judgments to the idea of drawing limitations. The concept of intensive magnitude incorporates all three interdependent categories. For Kant thinks of a determinate degree of intensity as a limitation on reality constructed by comparison with negation, the absence of the property.

---

[26] I do not know whether Kant was familiar with the notion of absolute zero for temperature.

One question that naturally arises concerns which aspects of sense qualities have intensive magnitudes. Kant assumes that all qualities have intensity, but he does not specify whether this is true of all of their aspects. For example, color can be analyzed in terms of hue, saturation, and brightness. Now the brightness of a color can vary in intensity, and so can its saturation, the degree to which it is free from admixture with white. But it is not so clear whether Kant thinks this is the way to describe hue. Hues of colors – red, blue, green, and so on – can be located on a continuum; red, for example, shades from the orange side to the purple side. In this sense we could designate degrees of redness, although this scale would have a maximum point (where red is pure) and two minimal points, unlike brightness and saturation. An examination of sound, taste, and odor shows that there is no general pattern exhibited by the aspects of all sense qualities. It may be that all Kant needs for his argument is that each type of sense quality have some aspect that admits of degrees of intensity.

We should also note that Kant does not claim that we "directly" perceive the real properties of objects causing our sensations. In the Postulates of Empirical Thought he uses the example of magnetic forces: "Thus we cognize the existence of a magnetic matter penetrating all bodies from the perception of attracted iron filings, although an immediate perception of this matter is impossible for us given the constitution of our organs" (A226/B273). Presumably the same is true of fundamental forces of repulsion and attraction: he postulates the force of repulsion to explain the impenetrability of bodies, which is sensed through the feeling of solidity. Kant understands the real properties of objects as those investigated by scientific theories, based on evidence given directly or indirectly in perception. What we directly sense is in part a function of the nature of our sense organs. Kant maintains, however, that no theoretical claim can be empirically meaningful unless it is testable by reference to empirical intuition.

Now we can address the relation between apprehension and the synthesis involved in measuring intensive properties. Paton, for example, thinks the idea of a continuous change from its absence to any determinate degree of sensation applies to the apprehension of qualities: "I think Kant does believe that when we open our eyes and look at a red colour, we pass from complete absence of colour through various degrees up to that particular shade of red."[27] But as Guyer points out, this contradicts the doctrine that all sensation is instantaneous.[28] Paton's reading confuses what happens in apprehension with what happens in measuring degrees of intensity. Recall that an intensive magnitude "can only be apprehended as a unity, and in which multiplicity can only be represented through approximation to negation = 0" (A168/B210). Now Kant says explicitly:

Apprehension, merely by means of sensation, fills only an instant (if I do not take into consideration the succession of many sensations). As something in the appearance, *the apprehension of which is not a successive synthesis*, proceeding from the parts to the whole representation, it therefore has no extensive magnitude. (A167/B209, emphasis added)

And at A168/B210: "the real in appearance always has a magnitude, *which is not, however, encountered in apprehension*, as this takes place by means of the mere sensation in an instant" (emphasis added). These two passages clearly separate the mere, instantaneous apprehension of sensation from the representation of its degree of intensity. In apprehension we instantaneously take up the sensation as a whole. By contrast, awareness of the degree of intensity, either through comparison or some measuring procedure, requires a synthesis in which the whole is divided into parts. The difference between this synthesis and that involved in extensive measurement is not the temporality of the process – all synthesis takes time – but rather the part-whole relation, since the degrees of the perceived quality or property are determined relative to one or more fixed points. Kant apparently thinks it possible simply to apprehend sense qualities without recognizing their degree of intensity.[29] Now he does say of the apprehension of sensation that "the empirical consciousness *can* grow in a certain time from nothing = 0 to its given measure" (B208, italics added). The fact that intensities can vary in apprehension does not mean apprehension is

[27] See *Kant's Metaphysic of Experience*, 2:142n2.
[28] See *Kant and the Claims of Knowledge*, 205. Guyer connects the intensity of sensation with the schema of filling time, but he does not distinguish between apprehension and the synthesis required to conceive of intensive magnitude.
[29] An analogous case is the indeterminate intuition of spatial extent Kant recognizes at A426–8n/B454–6n.

not instantaneous, but rather that we can become aware that a sound is becoming louder, for example, through the "succession of many sensations" mentioned at A167/B209. Thus I see no inconsistency between the views that sensations are apprehended instantaneously and that the synthesis required for measurement takes time.

It remains to consider whether Kant's argument depends on unwarranted assumptions about the causes of sensation, and whether, even granting his assumptions, his conclusion follows. I argued above that his proof is independent of his dynamical theory. But we have seen that he conceives of sensations as effects on sense organs caused by interactions with external bodies. It is not clear, however, that the causal assumption plays a role in the proof. The A edition version does not explicitly appeal to a causal connection between sensations and real properties of objects; the B edition version mentions it only in the conclusion. I agree with Paton that the only relation the Anticipations argument presupposes between sensations and real properties is an intentional or representative relation, namely that we take sensations to represent real properties of objects. Once Kant defends the principle of causality in the Second Analogy, he can then conclude that they must be caused by contact with external bodies.

I think, however, that Kant cannot escape the objection that his premises do not entail that every sensation must admit of a continuum of intensity. The premises claim merely that it is possible for sensation to diminish gradually, whereas the latter claims that sensations and real properties do admit of degrees of intensity. As Falkenstein points out, the argument does not rule out the possibilities that sensations (and hence real properties) have a unit value – either they are present or they are not – or admit of degrees that consist in discontinuous quantum states. Such a quality could be present at, for example, 50% or 60% of intensity, but not at intermediate states.[30] Even granting that consciousness admits of degrees of clarity, it does not follow that sensations must admit of continuous degrees of intensity.

---

[30] Both Béatrice Longuenesse and Jonathan Bennett recognize that Kant could have what I called the weaker conception of possibility such that any sensation could vary continuously in principle, although in fact some sensations might not do so. See Longuenesse, *Kant and the Capacity of Judge*, 314–15, and Bennett, *Kant's Analytic*, 172.

5. SUMMARY

In the Schematism, Kant describes the transcendental schemata –
sensible conditions – required to apply pure concepts of the understanding to objects of intuition. A schema is a procedure by which the
productive imagination constructs temporal features of objects. Thus
it provides the sensible content that turns a syntactic concept into a
real concept of an object. The Axioms of Intuition and the Anticipations of Perception are synthetic *a priori* principles of the understanding expressing the mathematical categories of quantity and quality.
The Axioms specify that spatiotemporal objects must have extensively
measurable properties; the Anticipations require that the real properties of objects must be intensively measurable. These transcendental
deductions thus justify synthetic *a priori* cognition of appearances,
while explaining why such knowledge does not apply to things in
themselves.

CHAPTER 7

The Analytic of Principles II

This chapter examines three of Kant's most important arguments, those responding to skepticism. From the Greeks up to Hume, skeptics attacked metaphysical claims about reality, especially regarding substance, causal connections, and the external world. Kant replies to these attacks in the Analogies of Experience and the Postulates of Empirical Thought, where he defends pure principles based on the relational and modal categories. According to Kant's proofs, these regulative principles supply the elements required to turn mere intuitions into perceptions of objects in the "weighty" sense, as subject-independent entities in unified space and time. The Analogies argue that the principles of substance and causal connection are necessary to locate events in objective time. The Postulates of Empirical Thought, which include the Refutation of Idealism, demonstrate the principles enabling subjects to judge the real possibility, actuality, and necessity of states of affairs. Here I first explain Kant's arguments for these principles, and then comment on Kant's success in answering skepticism.

I. THE ANALOGIES OF EXPERIENCE

The Analogies argue that the *a priori* concepts of substance and causality are required to order appearances in one time.[1] Although the text contains a distinct proof for each category, the introduction argues for a general principle emphasizing the notion of objective time-determination. The A edition principle states: "As regards their existence, all appearances stand *a priori* under rules of the determination of their relation to each other in **one** time" (A176/B218). The B

---

[1] This discussion is heavily indebted to Melnick's *Kant's Analogies of Experience*.

edition version reads: "**Experience is possible only through the representation of a necessary connection of perceptions**" (A176/B218). Despite their differences, both versions claim that a consistent ordering of states of affairs in global time requires thinking appearances by the relational categories.

As with the previous principles, Kant added a new proof to the beginning of the B edition. The brief A edition argument at A177/B220 proceeds by claiming that "original apperception is related to inner sense." This means that we can become aware that our representations exist in one unified time. Since performing the t.u.a. requires synthesis, and synthesis requires an *a priori* ground, the rules for ordering representations in one time must be *a priori*. Therefore, "all empirical time-determinations must stand under rules of general time-determination," namely the Analogies.

Unfortunately this does not explain why the intuitions being ordered in time must be of subject-independent objects. Kant addresses this defect in the B edition by emphasizing the notion of objective time-determination. The key is the contrast between a merely subjective order of representations in apprehension and the objective order of events in time. At B218 Kant defines experience as empirical cognition of objects through perception, which we know requires a synthesis in one consciousness. At B219 Kant states that in apprehension representations occur in a contingent, subjective order, which can be distinguished from the objective order of the perceived states in unified time. This latter order can be thought only by means of *a priori* rules expressing necessary temporal features of objective states. Insofar as they unify appearances in one time, these synthetic *a priori* principles ground our judgments of subject-independent states of affairs.

Some common experiences illustrate the distinction between the subjective order of apprehension and the objective order of events. The simplest case involves successive perceptions of coexisting states of affairs. In the Second Analogy at A191/B235 Kant uses the example of perceiving a house. Although the parts of the house coexist, our perceptions of them occur successively, the order contingent on where we begin. But this does not prevent us from recognizing that the parts exist simultaneously. A more subtle case occurs when we see lightning at a distance and hear thunder a few moments later. Knowing that light travels faster than sound, we can recognize that the lightning and thunder actually occur simultaneously, although we apprehend them successively. Finally, it is even possible to apprehend states of affairs in an order opposite to that in which they exist. Suppose one first sees a cat moving nearby, and then observes some distant astronomical event, such as a nova. Given the time it takes light to travel to the Earth, we can judge that the nova actually occurred long before the cat moved. Clearly we do in fact distinguish the objective order of events from their order in apprehension.

Kant's strategy is to show that locating states in objective time presupposes the principles of the Analogies. Put simply, an objective time-determination is a way of conceiving the order of appearances in global time, in terms of three modes: persistence (or duration), succession, and simultaneity. "Hence three rules of all temporal relations of appearances, in accordance with which the existence of each can be determined with regard to the unity of all time, precede all experience and first make it possible" (A177/B219). The "modes of time" are actually properties of appearances rather than time itself. Although global time persists, it cannot be either successive or simultaneous. Distinct parts of time exist successively, and only states can exist simultaneously. Thus all states of affairs have some objective duration, and distinct states exist successively or simultaneously. Objective time-determination involves measuring temporal intervals, as well as determining the orders of states of affairs.

Kant next emphasizes the regulative role of the principles. As we saw in chapters 4 and 6, Kant characterizes quantitative and qualitative categories and principles as "mathematical" or "constitutive," and relational and modal categories and principles as "dynamical" or "regulative." Whereas mathematical categories are required to represent distinct individuals and their properties, dynamical categories relate these representations to one another in time and to the subject (A178/B220–1). This has two important implications. First, the existence of appearances cannot be "constructed," that is, known *a priori* (A179/B222). The fact that anything is given at all in intuition, and when it exists, can be known only empirically. The second implication concerns their demonstrability. Kant says that although both types are *a priori*, they differ in "the manner of their evidence, i.e., with regard to their intuitiveness" (A180/B223). Unlike extensive and intensive properties, locations and relations in objective time and possibility, actuality, and necessity are not intuitable features of appearances. Now this distinction between the constitutive and regulative categories amounts to a distinction between principles establishing the mere intentionality of perception, and those establishing the robust objectivity of the intuited objects. Although merely intentional objects might present extensively and intensively intuitable features, the order of their existence could not be distinguished from their order of apprehension. The mark of real subject-independent objects is objective spatiotemporal location.

2. THE FIRST ANALOGY: THE PRINCIPLE OF SUBSTANCE

Kant intends the First Analogy to defend the belief in substances as permanent things underlying changing states. Historically there were many concepts of substance, but most philosophers subscribed to the view that transitory states must belong to something permanent. Since we are directly aware only of our own successive, fleeting perceptions, Hume denied we could know any kind of permanent entity, physical or mental. Although it does not become clear until the Second Analogy, for Kant substance can only be physical; he rejects Descartes's dualistic concept of mind as a substantial entity.

Each relational category corresponds to a particular mode of time. Kant correlates substance with duration or persistence, cause–effect with succession, and causal interaction with simultaneity. Like the other categories, the three relational concepts are interdependent, because the three modes of time are also interdependent. Duration (or persistence) is the fundamental mode, since all states last for some time. Different states of affairs exist either successively or simultaneously. But determining the objective succession and coexistence of states presupposes determining objective time intervals. As Melnick points out, knowing only that one state precedes another does not determine their exact locations in global time. Existing three minutes apart is a different order from existing three days apart. In the two cases, the states will bear different relations to all other states in time. Moreover, determining when a state begins or ends also depends on measuring time intervals. To use Melnick's example, if it starts to rain at some time t, there must be some definite time interval before t during which it was not raining. Although we do not have to determine how long before t it was not raining, we must be able to determine some time interval before it started to rain. Otherwise it would not be true that it began to rain at t.[2] Thus the ability to identify the beginnings, endings, and relations of states of affairs in objective time presupposes being able to measure temporal intervals. For Kant, this means that our notions of causal action and interaction presuppose the concept of substance.

Kant offers two versions of the principle of substance. The A edition states, "All appearances contain that which persists (**substance**) as the object itself, and that which can change as its mere determination, i.e., a way in which the object exists" (A182). The B edition says, "In all change of appearances substance persists, and its quantum is neither increased nor diminished in nature" (A182/B224). Although the A version emphasizes permanence, the B version includes the corollary principle of the conservation of substance. Both versions claim that all changes in appearance must be thought as states of some absolutely permanent substance. This principle is synthetic *a priori* since it asserts that permanent things exist. Its deduction depends on the assumption that we do in fact perceive states of affairs that endure and that are related successively and simultaneously in time.

Kant offers two proofs for the principle. The first, which Melnick calls the argument from time magnitude, occurs in the first paragraph, at A182/B224–5. Kant elaborates on it up to the second proof at A188/B231. These arguments raise three issues: first, whether substance must be absolutely permanent; second, what counts as substances for Kant; and third, how he defends the conservation principle.

The argument from time magnitude consists in the following steps:

1. Time is the substratum of all appearances; time itself cannot change.
   1a. We do in fact perceive successive and simultaneous states in time.
2. Time itself cannot be perceived.
3. Therefore, there must be something in appearance that represents time as the substratum of all change.

---

[2] See Melnick, *Kant's Analogies of Experience*, 60–1.

4. The substratum of everything real is substance; everything that belongs to existence can be thought only as a determination of substance.

5. Therefore, there must be real substance in appearance; all perceivable changes must be alterations of real substance. Moreover, the quantity of substance cannot increase or diminish. (A182/B224–5)

Allison calls steps 1–3 the "backdrop thesis," since they express Kant's view of time perception underlying all the Analogies. Let us now examine each step of the argument.

1. *Time is the substratum of all appearances; time itself cannot change.* Here Kant restates the Aesthetic view that time is the universal form of all appearances. The difference between the term 'substratum' and the term 'substance' is crucial. By a substratum Kant means a foundation or underlying structure. His point is that we can perceive succession and simultaneity only in time. But the Aesthetic also proves that there is only one time. Thus all appearances must be related to one another in the same unchanging, global time.

1a. *We do in fact perceive successive and simultaneous states in time.* This is the premise establishing the "fact" from which the principle follows. It is not stated explicitly but is presupposed in Kant's statements at A181/B225 that "succession and simultaneity can be represented" and "all change or simultaneity can be perceived" only in time.

2. *Time itself cannot be perceived.* It is an axiom of Kant's theory that neither empty space nor empty time is an object of perception. Only appearances in space and time are perceivable. But the absolute times of states are not given in the appearances. First, time is qualitatively homogeneous and so the nature of time provides no basis for distinguishing one moment or interval from another. Second, the qualities we sense are independent of their times (and places): they do not come "stamped" with objective temporal locations, and none can be inferred from them alone.

3. *Therefore, there must be something in appearance that represents time as the substratum of all change.* Since time itself cannot be perceived, something else must represent the underlying substratum against which to judge successive and coexisting states. The only other thing given in intuition is appearances. Therefore there must

be some feature of appearances functioning as the basis for ordering transitory states in time.

4. *The substratum of everything real is substance; everything that belongs to existence can be thought only as a determination of substance.* Here Kant connects substance with the substratum of change, but his claim involves two different notions of substance.[3] The correlation between the pure concept of substance and the subject-predicate form of judgment retains the traditional idea of substance as the subject which is not itself predicable of anything else. This substance, which Bennett dubs "substance$_1$," must endure only relative to its changing predicates. Another conception, Bennett's "substance$_2$," is of something absolutely permanent.[4] This is Kant's schematized concept of substance: "the proposition that substance persists is tautological" (A184/B227). This premise maintains that the only candidate in appearances to represent the persistence of time is the enduring subject of changing states, the "substratum of everything real." It involves two claims: first, that the only thing that can serve in appearance as the substratum of change is the subject of changing states (substance$_1$), which, second, must be absolutely permanent (substance$_2$) to represent the persistence of time.

5. *Therefore, there must be real substance in appearance; all perceivable changes must be alterations of real substance.* Finally Kant draws the synthetic *a priori* conclusion that permanent substances must exist as the subjects of the changes we perceive in appearances. At A187/B230–1 he clarifies the terms 'change' (*Wechsel*) and 'alteration' (*Veränderung*): "Arising and perishing are not alterations of that which arises or perishes. Alteration is a way of existing that succeeds another way of existing of the very same object. Hence everything that is altered is **lasting**, and only its **state changes**." That is, a change consists in a coming-to-be or ceasing-to-be of some state. The subject of this change undergoes an alteration, but does not itself change. Thus the conclusion asserts that all changing states perceived in appearances must be alterations of some permanent substance.

On this reading the debatable claims are evident. The backdrop thesis (steps 1–3) is uncontroversial, since premises 1 and 2 are based

---

[3] See Allison, *Kant's Transcendental Idealism*, 212–15.   [4] See Bennett, *Kant's Analytic*, 182.

on the Aesthetic. Now one might question step 1a, depending on what counts as a "state" in time. Certainly Kant cannot presuppose that the changing states we perceive must be fully objective in the sense of apprehension-independent states of affairs, since this is what he intends to prove. But he does not need that claim. Even Hume admits that "perceptions of the mind" occur successively. Taking these as states, it follows that in inner sense, we do perceive a succession of changing states. So the skeptic who admits steps 1, 1a, and 2, must also accept conclusion 3.

This puts the burden on steps 4 and 5, where Kant identifies the substratum of real changes with substance. Here I follow Melnick, who offers the most plausible account of step 4.[5] First, we must note something not expressed here, namely the empirical criterion of substance. In the Second Analogy Kant says this criterion is action: "Where there is action, consequently activity and force, there is also substance" (A204/B250). Later, in the Amphiboly of the Concepts of Reflection, Kant remarks: "We know substance in space only through forces that are efficacious in it" (A265/B321). In other words, the empirical basis for determining time intervals are actions of things we take to be enduring entities. Examples of such actions are the motion of the hands of a clock, the motion of the Earth around the Sun, and the decay of a radioactive particle. Steps 4 and 5 claim that only if an action is taken to be of something persisting through a change can we use it as a basis for measuring the time interval.

To defend this, Melnick describes a case in which an object used in measurement fails to persist through an interval. Imagine we are measuring an interval from t_1 to t_2 by the motion of the hands of a clock. Suppose at t_1 the hands read 4:00, and at t_2 the hands read 4:05. But further suppose that the substance of the clock (call it A) goes out of existence at some point t' between t_1 and t_2, and that its replacement (call it B) comes into existence at some later time t'' before t_2. Thus we have the following situation:

$$t_1 \text{-------}A\text{-------} t' \qquad t''\text{======}B\text{=======}t_2$$

Now measuring the interval t_1–t_2 requires measuring the component interval t'–t''. But we cannot do this by reference to the hands of

⁵ See *Kant's Analogies of Experience*, 62–6.

the clock. Let the reading at t′ be 4:02:25, and the reading at t″ be 4:02:27. Although we are tempted to say the interval t′–t″ is 2 seconds, we cannot do so, since the readings of the clocks are significant only insofar as they record the mechanical actions of the two clocks. In this case their significance is lost, since the time interval t′–t″ "is not marked off by the mechanical process" (66). In other words, the action used to measure a temporal interval must be the action of something existing continuously through the interval. Thus Kant's stated conclusion appears justified.

On the other hand, Melnick thinks Kant is wrong to claim that substances must be absolutely permanent. He should conclude only that the things serving as substrata for time measurement cannot go out of existence during the intervals being measured. On Melnick's view, if some substance had to be employed for all measurements, then that substance would have to be absolutely permanent. But that condition does not obtain, since we use many different kinds of physical processes for different cases. Near the end of the First Analogy, Kant defends his claim about absolute permanence based on the "unity of time": "The arising of some [substances] and the perishing of others would itself remove the sole condition of the empirical unity of time, and the appearances would then be related to two different times, in which existence flowed side by side, which is absurd" (A188–9/ B231–2). Kant thinks that if substances were not absolutely permanent, and time-determinations were based on actions of different substances, then conflicting measurements might result, disrupting the coherence of temporal ordering in global time (the "empirical unity of time"). Melnick agrees that measurements of the same interval based on two different substrates could differ. But he argues that the problem arises only when both substrata are employed at the same time.[6] As long as only one substratum is used to measure any particular temporal interval, the use of different physical processes for different intervals need not disrupt the unity of time.

Kant's second proof that substance exists is the argument from empirical verifiability, that the absolute coming into being or perishing of something is not a possible object of perception:

---

[6] *Kant's Analogies of Experience*, 67–9.

If you assume that something simply began to be, then you would have to have a point of time in which it did not exist. But what would you attach this to, if not to that which already exists? For an empty time that would precede is not an object of perception; but if you connect this origination to things that existed antecedently and which endure until that which arises, then the latter would be only a determination of the former, as that which persists. It is just the same with perishing: for this presupposes the empirical representation of a time at which there is no longer an appearance. (A188/B231)

As Melnick explains, Kant is arguing that it is impossible to iden- tify the absolute beginning or ceasing of a state of affairs unless one attaches it to an enduring substance.[7] He describes the situation in which we want to determine that something S came into existence at a certain time t. To do so we must show that S did not exist before t, say at t'. But if S is not connected to anything enduring before t, then to verify that S did not exist before t requires showing that for all possible locations, S did not exist at any location at t'. But this is not a possible perception, and so the claim is not verifiable. By contrast, if S is a state of some enduring thing x, then it is possible to verify that S did not exist at t', since we can verify that x was not S at t'. To illustrate, he describes the creation of an electron pair (electron– positron) from a photon. This is the creation of an electron because there are no laws connecting the existence of this electron at t with the existence of an electron at any other place before t. But there are laws connecting the electron being here at t with another phenomenon at an earlier time and a certain place, in this case with the actions of photons. Melnick points out that for Kant, being governed by spatial laws is essential to states of substance; this foreshadows the argument in the Refutation of Idealism that substances must be spatial. In fact, Kant added this marginal note to the A edition text: "Here the proof must be so conducted that it applies only to substances as phenomena of outer sense, consequently from space, which exists at all time along with its determination."[8] We examine the Refutation below.

By now the reader is no doubt wondering what counts as a sub- stance for Kant. Assuming substances must be physical, it is not obvious what they would be. First, they could not be macro-objects

---

[7] *Kant's Analogies of Experience*, 71–7.
[8] Cited in *CPR*, 299. Original source given as Erdmann, *Nachträge zu Kants Kritik der reinen Vernunft*, 32; Academy edition of *Kant's gesammelte Schriften*, 23:30.

such as trees, tables, and chairs, since these objects pass in and out of existence. Melnick's example of electron creation also shows that even sub-atomic particles of matter could not qualify as substances if they can be created or destroyed. In *MFNS*, Kant argues that matter must be composed of absolutely permanent centers of force. Accordingly, these centers would count as substances, and the particles and objects they give rise to would count as their states. In any case, only theoretical physics can decide the nature of substance.

Finally, we should consider Kant's corollary, that the quantity of substance is conserved. Kant offers no argument for it here. A marginal note in the A edition, however, specifies that substance can be conceived only in terms of quantity: "Now everything that can be distinguished from that which changes in experience is quantity (*grösse*), and this can only be assessed through the magnitude of the merely relative effect in the case of equal external relations (*Relationen*) and therefore applies only to bodies."[9] Allison points out that at A848/B876 Kant defines matter as "impenetrable lifeless extension," that is, a mere occupier of space. So the corollary hinges on the idea that the only conceivable property of substance is its quantity. Unfortunately Kant does not explain why this must be so.[10]

3. THE SECOND ANALOGY: THE PRINCIPLE OF CAUSALITY

The Second Analogy argues for the general principle that every event has a cause. Although commentators agree that Kant is responding to Hume's attack on belief in causal connections, they disagree about whether he also intends to guarantee the existence of empirical laws. Despite a majority opinion against this view, Melnick and Friedman present compelling reasons in its favor. We shall examine this issue after analyzing the argument and some objections to it.

The A edition principle states: "Everything that happens (begins to be) presupposes something which it follows in accordance with a rule" (A188). The B edition version says, "All alterations occur in accordance

---

[9] Allison's discussion of this topic is found at *Kant's Transcendental Idealism*, 210–12. The marginal note is cited in *CPR*, 299. Original source given as Erdmann, 32; *Ak.* 23:30–1.

[10] For Kant's conception of matter in the *MFNS*, see Allison, *Kant's Transcendental Idealism*, 210–12, Brittan, *Kant's Theory of Science*, chapter 6, and Friedman, *Kant's and the Exact Sciences*, 38–9.

with the law of the connection of cause and effect" (A188/B232). Whereas the B edition mentions only the general causal principle, the A edition refers to a rule, which, it appears, could only be an empirical law. As we have seen, the relational categories function to determine the position of states of affairs in objective time. The Second Analogy ties the concept of cause–effect to our experience of succession. Kant will argue that the perception of states as objectively successive presupposes that events are caused.

First we need to clarify the notions of an event and a cause. For Kant an event is a change of state, which, as the First Analogy argues, can only be the state of a substance. Thus an event is a coming to be in something of a state that did not already obtain. In general an event E consists in a succession of states of an object from S_1 to S_2 (hereafter 'S_1–S_2'). Events are objective happenings: they have a determinate position in global time. Examples of events are the freezing or melting of water, the radioactive decay of a particle, and a stationary billiard ball beginning to move. Note also that the change of representations in a subject would be an event, albeit a "mental event." Kant uses the example of a ship moving downstream at A192/B237, but according to the law of inertia, only accelerations, not uniform motions, are changes of state. Kant in fact recognizes this in a footnote at A207/B252: "Hence if a body is moved uniformly, then it does not alter its state (of motion) at all, although it does if its motion increases or diminishes." Now this analysis of an event makes no reference to causal connections or rule-governed succession. Thus Arthur O. Lovejoy is wrong to claim that for Kant the causal principle is analytic since an event is defined as "a phenomenon that follows another phenomenon according to a rule."[11] To the contrary: Kant clearly recognizes the synthetic *a priori* nature of the causal principle.

A second confusion concerns the relation between events and their causes. Philosophers often take the successive states S_1–S_2 composing the event to be respectively the cause and the effect. As Melnick shows, however, this is not Kant's view, and it is generally not true of events as we understand them.[12] Consider the freezing of water: clearly the state of being liquid is not the cause of the water becoming solid. The event consists in the change S_1–S_2, but the cause is some other

---

[11] See Lovejoy, "On Kant's Reply to Hume," 295.
[12] *Kant's Analogies of Experience*, 100–1.

event or condition, such as lowering the temperature. Kant conceives of the cause as a condition that brings about the change according to a rule: "there must therefore lie in that which in general precedes an occurrence the condition for a rule, in accordance with which this occurrence always and necessarily follows" (A193/B238–9). In sum, the event is the effect, and the cause is some other event.

The first statement of the proof occurs at B233–4; Kant then elaborates the argument several times. Here are the main steps, not in their order of presentation:

1. All apprehension is successive. (A189/B234; A192/B237)
2. I perceive events, and thus can distinguish an objective succession of states in time from a merely subjective succession of apprehensions. (B233; A190/B235–6; A192/B237)
3. Perceiving an objective succession of states requires the imagination to connect and order perceptions in global time. (B233)
4. The "backdrop thesis": the objective position of states in global time cannot be determined by mere perception, since: (a) time itself cannot be perceived; (b) the manifold given in intuition is not "stamped" with its objective time position; and (c) the order of apprehension does not yield objective time positions. (B233–4; A190/B235)
5. Therefore, the only alternative is to think the succession of states as necessarily determined or irreversible. (A188/B234; A192–3/B237–8)
6. The concept required to think the irreversibility of states is cause-effect, that is, the concept of a condition upon which something else follows necessarily according to a rule. (A193/B238)
7. Therefore, event perception presupposes that all events are caused.
8. Corollary: the subjective sequence of apprehension is "bound to" or derived from the objective order of the states. (A192/B237–8)

Kant wants to derive the principle that all events are caused from the fact that we perceive events or objective successions in time. Like the First Analogy, the proof depends on the backdrop thesis, that the objective times of appearances are not given in "mere perception," but must be thought. Judging that a succession of states is necessary means thinking it as irreversible. Kant believes that cause–effect is the *a priori* concept required to think successions as irreversible. From this he concludes that all events are governed by causal laws. Let us now examine each step in turn.

1. *All apprehension is successive.* This follows from the Aesthetic analysis of time as the form of inner sense.

2. *I perceive events, and can thus distinguish an objective succession of states in time from a merely subjective succession of apprehensions.* Kant's argument is based on the fact that we distinguish between a mere succession of perceptions and the perception of a succession. As the example of perceiving a house shows (A190/B235), that two states are perceived successively does not entail that they exist successively. Now we must consider whether a skeptic like Hume could object to this premise. Allison maintains that Hume cannot reject this premise since "event awareness is presupposed by his own well-known account of how we come to form the belief that future sequences of events will resemble past sequences."[13] Moreover, Hume's theory that impressions precede their corresponding ideas evidently requires him to distinguish between objective and subjective successions.

3. *Perceiving an objective succession of states requires the imagination to connect and order perceptions in global time.* Recognizing an event requires one to perceive (judge) the component states as having a determinate order in global time. Now commentators disagree over what Kant is claiming about this temporal ordering. Allison believes Kant is arguing only that we must be able to determine the relative order of states in time.[14] By contrast, Melnick takes Kant to argue that it must be possible to locate an *event* in relation to all other events in global time. In support, he cites passages such as A177/B219, where Kant describes the principles as rules "in accordance with which the existence of each [appearance] can be determined with regard to the unity of all time."[15] Melnick's reading offers a more coherent interpretation of Kant, one reinforced by the Postulates of Empirical Thought, as well as the First Analogy.

4. *The "backdrop thesis:" the objective position of states in global time cannot be determined by mere perception.* In discussing the First Analogy we accepted this view, that neither the data of intuition nor the mere order of apprehension can determine the objective times

[13] *Kant's Transcendental Idealism*, 228.   [14] See Allison, *Kant's Transcendental Idealism*, 229.
[15] Melnick, *Kant's Analogies of Experience*, 85–8.

of the intuited states. Lovejoy objects, however, that it is possible to perceive the succession of states constituting an event. Citing Kant's example of the ship floating downstream, Lovejoy says, "I can, in the language of common sense, *see* the ship move." From this he concludes that the principle of causality (he says sufficient reason) is not required to distinguish between objective successions and coexisting states.[16] Lovejoy is right, of course, that one can perceive successive states of an object (this is consistent with premise 2). But it does not follow from mere perception that these are states of the same substance, or that we can locate the states in global time. Consider the ship case: what guarantees that the substance of the ship upstream is the same substance as the ship downstream? It will turn out that one function of causal laws is precisely to justify assumptions about the identity of the objects whose states are being perceived. The discussion of time determination above also shows that mere perception is not sufficient to locate successive states in global time. Thus Lovejoy's example does not refute Kant's argument.

5. *Therefore, the only alternative is to think the succession of states as necessarily determined or irreversible.* This is the famous "irreversibility thesis," about which there is much confusion. What Kant actually says is that in order to determine the objective relation of the appearances, "the relation between the two *states* must be thought in such a way that it is thereby necessarily determined which of them must be placed before and which after rather than vice versa" (A188/B234, my italics). And at A192–3/B237–8 he distinguishes event perception from the successive perception of coexisting states: "if in the case of an appearance that contains a happening I call the preceding *state* of perception A and the following one B, then B can only follow A in apprehension, but the perception A cannot follow but only precede B" (my italics). By contrast, in the successive apprehension of coexisting states, the order of perceptions has no necessity: "In the previous example of a house . . . there was therefore no determinate order that made it necessary when I had to begin in the apprehension in order to combine the manifold empirically" (A193/B238). Thus what characterizes event perception is the irreversibility of the perceptions; as Strawson puts it, perceptions of coexisting states have

---

[16] See Lovejoy, "On Kant's Reply to Hume," 297–8.

"order-indifference."[17] The question arises whether Kant is attributing irreversibility to the states perceived or to our apprehensions of them, since the term "perception" is ambiguous. As I emphasized above, however, irreversibility must be attributed originally to the appearances. In consequence (I list this as a corollary in step 8), we must think the order of apprehension as "bound to" the order of the states perceived. Here, then, Kant identifies the feature characterizing event perception as the thought that the sequence S_1–S_2 constituting the event is irreversible. As both Melnick and Allison emphasize, Kant is *not* arguing that irreversibility in apprehension is a datum from which we infer the irreversibility of states of appearances.[18]

A second issue concerns whether Kant's claim that one must think the succession as necessary is analytic. Several commentators argue that given that one perceives an event E constituted by S_1–S_2, it is logically necessary that the states occur in the order S_1–S_2. If they occurred in the order S_2–S_1, by definition one would perceive a different event.[19] But as James Van Cleve has shown, this objection commits two fallacies.[20] First is a scope error: Kant is arguing that the necessity attaches unconditionally to the existence of the event rather than to the consequent of a conditional. That is, event perception is characterized by the thought "Necessarily S_1 is followed by S_2," rather than "If I perceive E, necessarily S_1 is followed by S_2," which is analytic. A related error is construing the necessity here as logical rather than real. Clearly the sequence S_1–S_2 has a real necessity, which Kant attributes to the necessity of causal laws. Kant is offering a transcendental deduction to show that the real necessity of metaphysical principles is grounded in their "epistemic" status.

6. *The concept required to think the irreversibility of states is cause–effect, that is, the concept of a condition upon which something else follows necessarily according to a rule.* Finally, Kant connects the idea of irreversibility to causal laws. As we saw earlier, the event being perceived is the effect, and the cause is some condition that initiates the change

[17] See Strawson, *The Bounds of Sense*, 133.

[18] See Melnick, *Kant's Analogies of Experience*, 82–3, and Allison, *Kant's Transcendental Idealism*, 225.

[19] Among those raising this objection are Strawson, *The Bounds of Sense*, 137, Wolff, *Kant's Theory of Mental Activity*, 268, and Bennett, *Kant's Analytic*, 221.

[20] See Van Cleve, "Four Recent Interpretations of Kant's Second Analogy," 82–3.

from S_1 to S_2. It is essential to causality that the relation between cause and effect be rule-governed: "This connection must therefore consist in the order of the manifold of appearance in accordance with which the apprehension of one thing (that which happens) follows that of the other (which precedes) **in accordance with a rule**" (A193/B238).[21]

As Melnick explains, Kant sees causal laws as rules for ordering states, based on features of appearances.[22] Since the sequence is irreversible, the law must be asymmetrical: Kant says that being rule-governed entails "that I cannot reverse the series and place that which happens prior to that which it follows" (A198/B243). But causal laws are complex, and it is an oversimplification to represent them in the form, "Whenever C occurs, E occurs." For in addition to describing the cause and the effect, they must take into account other relevant factors called boundary conditions. For example, it is not the case that water invariably freezes at a temperature of 32° Fahrenheit; other factors come into play, including the volume and shape of the liquid mass and the pressure acting on it. Thus the rules relating cause to effect must always refer to the circumstances in which the event takes place. To cite Melnick's more elaborate example, an automobile can be rust-free (P_1) at t, and corroded (P_2) at t'. How we order these states depends on the circumstances. The event could be the change P_1–P_2 if oxidation occurs; or it could consist of P_2–P_1 if the automobile is repainted. Causal laws, then, take the form, "Given circumstances B, whenever event C occurs, S_1 will be followed by S_2."

Whether step 6 is acceptable, then, depends on whether ordering successive states requires us to think them as governed by causal laws. Given the backdrop thesis, the conclusion that this objective ordering depends on features of appearances appears undeniable. But as Melnick points out, nothing about appearances determines their order "except in terms of some rule that orders the appearances on the basis of these features."[23] As we saw above, ordering the states as non-coexistent means that the rule must be asymmetrical: given the circumstances, S_1 is followed by S_2 and not vice versa. Thus Kant can reasonably conclude that perceiving states as necessarily successive requires thinking them as subject to causal laws. Causal laws

---

[21] Additional passages occur at A193/B238–9, A195/B240, and A201/B247.
[22] *Kant's Analogies of Experience*, 89–90. [23] *Kant's Analogies of Experience*, 89.

function as rules for ordering states as successive based on features of
the states.[24]

7. *Therefore, the perception of events in time presupposes that all events
are caused.* Kant's conclusion is the general principle that all events are
caused. This follows from steps 5 and 6, for if it is true that we must
think of the states making up an event as necessarily successive, and
if causal laws are required to order states in this way, then all events
must be subject to causal laws.

As I mentioned, commentators question whether Kant also intends
to prove the existence of particular empirical laws. On the above
interpretation, the causal principle must be true because we must
think of events as governed by empirical laws. Friedman defends
this reading in discussing Kant's view of empirical laws.[25] Friedman
argues that for Kant, causality is a rule-governed relation between two
events, such that given the cause, the succession of states constituting
the effect follows necessarily. Moreover, the universality of a rule
entails that it applies to types of events (e.g., lowering temperature
with the freezing of water).[26] Thus he agrees with Melnick that Kant
justifies the causal principle by showing that all events are governed
by empirical laws; in other words, "the universal causal principle
must assert the existence of particular causal laws."[27] Now as Melnick
explains, this does not guarantee that we can discover these causal
laws. The Second Analogy argues only that there must be causal
laws governing changes of state, not that we must know them. For
one thing, we may need the repetition of types of events to discover
causal laws, but the Second Analogy does not imply anything about
the frequency of types of events.[28]

Friedman also argues that Kant does not construe particular causal
laws as inductive generalizations. Of course empirical laws are more
specific than the causal principle because they employ empirical concepts (e.g., matter as the movable in space). Although "empirical laws
can only obtain and be found by means of experience" (A216/B263),
it does not follow that they are *a posteriori*. Throughout the Analytic,

[24] See Melnick, *Kant's Analogies of Experience*, 89–90.
[25] See "Causal Laws," especially 165–75.
[26] See "Causal Laws," 192n4 and 193n6. Obviously the general causal principle does not specify
the kind of rule Kant is arguing for.
[27] "Causal Laws," 171.   [28] See Melnick, *Kant's Analogies of Experience*, 91–3.

Kant emphasizes the necessity of causal connections. At A91/B124 he says the concept of causality requires that the effect follow from the cause

necessarily and **in accordance with an absolutely universal rule** . . . thus to the synthesis of cause and effect there attaches a dignity that can never be expressed empirically, namely that the effect does not merely come along with the cause, but is posited **through** it and follows **from** it.

And at A159/B198 he says laws of nature "carry with them an expression of necessity, thus at least the presumption of determination by grounds that are *a priori* and valid prior to all experience." For Kant, empirical laws have a mixed necessity, which Friedman describes as "*a priori* in a derivative sense."[29] Although empirical laws are not deducible from the principle of causality, that principle makes possible particular causal laws.[30] Friedman describes the three-stage procedure for deriving the law of gravitation from Kepler's laws, which subsumes both the latter and the theory of gravitation under the necessary transcendental principles. Melnick's and Friedman's analyses should put to rest doubts that Kant intends to demonstrate the existence of particular causal laws.

8. *Corollary: the subjective order of apprehension is "bound to" or derived from the objective order of the states.* Finally we come to Kant's claim concerning the order of apprehension in event perception. As I see it, this is not a premise, but an implication of the conclusion. One could interpret it to mean that to represent states as necessarily successive, our apprehensions of those states must also be necessarily successive. But a careful reading shows that Kant never says this: he claims only that the subjective order is "bound to" or "derived from" the objective order. A better construal is based on a causal theory of perception, according to which our apprehensions are mental events themselves subject to the principle of causality. Thus the order of our apprehensions a–b of an event A–B is determined by the location of the event A–B in time. Whether the subjective order reproduces the objective order depends on the circumstances. Under ordinary circumstances, such that the way a depends on A does not differ from

---

[29] "Causal Laws," 174.
[30] Friedman sketches how the law of universal gravitation is "grounded" in the *MFNS* in section IV of "Causal Laws," 175–80, and *Kant and the Exact Sciences*, 165–210.

the way b depends on B, the order of apprehension would reproduce the order of the states.[31] Moreover, since this is only a corollary
of the causal principle, there is no circularity in basing this claim on a
causal theory of perception. Demonstrating the truth of the principle
of causality *a fortiori* justifies a causal theory of perception and this
corollary claim.

Throughout the Second Analogy, Kant claims that only transcendental idealism, and not transcendental realism, can account for
the distinction between objective and subjective temporal orders.
Although this does not play a role in the proof, it does bolster the
case for transcendental idealism. Kant explains the inadequacy of
transcendental realism thus:

> If appearances were things in themselves, then no human being would be
> able to assess from the succession of representations how the manifold is
> combined in the object. For we have to do only with our representations;
> how things in themselves may be . . . is entirely beyond our cognitive
> sphere. (A190/B235)

For the transcendental realist, all representations are empirical and
provide no basis for distinguishing the subjective order of apprehension from the objective order of events. Only by taking appearances to
be constituted by the act of judging, can we recognize features essential to experience of objects: "If we investigate what new characteristic
is given to our representations by the **relation to an object**, and what
is the dignity that they thereby receive, we find that it does nothing
beyond making the combination of representations necessary in a
certain way, and subjecting them to a rule" (A197/B242–3).[32]

One last question concerns the simultaneity of cause and effect.
At A202–3/B247–9 Kant denies that the cause necessarily precedes
the effect, or that the necessary succession obtains between cause and
effect. Kant's examples of the stove heating a room and the lead ball
creating a depression in the pillow illustrate that "The majority of
efficient causes in nature are simultaneous with their effects, and the
temporal sequence of the latter is occasioned only by the fact that the

---

[31] Van Cleve calls this condition "perceptual isomorphism" in "Four Recent Interpretations of
Kant's Second Analogy," 81–2.
[32] See also A191/B236, A196–7/B241–2, and A199–200/B244–5.

cause cannot achieve its entire effect in one instant" (A203/B248). As we have seen, causal laws imply not that causes must precede their effects, but that given the cause, the succession of states constituting the effect is necessary. Now one relation that must obtain between cause and effect is that the effect could not precede its cause: "For if I lay the ball on the pillow the dent follows its previously smooth shape; but if (for whatever reason) the pillow has a dent, a leaden ball does not follow it" (A203/B248–9). In Kant's view, the actual temporal relations between cause and effect will depend on the nature of the interaction.

4. THE THIRD ANALOGY: THE PRINCIPLE OF CAUSAL INTERACTION

In the Third Analogy, Kant argues that our ability to determine that states of distinct substances coexist presupposes laws of causal interaction. This completes his analysis of the necessary conditions for determining objective time relations of appearances. As Melnick points out, however, the Second and Third Analogies are actually two sides of the same coin. This is not surprising since, according to Newton's third law of motion, every causal action also involves an interaction. Melnick argues that Kant's distinction between the schemata of causality (succession) and that of mutual interaction (coexistence) is mistaken. By generalizing the notion of causal law to include dynamical interactions, Kant can combine the two arguments. Thus the weakness is in the detail rather than the substance of the arguments.[33]

As usual, Kant presents two versions of the Third Analogy principle, which the B edition labels the "**Principle of simultaneity, according to the law of interaction, or community**." The A edition version states, "All substances, insofar as they are **simultaneous**, stand in thoroughgoing community (i.e., interaction with one another)" (A211). The B edition reads: "All substances, insofar as they can be perceived in space as simultaneous, are in thoroughgoing interaction" (B256). Since substances are absolutely permanent, simultaneity must

---

[33] Here I follow Melnick in *Kant's Analogies of Experience*, 94–7 and 102–10.

be a feature of their states. The point, then, is to show that judging states of (distinct) substances to be simultaneous requires that they fall under laws of dynamical interaction.

The official argument is given at B257–8, and closely parallels the argument of the Second Analogy. The main steps are these:

1. Things (states) are simultaneous when their perceptions are reciprocal or reversible. For example, perceptions of coexisting states of the moon and the earth can occur in any order.
2. Simultaneity is the existence of the manifold at the same time.
3. The backdrop thesis: objective simultaneity is not given in intuition.
4. Therefore, the understanding must think the perceived states as simultaneous and thereby as reversible in perception.
5. The concept required to do this is mutual dynamical interaction.
6. Therefore, the perception of simultaneous states presupposes laws of dynamical interaction.

The problem is how to distinguish causal actions determining objective successions from the dynamical interactions correlated with objective simultaneity. Melnick thinks this is not serious, since it is possible to unify the arguments of the Second and Third Analogies. The Second Analogy principle applies to successive states of one substance, the Third Analogy to simultaneous states of distinct substances. Melnick shows that determining a succession of states of distinct substances requires both causal action and mutual interaction. Had Kant generalized his approach, the two arguments could be combined as follows:[34]

1. We can determine the objective times of events or states of affairs only relative to other events or states of affairs, and presupposing that the position of an event can be determined relatively to all other events.
2. Objective time-determinations are not given in perception.
3. Therefore temporal determinability must be based on features of appearances.
4. Features of appearances can be used to locate events and states of affairs only by presupposing rules licensing such inferences.

[34] I paraphrase Melnick at *Kant's Analogies of Experience*, 95–7.

5. Rules licensing inferences from features of appearances to their temporal locations are laws describing real connections, both asymmetrical and mutual, among substances.
6. Therefore, the objective determination of states as successive or simultaneous requires the application of causal laws or rules describing necessary connections among states of affairs.

Melnick defends his view by analyzing the impact motion of billiard balls described by laws of collision. Consider an impact law L that describes the motions of bodies following a collision as a function of the magnitude and direction of force, their elasticity, the coefficient of friction, and so on. Melnick argues that such a law can be used to determine both successive and simultaneous states of the balls.[35] Suppose a billiard ball a simultaneously strikes two billiard balls at rest, b and c. If we are interested only in the positions of b and c relative to each other, but not with respect to a, we can use L to determine the simultaneous positions of b and c after the collision. By the same token, we can use L to determine that b is at p before c is at p' following the collision. In neither case are the positions of the two balls a function of each other, nor does any mutual interaction between them play a role. Thus where there is a causal interaction involving a change of state(s) brought about by an initiating condition, the same law can be used to determine both the objective succession and coexistence of states, in the same and distinct substances.

Melnick concludes that although Kant wrongly correlates causality with succession and interaction with simultaneity, he is right that objective time-determination requires us to apply causal laws of action and interaction to the things whose states they are.[36] In the absence of dynamical interactions among substances, we could not make objective temporal claims about their states, since we could not determine whether the two states are objectively successive or simultaneous. In concluding, Kant claims that "There are therefore certain laws, and indeed *a priori*, which first make a nature possible" (A216/B263). By "nature" he means the necessary unity of all appearances in one space-time. "Thus together [the Analogies] say: All appearances lie in one nature, and must lie therein, since without this *a priori* unity no unity

---

[35] See Melnick, *Kant's Analogies of Experience*, 102–10 for the full discussion.
[36] Melnick, *Kant's Analogies of Experience*, 109.

of experience, thus also no determination of the objects in it, would
be possible" (A216/B263).

5. THE POSTULATES OF EMPIRICAL THOUGHT

Up to this point the Principles describe conditions that constrain
the *content* of our experience of objects. By contrast, the Postulates
govern the mode in which the subject holds objective judgments, as
to their real possibility, actuality, or necessity. At A219/B266 Kant says
the modal categories are peculiar insofar as "they do not augment the
concept to which they are ascribed in the least, but rather express only
the relation to the faculty of cognition." Rather than contributing
to the concept of an object, the modal categories relate objects "to
the understanding and its empirical use, to the empirical power of
judgment, and to reason." In other words, the modal categories are
required to create a coherent system of knowledge.

The categories of modality are schematized versions of the logical
concepts of modality discussed in the Metaphysical Deduction. In
chapter 4 we saw that the latter concern the illocutionary or assertive
force of judgments: logical possibility expresses the mode in which
the subject merely considers a proposition; logical actuality expresses
assertion; and logical necessity expresses the assertion of a proposition
as following from other propositions. In the Postulates, Kant claims
our ability to judge states of affairs as really possible or impossible,
actual or non-actual, and necessary or contingent, requires us to think
appearances under these modal concepts.

Kant's discussion does not so much justify as explain the application
of the Postulates. The interesting argument here is the Refutation of
Idealism, which Kant added to the B edition, along with a long footnote in the B edition Preface at Bxxxix–xli. As previously mentioned,
this argument responds to Descartes's view that self-knowledge is
more certain than knowledge of external objects. Kant inserted this
proof, one of his key arguments against skepticism, in the middle
of his analysis of actuality. In spite of its location, the argument is
significant enough to stand on its own. Here I shall discuss Kant's
general claims about the modal categories. The next section examines
the Refutation.

Judgments about real possibilities are governed by the postulate that objects conform to the formal conditions of experience in general, that is, to conditions of synthesis required for empirical cognition (A220/B267). These conditions include both the forms of intuition, and the categories defended previously. Hence for a state to be a possible object of experience, it must first be located in the global space-time of human intuition. Moreover, it must be both extensively and intensively measurable (Axioms and Anticipations), and governed by the principles of substance and causality (Analogies). Clearly these are stronger constraints than the mere notion of logical possibility expressed in the principle of non-contradiction. Kant says the impossibility of a figure enclosed between two straight lines "rests not on the concept in itself, but on its construction in space" (A220–1/B268). Given our form of spatial intuition, such a plane figure is not a possible object of experience. Similarly, invented concepts not derived from the formal conditions of experience have no *a priori* possibility.

Because assertions about the actual make stronger claims, they depend on not only formal but also material conditions of experience, namely sensation. At A225/B270 Kant says this does not require "immediate perception of the object itself" but rather "its connection with some actual perception in accordance with the analogies of experience." That is, one can assert the existence of a state of affairs that is not immediately perceived, as long as it is connected by laws with what is given in intuition. This permits us to assert the existence of theoretical or unobserved entities such as electrons, dinosaurs, and so on. Kant uses the example of a magnetic field: "Thus we cognize the existence of a magnetic matter penetrating all bodies from the perception of attracted iron filings, although an immediate perception of this matter is impossible for us given the constitution of our organs" (A226/B274). And in the Antinomies he says:

That there may be inhabitants in the moon, although no one has ever perceived them, must certainly be admitted. This, however, only means that in the possible advance of experience we may encounter them. For everything is real which stands in connection with a perception in accordance with the laws of empirical advance. (A493/B521)

This postulate also provides a criterion for distinguishing between dreams and waking experience, since dream states are not integrated into experience by causal laws.

Finally, the concept of empirical necessity applies only to states perceived as following from other states according to causal laws. As Kant puts it at A226/B280, real necessity is neither logical necessity, nor the formal necessity of a valid inference (Kant's logical form of necessity), nor absolute metaphysical necessity. Instead it is a hypothetical or material necessity of a state of affairs, given certain conditions, according to a universal law. Consequently, real necessity attaches not to substances, but only to their states: "Hence we cognize only the necessity of **effects** in nature, the causes of which are given to us . . . and even in this it does not hold of the existence of things, as substances, since these can never be regarded as empirical effects, or as something that happens and arises" (A227/B280). No substance exists necessarily; as the Second Analogy shows, empirical necessity attaches only to states of substances.

Finally Kant explains why he calls the modal principles postulates. Although 'postulate' sometimes means a proposition assumed without justification, this is not Kant's definition. As pure principles of the understanding, the Postulates express "the synthesis through which we first give ourselves an object and generate its concept" (A234/B287). Here Kant is thinking of propositions describing the construction of figures in space. These mathematical postulates cannot be proved "since the procedure that it demands is precisely that through which we first generate the concept of such a figure." Similarly, the Postulates of Empirical Thought cannot be proved since they do not add content to the concept of an object, but only indicate how it "is combined with the cognitive power" (A235/B287). In expressing *a priori* conditions for judging real states of affairs, the Postulates make it possible to construct a coherent system of empirical cognition.

6. THE REFUTATION OF IDEALISM

Kant inserts the Refutation in the discussion of actuality, since he intends to show that we must have actual knowledge of the external world. Along with the revised Transcendental Deduction, this is a major change in the B edition, added to clarify Kant's idealism. In the

A edition Kant tackled the problem of the external world in the fourth paralogism. There he claimed that transcendental idealism solves the problem by showing that external objects "are merely appearances, hence also nothing other than a species of my representations" (A370–1). It is no wonder many readers confused his position with empirical idealism, according to which physical objects are merely collections of perceptions. The Refutation also makes an important correction to Kant's treatment of space and time. Whereas the Aesthetic treats outer and inner sense as parallel, the Refutation establishes the priority of outer sense to inner sense.

The argument is aimed against empirical idealism, "the theory that declares the existence of objects in space outside us to be either merely doubtful and **indemonstrable**, or else false and **impossible**" (B274). Kant attributes the first variant, which he calls problematic idealism, to Descartes. The second he labels dogmatic idealism, which he attributes to Berkeley, who claims that the ideas of mind-independent space and matter are incoherent.[37] Kant agrees with Berkeley if one takes space to pertain to things in themselves, "for then it, along with everything for which it serves as a condition, is a non-entity" (B274). Since space is neither a substance nor a property of substances, it could have no clear metaphysical status as a thing in itself. But the conclusions that space is merely a form of intuition and not a thing in itself refute dogmatic idealism in two ways. First, they show that space and spatial things are possible as appearances; second, they prove that space is a necessary condition for experience of particulars distinct from the subject.

These arguments do not, however, address the possibility that whereas experience may actually be temporal, it may only seem to be spatial. Put another way, perhaps only inner sense is real, and outer sense is imaginary. This is Descartes's position in the second *Meditation*, where he argues that his mental states are immediately knowable and certain, while experience of physical things could be illusory. Not until the sixth *Meditation* can he argue for the existence of physical reality, based on his proofs of the existence of God. Although he concludes that physical objects exist, Descartes maintains this knowledge

---

[37] This discussion is drawn largely from my article, "On Kant's Proof of the Existence of Material Objects."

is based on inference from perception, guaranteed by God's benevolence. Thus knowledge of the external world is in principle less certain than self-knowledge.

In the Refutation, Kant will prove that knowledge of the external world is just as certain as knowledge of one's mental states. His strategy is *ad hominem*: that is, Descartes could not have certain and immediate knowledge of his mind unless he also had certain and immediate knowledge of spatial objects. Now we must be clear on what Kant is claiming about "outer" objects. According to transcendental idealism, both the objects of outer sense and the self known through inner sense are merely appearances and not things in themselves. Although Descartes was a transcendental realist, the issue here is not transcendental realism vs. idealism, but the certainty of physical knowledge compared to knowledge of the self. In the *cogito*, Descartes claims certain knowledge of his thoughts while doubting that external objects exist. In the order of experience, knowledge of the self is prior to knowledge of physical objects. Regarding evidence, the external world is not known directly, but only by inference from what is directly perceived.

In a long footnote to the B edition Preface, Kant says it is a "scandal of philosophy and universal human reason that the existence of things outside us . . . should have to be assumed merely **on faith**" (Bxxxix). The only way to prove that external objects are (empirically) real is as a condition of inner experience. Hence the thesis to be proved is: "**The mere, but empirically determined, consciousness of my own existence proves the existence of objects in space outside me**." In Kant's terms, the possibility of determinate inner sense presupposes immediate awareness of objects through outer sense.

His proof at B275–6 (with an emendation at Bxxxix) consists of five steps:[38]

1. Descartes's premise: "I am conscious of my existence as determined in time" (B275). Descartes's claim involves at least two capacities: first, to judge concerning any two mental states that they are both mine; and second, to recognize the order in which such states occur in consciousness.

---

[38] Here I follow the accounts in Strawson, *The Bounds of Sense*, 125–8; Gochnauer, "Kant's Refutation of Idealism"; and Allison, *Kant's Transcendental Idealism*, 297–304.

2. The First Analogy principle: "All time-determination presupposes something **persistent** in perception" (B275). As we saw, the First Analogy argues that determining objective temporal intervals pre-supposes the existence of substance enduring through changes of state. But since the proof establishes nothing about the nature of these substances, Kant must show here that they are spatial.

3. The third step is stated in the B edition Preface this way:

> But this persisting element cannot be an intuition in me. For all the determining grounds of my existence that can be encountered in me are representations, and as such they themselves need something persisting distinct from them, in relation to which their change, and thus my existence in the time in which they change, can be determined. (Bxxxix)

Here Kant rules out for the substantial basis in perception both aspects of the self, the representations and the thinking thing that has them. Representations cannot qualify, since the issue is precisely how I locate my representations in time. On the other hand, the thing serving as the permanent substratum cannot be the thinking self, since the only awareness of the self given in perception just is of its temporary states. This is why Kant says there is no perma-nent representation in intuition, that even representation of the permanent is itself transitory (Bxli and B291–2).

4. Therefore the permanent must be "a **thing** outside me" and not "the mere **representation** of a thing outside me" (B276). By a "thing outside me" Kant means first, something numerically distinct from the thinking self and its representations. But the thesis leaves no doubt that this thing must be in space; its otherness guarantees its physical nature.

5. Therefore determinate experience of myself as a particular thinker proves that I immediately perceive physical objects; only by means of this awareness can I know myself as the owner of my represen-tations.

This argument has never been taken seriously. In particular, commentators raise three issues: first, why the enduring objects required to know oneself must be spatial;[39] second, how the argument

---

[39] Included among these objectors are Allison, *Kant's Transcendental Idealism*, 303, and Ameriks, *Kant's Theory of Mind*, 121–2.

guarantees that these objects exist as opposed to being merely imagined;[40] and third, in what sense experience of spatial things is immediate, especially given the role of concepts in experiencing objects.[41] Here I shall respond to these three objections.

A. Why enduring objects must be spatial

Kant's strategy depends on what Descartes claims to know about himself. This includes awareness of first, a succession of temporary representations; second, the enduring self that has them; and third, the coexistence of this permanent self with its changing representations. Thus Descartes claims certain and direct knowledge of things having all three temporal characteristics: duration, succession, and coexistence.

Now Kant does not dispute Descartes's belief that he intuits something enduring. What he questions are Descartes's identification of the object as the thinking self, and his claim to intuit this self by the intellect. The Aesthetic has shown that human intuition of existing particulars, including themselves, is sensible. Moreover, as the Transcendental Deduction shows, the 'I think' of transcendental apperception is a purely formal consciousness and cannot represent the particular self: "in the synthetic original unity of apperception, I am conscious of myself, not as I appear to myself, nor **as** I am in myself, but only **that** I am. This **representation** is a **thinking**, not an **intuiting**" (B157–8). Descartes can recognize himself as a particular thinker with his particular thoughts only through inner sense. The *cogito* confuses the 'I think' of transcendental apperception with cognition of the empirical self.

Moreover, intuition of the self in time presents only the succession of mental states and not the permanent thinker who has them. As Kant remarks at A107, consciousness of oneself "in internal perception is merely empirical, forever variable; it can provide no standing or abiding self." At Bxli Kant distinguishes between the representation of something permanent and a permanent representation. In fact, "there is no persistent intuition to be found in inner sense" (B292). Everything given in inner intuition is merely transitory and successive. Since distinct parts of time exist only successively, their occupants must exist one after the other. Consequently, when I intuit my representations as "in me," the only temporal feature I am given is succession. The formal features of inner intuition cannot provide the awareness of duration and coexistence required to recognize oneself as their owner.

Now as Descartes recognizes, in addition to their formal reality, representations also have an objective reality: they represent some thing to the thinker. So if the formal features of representations cannot provide consciousness of myself as a persisting thing, then this awareness must be achieved through the objects represented. Therefore I must intuit through my representations something permanent, distinct from my mental states. In the Preface, Kant says this permanent must be "a thing distinct from all my representations and external, the existence of which is necessarily included in the **determination** of my own existence . . . which could not take place even as inner if it were not simultaneously (in part) outer" (Bxli). The "outer" part can only be the reality presented in intuition, since representations are, considered formally, "in me." The objective reality of my immediate consciousness must include things outside me where "outside" means numerically distinct from my mental states.

Kant maintains that the only way to perceive an object as other than myself is to locate it in space. The key is the contrast between space, as a framework of permanent, coexisting locations, and time. Because distinct parts of time exist successively, no temporal location, and hence no occupant of a merely temporal location, is re-identifiable through time. But spatial locations exist non-successively. Although both space and time as wholes are permanent, space alone is determined as permanent (B291). Unlike time, space can be divided into numerically distinct, coexisting parts. It is the nature of distinct spatial locations that they exist permanently. Consequently, each spatial location, and hence its occupant, can in principle be re-identified from one time to another. The permanence of coexisting parts of space makes possible our consciousness of permanent and distinct objects coexisting throughout our transitory perceptions. The crucial features of objectivity – independence of mere representation and re-identifiability through time – are possible only through the permanence of space.

B. *Why space of our experience cannot be merely imaginary*

The above argument also explains why we can be certain that space is real and not merely imaginary. Like many of his predecessors, Kant believes that the ability to imagine external objects presupposes perception of them. He says this at B276–7n: "in order for us even to imagine something as external, i.e., to exhibit it to sense in intuition, we must already have an outer sense, and by this means immediately distinguish the mere receptivity of an outer intuition from the spontaneity that characterizes every imagining." Unfortunately this cannot be the reason that outer sense could not be merely imaginary, since it begs the question. The real reply concerns what experience would be like if space and spatial objects were merely imaginary. A merely imaginary object is one that exists only through the subject's representing, as in dream states, hallucinations, and after-images. The objects of these states do not in fact exist independently of their representation by the subject. Since representations are only temporary, a merely imaginary space and its occupants would last only as long as each representation of them. That is, each new representation would present a new, numerically distinct spatial framework. If there were no continuity of the spatial framework from one representation to another, there could be no consciousness of enduring, continuous existence in time. We could not recognize our passing states as thoughts, nor ourselves as thinking things. The empirical reality of space is guaranteed by its permanence. In being re-identifiable through time, space and spatial objects exhibit their independence of momentary representations, including mere imaginings. To claim that one can imagine a permanent space is to erase the distinction between real and imaginary space.

This is why Kant says, "For even merely to imagine an outer sense would itself annihilate the faculty of intuition, which is to be determined through the imagination" (B277). Notice that not just outer intuition, but the very faculty of intuition, would be annihilated were we to lack outer sense. Intuition is the means by which we are immediately related to objects (A19/B33). And objects are things that correspond to and yet are distinct from our representations of them (A104). But only outer sense presents awareness of enduring objects distinct from the subject. The Cartesian hypothesis that I can know my thinking self and merely imagine spatial things is not a possible state of affairs after all.

C. The immediacy of spatial perception

The Refutation attempts to refute two Cartesian views: first, that self-knowledge is prior to knowledge of the external world; and second, that knowledge of physical reality is based on inference. Descartes claims that only self-knowledge is immediate as both given directly in consciousness, and as first-order consciousness of existence. To appreciate Kant's argument, we need to specify two distinctions between immediate and mediate knowledge, the first concerning *the evidence justifying a belief*, the second concerning *the order of knowledge*. Let us designate "the immediate$_1$" as a judgment non-inferentially justified by intuition, as contrasted with one requiring an inference from that data. Let us define "the immediate$_2$" as original consciousness of existence, as opposed to consciousness derived from it. Now although these two senses are closely linked, they are not equivalent if one allows for a second-order or derivative consciousness that is given in intuition. In that case a belief can be known "immediately$_1$" (sufficient evidence is available in intuition) but nevertheless be "mediate$_2$," (not original consciousness of existence). This is in fact Kant's view of self-knowledge.

Kant argues in the Refutation that the permanent substratum of objective time-determination must be spatial, that one must perceive material objects in order to know oneself as a thinking subject. But the Aesthetic has shown that space is a pure form of intuition, where intuition is the means by which objects are immediately given to the subject. When Kant concludes that spatial experience is immediate, he means that the abiding spatial framework presented in intuition provides sufficient evidence for our belief in material existence. Unlike Hume, Kant does not identify the content of a belief with its evidential basis, since for Kant all perception of particulars (including space and time) also requires concepts of the understanding. But concepts do not establish the existence of their objects: "In the **mere concept** of a thing no characteristic of its existence can be encountered at all" (A225/B272). If existential beliefs are not based on concepts, then there are only two ways such beliefs can be justified: either directly by intuition or indirectly by inference from it. But if knowledge of external reality is guaranteed by the intuition of space, then the Cartesians are wrong to claim that such knowledge is only inferential. Thus Kant can conclude that knowledge of space is immediate$_1$.

Now Kant agrees with Descartes that self-knowledge through inner sense is also directly given, and hence immediate$_1$. Because intuition provides direct awareness of both external and internal existence, Kant says in the second edition Preface: "I am just as certainly conscious that there are things outside me, which are in relation to my sense, as I am conscious that I myself exist as determined in time" (Bxli). Kant diverges most sharply from Descartes with respect to the order of consciousness: the Refutation shows that perception of spatial objects is epistemically prior to knowledge of the self. Thus first-order objective consciousness – the immediate$_2$ – must be of physical reality. It is from things outside us, Kant notes, that "we derive the whole material of knowledge, even for our inner sense" (Bxxxix). And in the Aesthetic: "the representations of **outer sense** make up the proper material with which we occupy our mind" (B67). That outer sense supplies the proper material of experience implies that inner sense presupposes outer sense.

For Kant, awareness of our mental states is a second-order or derivative consciousness, produced not by inference, but by reflection. When he says "inner experience itself is consequently only mediate and possible only through outer experience" (B277), he means that self-awareness is mediate$_2$, that it requires prior awareness of external objects. But this is consistent with the idea that both kinds of reality, given in sensible intuition, are known immediately$_1$. In the Refutation, Kant argues that had Descartes no experience as a person in a world of physical objects, he could never have discovered his thinking self at all.

Taken together, the Analogies and the Refutation also refute Descartes's dualism, for they entail that there could be no purely mental substance. Not only are the fundamental objects of experience spatial, but all substance must be spatial, and hence corporeal. Since the criterion of substance is action, and only physical actions are perceivable, the only entities that can count as substantial for Kant are physical objects. This also implies that the empirical self, known as an individual distinct from others, must be embodied. Even one's "mental" states must be located in space in two senses: first, they must belong to a self who is a physical object, and second, the objects we intuit through them must be physical. As we shall see in chapter 8, Kant explicitly criticizes Descartes's notion of the substantial soul in the Paralogisms of the Transcendental Dialectic.

7. KANT'S RESPONSE TO SKEPTICISM

Kant's transcendental idealism embraces one form of skepticism, that concerning knowledge of things in themselves. But Kant is not an empirical idealist: for him, spatiotemporal appearances are more than ideas in individual perceivers' minds. He also believes synthetic *a priori* knowledge makes it possible to know necessary features of these objects. This puts him at odds with traditional skeptics, who deny that we can know anything other than our own mental states. On their view all beliefs about things that exist independently of representation, including the enduring subject, are doubtful. Kant's answers to metaphysical skepticism also address skepticism about mathematics, logic, and reason in general. For all forms of skepticism the only solution is to appeal to the necessary conditions of thought and experience. And thus was born Kant's innovative strategy, the transcendental deduction.

The method of transcendental deduction is *ad hominem* in beginning with premises acceptable to the skeptic. These include the following claims:

1. I can recognize my own mental states, ascribing them to myself, in "I think."
2. I can identify the content of these states, and recognize the order in which I apprehend them.
3. I can think the difference between a subjective order of apprehension and an objective order of states of affairs.
4. My sensory impressions occur in a unified time and a unified space.
5. I can make judgments that purport to be true.

Notice that none of these claims expressly commits one to knowledge of anything except one's mental states and a self that has them. Clearly

Hume accepts all of them, either explicitly or implicitly. First, his theory of ideas presupposes the first three claims. Both impressions and ideas are "perceptions of the mind." And even though Hume attacks belief in an enduring self in the *Treatise*, in the Appendix he apparently recognizes that his own account of mental faculties commits him to the existence of something having perceptions. Not only can Hume identify the content of perceptions, his theory of the process of association assumes that he can recognize the order of apprehension, as well as distinguishing subjective from objective orders. Like empiricists generally, Hume has difficulty explaining space and time, but there is no reason to think he would reject claim 4. And of course his entire theory commits him to proposition 5.

Kant's strategy is to bootstrap his arguments for objective knowledge on the above assumptions about one's representations. Transcendental deductions show that recognizing certain features of "subjective" states presupposes cognitive processes importing objectivity into experience. In the Aesthetic, Kant bases his theory of the forms of intuition in part on the fact that experience occurs in a unified spatiotemporal framework. The Transcendental Deduction of the categories incorporates all of the above claims. The arguments of the Analogies and the Refutation also assume that we are capable of locating apprehended states of affairs in objective time. Given Hume's theory of association, it is hard to see how he could deny these assumptions. In short, Kant tries to show that the skepticism implied by empirical idealism is self-defeating.

Kant's strategy depends essentially on the relation between judgment and the notion of objectivity. As chapter 4 explains, Kant was the first philosopher to analyze concepts in terms of their judgmental function. The logical forms of judgment as well as the very notion of an object of judgment are presupposed in taking sensory experience to be of objects. The key move is to connect the notion of an object, and the distinction between the objective and the subjective, with the objective validity of judgment. This consists in two features: first, judgments are complex representations of objects or states of affairs, and second, they are capable of truth values. Anyone who judges, including the skeptic, implicitly recognizes the notions of truth and falsity. These notions are essentially objective, since even assertions about one's subjective states are true or false for everyone.

Further, objective states of affairs must be rule-governed. Representations of states that obtain for everyone must conform to something outside my representation of it. Thus the objectivity of judgment entails that the states about which one judges must be subject to rules importing necessity into our thought. Now in order for judgments to provide knowledge, they must also have objective reality. And to do this they must be connected to experience that is intersubjectively available. Kant argues that the intersubjective nature of experience depends on the fact that it is, at the first order, of spatial objects. The permanence of space guarantees that things given in it are more than any individual perceiver's apprehension of them. By virtue of their spatial properties and locations, appearances are not reducible to any (finite) collection of representations.

The issues raised by skepticism and Kant's response to them are complex. However one evaluates his arguments, Kant's brilliance lies in seeing that what is usually considered "subjective" experience has its own objectivity. The genius of the Transcendental Deduction consists in "bootstrapping," that is, justifying first-order beliefs on second-order, reflective claims about mental states. Whether Kant puts skepticism to rest, he certainly presents a viable alternative to the failed methods of foundationalism and the infinite regress.

8. SUMMARY

In completing Kant's deductions of the pure principles of the understanding, the Analogies of Experience and the Postulates of Empirical Thought offer his strongest arguments against skepticism. In the Analogies, the principles correlated with the relational categories, Kant justifies the metaphysical concepts of substance, cause, and causal interaction by showing that they are required to locate states of affairs in global, objective time. The Postulates describe the conditions required to apply the modal concepts in judging the real possibility, actuality, and necessity of states of affairs. This section also contains the Refutation of Idealism, added in the B edition, where Kant argues against the Cartesian view that self-knowledge is more certain than knowledge of the external world. These arguments taken together constitute a direct response to skeptical attacks on metaphysical knowledge of objects independent of perceivers. By showing that principles of substance and causation are required to produce a coherent system of empirical knowledge, Kant completes his positive account of the functions of the understanding. At the same time he demonstrates why legitimate metaphysical principles cannot provide knowledge of things in themselves, thus reinforcing the case for transcendental idealism.

CHAPTER 8

Transcendental illusion I: rational psychology

In the remaining sections of the *Critique*, Kant has two main purposes. Most of the text concerns errors arising from the misuse of
the understanding and reason, the basis of the traditional disputes
of metaphysics. This discussion begins with two bridging sections
at the end of the Transcendental Analytic, one clarifying the distinction between phenomena and noumena, the other titled On the
Amphiboly of the Concepts of Reflection. It then proceeds with the
Transcendental Dialectic, containing Kant's theory of transcendental illusion. The main discussion concerns the arguments of rational
psychology (the Paralogisms), rational cosmology (the Antinomies),
and rational theology (the existence of God). In an Appendix at the
end of the Transcendental Dialectic Kant then turns to his second
purpose, his theory of the legitimate functions of theoretical reason
as the highest intellectual faculty. Here he explains the role of transcendental ideas and maxims of reason in scientific knowledge. The
last part of the *Critique*, the Transcendental Doctrine of Method,
discusses the methods of mathematical construction, and serves as a
transition to Kant's account of practical reason. Chapters 8, 9, and
10 will treat Kant's theory of error. Chapter 11 discusses Kant's positive accounts of the role of reason in empirical and mathematical
cognition.

I. ERRORS OF THE UNDERSTANDING

In the section On the Ground of the Distinction of all Objects in
General into *Phenomena* and *Noumena*, and the Appendix On the
Amphiboly of the Concepts of Reflection, Kant explains how extend-
ing pure concepts of the understanding beyond appearances leads to

spurious metaphysical conclusions. Although adding nothing new, he offers an interesting critique of Leibniz's rationalist metaphysics. In particular, Kant shows how Leibniz's application of the principle of the Identity of Indiscernibles to things in general misapplies the pure concepts, an error arising from a mistaken view of the relation between the sensibility and the understanding.

Leibniz used the terms "phenomena" and "noumena" to distinguish between objects of the senses and objects of the intellect. According to Leibniz's theory of ideas, sense perceptions are merely confused or indistinct concepts. But there is a correspondence between our sensory representations and the noumenal objects as they are in themselves. Leibniz calls space and time "well-founded phenomena" to mark this correspondence.[1] For Leibniz it is possible to know noumena, the intelligible substances or monads giving rise to appearances, through intellectual intuition. Thus like all rationalist metaphysics, Leibniz's monadology is a form of transcendental realism.

Kant begins the section on phenomena and noumena by distinguishing between transcendental and empirical uses of pure concepts. In its transcendental use, a concept is applied to things in general and in themselves; in its empirical use it applies only to objects of experience (A238–9/B298). In his previous arguments Kant established three essential conclusions. First, human intuition is sensible; only through the sensibility are objects given to us. Second, human understanding is discursive and not intuitive; our intellect has no independent access to existing things. And third, pure concepts of the understanding acquire cognitive significance only when schematized in spatiotemporal terms. Hence any use of them beyond spatiotemporal objects is illegitimate. Kant sums up these points at A248/B305: "The pure categories, without formal conditions of sensibility, have merely transcendental significance, but are not of any transcendental use." The point turns on distinguishing two senses of "transcendental." The *transcendental significance* of pure concepts refers to their role as necessary conditions of experience. Their *transcendental use*, however, refers to their application beyond appearances. This latter gives rise to transcendental realism, that is, meaningless claims about things in themselves or objects "in general."

---

[1] See my *Space and Incongruence*, 31–8, for a discussion of these views.

Contrasting legitimate with illegitimate uses of pure concepts produces two notions of the noumenon: one negative or "limiting," the other positive. In essence, Kant's negative notion of the noumenon is his notion of the thing in itself. This is the legitimate correlate to the notion of appearance. Recall that in the B edition Preface, Kant claims that although we cannot know things in themselves, "we at least must be able to think them . . . For otherwise there would follow the absurd proposition that there is an appearance without anything that appears" (Bxxvi). Here he repeats the point: "it also follows naturally from the concept of an appearance in general that something must correspond to it which is not in itself appearance" (A251–2).[2] Since things in themselves are unknowable, however, this notion has no cognitive content. It is the completely indeterminate thought of whatever exists considered independently of all relations to knowers. Kant labels it "negative" and "problematic" to indicate that we cannot make any meaningful predications of such things.

Now this negative notion has to be distinguished from two others: the idea of the transcendental object and the positive notion of the noumenon. The former is the legitimate thought, through pure concepts, of the object of sensible intuition. As we have seen, it is not an object of cognition but only "the concept of an object in general, which is determinable through the manifold of those appearances" (A250–1). As the correlate of the t.u.a., the idea of the transcendental object is the merely formal thought of the object of the manifold about which one judges.

A more serious error confuses the negative notion of the noumenon with the positive notion of an object of a non-sensible intuition. This is the basis of all rationalist metaphysics, which presupposes that the intellect can intuit things in themselves. In the B edition, Kant says this error occurs when the understanding takes the "undetermined concept of a being of understanding," for a determinate concept of something the understanding could know (B307). In short, illegitimate metaphysics commits a scope error, shifting the negation from the (legitimate) notion of the noumenon as "*not* an object of our sensible intuition" to the positive notion of "an object of

---

[2] I discuss this point in *Space and Incongruence*, 105–12. On my reading, Kant errs in relating the thing in itself to the cause of appearance or the transcendental object, as at A288/B344.

a *non*-sensible intuition" (emphases mine, B307). As a corollary, Kant argues that it is a mistake to divide objects into two worlds, objects of the senses and objects of the understanding: "The division of objects into *phaenomena* and *noumena*, and of the world into a world of sense and a world of understanding, can therefore not be permitted at all" (B311).[3]

The Appendix On the Amphiboly of the Concepts of Reflection develops this analysis in terms of four distinctions Kant attributes to transcendental reflection. In the first *Critique*, Kant treats transcendental reflection primarily as the process enabling one to perform the critique of pure reason. Not until the *Critique of the Power of Judgment* of 1790 does he explain the role of reflective judgment in aesthetics and science. Here Kant's main point is to show how Leibniz misuses the concepts of transcendental reflection.

Kant criticizes Leibniz by analyzing concepts of reflection fundamental to all philosophical analysis. In logical reflection the understanding considers concepts by four distinctions: identity and difference; agreement and opposition; inner and outer; and matter and form. Identity and difference concern the content of concepts. By agreement and opposition Kant means whether they are logically compatible. Inner and outer have to do with whether a concept is relational or not. Connected to this is the distinction between matter and form, or the determinable and the determinate. As we have seen, the form is the way in which the matter is related, which is also equivalent to giving the matter specification, or determining a determinable. In the logic of concepts, the determinable is that which can be made more specific. A genus, for example, is determined by enumerating the species falling under it. In logical reflection these comparisons bear only on concepts rather than on objects.

Transcendental reflection consists in comparing "representations in general with the cognitive power in which they are situated," and distinguishing "whether they [belong] to the pure understanding or to pure intuition" (A261/B317). Kant's analyses of the forms of intuition and the categories are exercises of transcendental reflection. In this

---

[3] This passage apparently rules out the "two-worlds" reading of Kant's distinction between appearances and things in themselves, espoused by Kemp Smith and others.

act the faculty doing the comparing is reason rather than the understanding. And because the representation is referred to the source of the cognition, Kant says the comparison "goes to the objects themselves" since it "contains the ground of the possibility of the objective comparison of the representations to each other." He also emphasizes that "transcendental reflection is a duty from which no one can escape if he would judge anything about things *a priori*" (A263/B319). Kant has shown, for example, that sensible intuition yields both a matter (sensation) and the pure forms in which the matter is given, whereas the understanding provides the determining concepts through which this manifold is related to objects.

Leibnizian metaphysics illustrates the errors that arise when concepts of reflection are mistakenly applied to things in themselves. Leibniz's system depends on the principle of the Identity of Indiscernibles, that things that are indiscernible in all their properties are numerically identical. Thus there cannot be two numerically distinct things that are similar in all respects. On Kant's view this principle is true of concepts: concepts that are entirely similar in their contained concepts are identical. He makes the point with reference to objects of the understanding: "If an object is presented to us several times, but always with the same inner determinations (*qualitas et quantitas*), then it is always exactly the same if it counts as an object of pure understanding" (A263/B319). But the principle does not apply to appearances because of the sensible forms in which they are given. Space and time are homogeneous wholes whose parts are numerically distinct although qualitatively similar. Kant says

multiplicity and numerical difference are already given by space itself as the condition of outer appearances. For a part of space, even though it might be completely similar and equal to another, is nevertheless outside of it, and is on that account a different part . . . and this must therefore hold of everything that exists simultaneously in the various positions in space. (A264/B320)

Thus two particles of matter could be entirely similar in all their properties, but numerically distinct by virtue of their distinct spatiotemporal locations.

Leibniz misuses other concepts of reflection, in assuming that inner determinations always precede outer determinations, and that matter always precedes form. The former claim means that relations of things presuppose their non-relational properties. The latter means that the determinable matter is independent of its organization. Leibniz expressed both views in his theory that relations among things are ideal, meaning they depend on non-relational properties, and have no independent metaphysical status. This is the reason Leibniz describes space and time as "well-founded phenomena." As with the Identity of Indiscernibles, Kant claims these principles would be true were we able to know things by intellectual intuition: "As object of the pure understanding . . . every substance must have inner determinations and forces that pertain to its inner reality" (A265/B321). The same holds for matter and form: "The understanding . . . demands first that something be given (at least in the concept) in order to be able to determine it in a certain way. Hence in the concept of pure understanding matter precedes form" (A267/B322–3). Because relations between concepts depend on their non-relational content, for concepts the inner precedes the outer, and matter precedes form. But pure concepts apply only to objects of intuition, which appear in space and time. Now as the Aesthetic shows, space and time are logically independent of the manifold given in them. For appearances, then, form precedes matter. Moreover, because space and time are systems of relations underlying all properties of appearances, "We know substance in space only through forces that are efficacious in it" (A265/B321). In other words, all knowledge of objects is of relations: "a persistent appearance in space (impenetrable extension) contains mere relations and nothing absolutely internal, and nevertheless can be the primary substratum of all outer perception" (A284/B340). The Remark to the Amphiboly of the Concepts of Reflection develops these ideas in more detail.

Like all rationalist metaphysics, Leibniz's monadology rests on two fundamental errors. First, he makes cognitive claims about things in themselves or noumena in the positive sense. And second, he attempts to derive *a priori* truths about noumenal reality by misapplying concepts originating in the understanding and in logical reflection. In the Dialectic, Kant explains the transcendental illusion motivating these errors, and applies his analysis to metaphysical disputes concerning the soul, the world, and God.

2. TRANSCENDENTAL ILLUSION

Transcendental illusion arises from the misuse of theoretical reason. As the highest intellectual function, theoretical reason unifies the judgments of the understanding in empirical cognition. Like the understanding, theoretical reason has both a logical and a real use. In its logical or justificatory use, reason infers conclusions from premises. In its real use, reason provides principles directing the search for empirical knowledge. Scientific reasoning involves explaining natural phenomena and subsuming empirical generalizations or laws under higher laws. Although Kant postpones the details of its legitimate function until the Appendix of the Dialectic, here he briefly sketches how the misuse of reason leads to illegitimate metaphysics.[4]

The Transcendental Dialectic begins with a general account of error. Because the understanding, if left to its natural operations, could not make erroneous judgments, all error or illusion involves some interfering factor, namely "the unnoticed influence of sensibility on understanding, through which . . . the subjective grounds of the judgment join with the objective ones, and make the latter deviate from their destination" (A294–5/B350–1). Kant uses the analogy of opposing forces to illustrate how the sensibility can cause the understanding to go astray. At A295/B352 he remarks that in empirical illusions, such as optical illusions, the imagination interferes with "the empirical use of otherwise correct rules of the understanding." Although transcendental illusion does not always directly involve the sensibility, it arises from conflating subjective with objective grounds of judgment.

Kant next makes some confusing distinctions between the immanent and transcendental uses of principles, and between the transcendental use of a principle and a transcendent principle. The categories and principles of the understanding are "objective" rather than transcendent, because they apply to objects. In their immanent

---

[4] My discussion of the Dialectic relies heavily on Grier's *Kant's Doctrine of Transcendental Illusion*.

(legitimate) use, they are restricted to objects of possible experience. To apply them beyond experience, to things in themselves, would be a (positive) *transcendental use*, which of course is illegitimate. A *transcendent principle*, by contrast, is one "that takes away these limits, which indeed bids us to overstep them" (A296/B353). As we shall see, the ideas of reason and the principle(s) directing their use are "transcendent principles" because they do not directly apply to objects. Taking them to represent objects of any kind, whether appearances or things in themselves, is an error. But because these transcendent principles of reason are indispensable for empirical cognition, Kant says they have a "subjective necessity." Transcendental illusion occurs when this subjective necessity is mistaken for the objective necessity of principles of the understanding.

The section ends with the claim that transcendental illusion is as "natural and unavoidable" as the optical illusions that the sea is higher away from the shore than at the shore, and that the moon is larger at the horizon. To some commentators this appears at odds with his claim that the dialectical fallacies infecting metaphysical disputes can be corrected by a critique of reason. As Michelle Grier argues, however, it is possible to reconcile Kant's claims by distinguishing the inevitable transcendental illusion from the avoidable fallacies of the understanding to which it gives rise.[5] We shall return to this point below.

Finally Kant turns to the analysis of theoretical reason. Recall that in the metaphysical deduction Kant derives the categories from the logical forms of judgment. Here he intends to show a similar relation between the pure transcendent ideas of reason and the logical forms of syllogistic inference. Like the forms of judgment, rules of inference are universally valid because they abstract from all content. Equally, Kant will argue at A333–8/B390–6, these logical forms of inference yield transcendent principles or ideas of reason when appropriately "schematized." The difference, of course, is that the principles of reason are regulative rather than constitutive. Rather than applying directly to objects, they operate to unify the judgments of the understanding:

---

[5] See chapter 1 of Grier, *Kant's Doctrine of Transcendental Illusion*, for both the criticisms and the solution to them.

If the understanding may be a faculty of unity of appearances by means of rules, then reason is the faculty of the unity of the rules of understanding under principles. Thus it never applies directly to experience or to any object, but instead applies to the understanding, in order to give unity *a priori* through concepts to the understanding's manifold cognitions. (A302/B359)

In other words, the role of reason is to unify and systematize judgments of the understanding. This occurs formally when one logically derives a conclusion from premises. The legitimate real use of reason consists in explaining phenomena or subsuming an empirical law under a higher law.

The next step characterizes the unifying function of reason in logical inferences. Every syllogism consists of a major premise, a minor premise, and the conclusion. At A304/B360–1 Kant explains that the major is a general rule thought through the understanding. The minor premise subsumes a cognition under the condition (subject) of the rule given in the major premise. Finally, reason determines the subsumed cognition through the predicate of the rule. Kant discusses examples at A322/B378 and at A330/B387.

Transcendental illusion occurs when a legitimate regulative principle of reason is confused with an objective claim about reality. Kant derives the legitimate principle as follows: in logical inferences where one attempts to justify a conclusion, the premises are the conditions (evidence) for the truth of the conclusion. In proving a conclusion, then, one identifies the conditions for the given conditioned. But the process of justification can continue indefinitely: one can demand a justification for each premise. This process could end only if one could arrive at premises that were self-justifying, their truth unconditioned by other judgments. The logical task of reason, then, is "to find the unconditioned for conditioned cognitions of the understanding, with which its unity will be completed" (A307/B364). If one could arrive at a complete proof of a given judgment, one would have succeeded in this logical task of reason.

On Kant's view, this logical "maxim" in fact presupposes an objective claim: "But this logical maxim cannot become a principle of pure reason unless we assume that when the conditioned is given, then so is the whole series of conditions subordinated one to the other, which is itself unconditioned, also given" (A307–8/B364). Grier calls the regulative principle expressing the legitimate task of reason P_1: "To find the unconditioned for conditioned cognitions of the understanding, with which its unity will be completed" (A307/B364). Principle P_1, which Kant calls a "logical maxim," is *subjectively necessary* because it does not supply concepts of objects, and yet is indispensable for empirical cognition. The error occurs when one conflates P_1 with the "objective" or "transcendental" principle P_2: "when the conditioned is given, then so is the whole series of conditions" (A307–8/B364). Unlike P_1, which expresses an imperative or maxim for seeking knowledge, P_2 makes a synthetic (factual) claim about objects.

Although P_2 is illegitimate, Kant says it is "unavoidable" since it is presupposed by P_1. At A650–1/B678–9, he discusses the regulative function of pure reason: "In fact it cannot even be seen how there could be a logical principle of rational unity among rules unless a transcendental principle is presupposed, through which such a systematic unity, as pertaining to the object itself, is assumed *a priori* as necessary." And at A645/B673 he says, "This unity of reason always presupposes an idea, namely that of the form of a whole of cognition, which precedes the determinate cognition of the parts and contains the conditions for determining *a priori* the place of each part and its relation to the others." According to Grier, the "transcendental" principle P_2 is necessary as an "application principle" for P_1, analogous to the schemata of pure concepts.[6] Transcendental illusion, then, occurs when the "need of reason" to ascend to higher conditions in order to bring unity to cognition is mistaken for a transcendental principle that postulates "an unlimited completeness in the series of conditions in the objects themselves" (A309/B366).

The idea of reason underlying both principles is the idea of the unconditioned or the totality of conditions: "since the unconditioned alone makes possible the totality of conditions, and conversely the totality of conditions is always itself unconditioned, a pure concept of reason in general can be explained through the concept of the unconditioned" (A322/B379). This idea has three forms. As Kant explains at A323/B379, the unconditioned can be thought with respect to the subject as well as the object of the judgment. The latter can further be distinguished as the object in appearance as opposed to the object of thought in general. Thus he concludes that there are

---

[6] See Grier, *Kant's Doctrine of Transcendental Illusion*, especially 127–30 and chapter 8.

three transcendental ideas: "the absolute (unconditioned) unity of the thinking subject, . . . the absolute unity of the series of conditions of appearance, [and] . . . the absolute unity of the condition of all objects of thought in general" (A334/B391). The following paragraph identifies these ideas as the basis, respectively, of rational psychology, rational cosmology, and rational theology. Rational psychology concerns the soul, that which ultimately underlies the thinking subject. Rational cosmology is the "science" of the ultimate nature of appearances. Finally, rational theology makes claims about the ultimate foundation of all objects in general, namely God.

Kant's "metaphysical" deduction of these ideas of reason occurs in the third section, where he connects them with the three forms of syllogism. This account is so cryptic that it is unintelligible apart from his earlier discussion of the forms of judgment in the Analytic. At A336/B393 he explicitly correlates the ideas of the soul, the world, and God with the respective logical relations of inherence, dependence, and concurrence characterizing categorical, hypothetical, and disjunctive judgments. Referring back to his discussion of these forms of judgment at A73–4/B98–9 suggests the following "derivation."

First, the major premise in the categorical syllogism is a categorical judgment. This is the simplest (atomic) form of judgment, in which a predicate is thought as inhering in a subject. When applied to cognition, this yields the idea of a thinking subject in which the thought inheres. The notion of the soul is the hypostatized or objectified notion of the totality of conditions underlying the thinking subject. Second, the major premise in the hypothetical syllogism is a hypothetical or conditional judgment. This complex form connects two or more judgments, so that the consequent is thought as logically dependent on the antecedent. This logical dependence, as we know, has its real counterpart in causal dependence. The totality of conditions underlying appearances is the completed causal series of events in time. Finally, disjunctive syllogisms have a disjunctive judgment as the major premise. Kant thinks of disjunctive judgments as dividing a concept into its complete set of possibilities, each of which mutually excludes the others, but which together exhaust the whole. The concept of the ultimate ground of this whole of possibilities Kant calls the "rational concept of a being of all beings" (A336/B393). In other words, the thought of the totality of objects in general leads to the idea of the ultimate condition of all existence, traditionally God.

On Kant's view, then, rational metaphysics results from the illusory attempt to arrive at ultimate explanations of the thinking subject, the world as appearance, and the totality of objects in general. This occurs when reason erroneously extends the "logical maxim" to seek the unconditioned for the conditioned, which legitimately applies within experience, to "totalities" that are not objects of possible experience. Since the only concepts reason has at its disposal are concepts of the understanding, the search for metaphysical knowledge inevitably results in misapplying concepts of appearances beyond experience. In this way transcendental illusion is one motivation behind the dialectical fallacies of the understanding.

As Kant points out, this illusory use of reason reveals itself only in the regressive or "ascending" series: "pure reason has no other aim than the absolute totality of synthesis **on the side of conditions** . . . and [it] has nothing to do with absolute completeness **from the side of the conditioned**. For it needs only the former series in order to presuppose the whole series of conditions" (A336/B393). That is, metaphysics always works backwards from what is given to its necessary conditions. By contrast, the thought of the "descending series" or the totality of consequences following from the given is not a necessary idea, but "a thing . . . which is thought up only arbitrarily, and not presupposed necessarily by reason" (A337/B394). Furthermore, the laws of the understanding are sufficient for knowing the consequences of the given appearances, although of course we cannot know the totality of consequences.

Before turning to the arguments based in transcendental illusion, we should note Kant's remark in a footnote at B395:

Metaphysics has as the proper end of its investigation only three ideas: God, freedom, and immortality . . . Everything else with which this science is concerned serves merely as a means of attaining these ideas and their reality. The insight into these ideas would make theology, morals, and, through their combination, religion, thus the highest ends of our existence.

He believes that the metaphysical drive to give ultimate explanations of existence leads to three concepts of the highest good. The idea of immortality belongs to the doctrine of the soul, and is the basis of religion. The idea of free will is the basis of morality; Kant will argue that although recognition of the moral law presupposes freedom, it does not yield metaphysical knowledge of freedom. The idea of God as the "being of all beings" is of course the basis of theology. Although Kant sees the idea of immortality as following in some sense from the ideas of God and freedom, his own discussion of the arguments treats them in "the analytic order," beginning with the idea of the soul in the Paralogisms, moving to the doctrine of the world in the Antinomies, and ending with the proofs for the existence of God. The rest of this chapter examines Kant's analysis of the Paralogisms. Chapter 9 discusses the Antinomies and chapter 10 treats the proofs of rational theology.

3. THE PARALOGISMS OF PURE REASON

Kant labels the metaphysical arguments about the soul the Paralogisms of reason. These commit fallacies based on the transcendental illusion taking the totality of conditions of the thinking subject as a "given" object, a mind or soul. In attempting to determine the nature of this object underlying all consciousness, rationalist metaphysicians erroneously apply to the thinking subject pure concepts that have significance only for appearances. Thus the illusion inherent in reason leads to errors of the understanding. Here the arguments are based on the "I think" or the t.u.a. From this purely formal thought, rationalists attempted to derive synthetic conclusions concerning the substantiality, simplicity, numerical identity, immateriality, and incorruptibility of the soul. Thus they hypostasized or objectified purely formal self-consciousness as a thing, the subject in itself.[7]

Kant significantly altered both the content and presentation of the Paralogisms in the B edition. Both editions treat four arguments about the soul, correlated with the categorical headings in this order: relation, quality, quantity, and modality.[8] The first three arguments, which are unchanged, conclude that the soul is a substance, is simple, and is numerically identical through time. In the A edition the Fourth Paralogism concerns Descartes's view that knowledge of the mind is prior to knowledge of spatial objects. Because this makes knowledge of the external world less certain than self-knowledge, Kant calls this

[7] For a detailed discussion of the Paralogisms see Ameriks's *Kant's Theory of Mind.*
[8] This is a case where the traditional arguments appear to drive the Architectonic. Kant gives no explanation for correlating the Paralogisms with these categories and in this order.

the "paralogism of the ideality (of outer relation)" (A366). As we saw in chapter 7, in the B edition Kant responds with the Refutation of Idealism. In the revised Paralogisms he substitutes a discussion of the immateriality of the soul. In addition to this change, Kant also condenses his treatment, focusing on the errors underlying all four arguments. Since we have already examined the Refutation of Idealism, this discussion will ignore the Fourth Paralogism of the A edition. I shall also follow Kant's lead by emphasizing the general criticism of all the arguments.

At A341/B399 Kant explains that a logical paralogism "consists in the falsity of a syllogism due to its form . . . A transcendental paralogism, however, has a transcendental ground for inferring falsely due to its form." In both cases the arguments are formally invalid. At A402 and B411 he says the arguments commit a *sophisma figurae dictionis* (sophistry of a figure of speech), specifically an equivocation on a term occurring in both the major and minor premises. Despite some confusion in locating the equivocation, Kant does offer a consistent account of the invalidity in the arguments.

Because the four arguments share the same "schema," an analysis of the first argument sets the pattern for the others. Kant states the First Paralogism in the A edition as follows (I have inserted line numbers):

[1] That which is represented only as the **absolute subject** of our judgments, and cannot be predicated of another thing, is **substance**.
[2] I, as a thinking being, can be represented only as the **absolute subject** of all my judgments, and cannot be predicated of another thing.
[3] Thus I, as thinking being (soul) am **substance**. (A348)

The B-edition version rewords the same argument (line numbers inserted):

[1] What can be thought only as subject exists only as subject, and is therefore substance.
[2] Now a thinking being, considered as such, can be thought only as subject.
[3] Therefore it also exists only as substance. (B410–11)

In both versions the first premise is the major premise; it makes the synthetic claim that the "absolute subject" of judgment, which can be represented only as subject, is substance. The second premise, the minor premise, identifies the "I" of "I think," or the thinking being "as such" with the absolute subject of judgment. The conclusion then predicates being a substance of the "I" of "I think."

Unfortunately Kant's explanation of the equivocation differs in the two editions. In the A edition, he says the term equivocated on is 'substance': "the major premise makes a merely transcendental use of the category in regard to its condition, but . . . the minor premise and the conclusion . . . make an empirical use of the same category" (A402–3). But since the term 'substance' does not appear in the minor premise, it is unlikely to be the source of the equivocation. In a B edition footnote Kant locates the ambiguity in the term 'thinking,' which signifies differently in the two premises: "in the major premise, as it applies to an object in general (hence as it may be given in intuition); but in the minor premise only as it subsists in relation to self-consciousness," which is not an object but the mere form of thinking (B411n). Although this seems more plausible, the term 'thinking' does not appear *per se* in the major premise of either version. Allison suggests Kant should locate the ambiguity in the subject-term of the major premise, "That which cannot be thought otherwise than as subject" (in the A edition, "the absolute subject of judgment").[9] This is reasonable, since it occurs in both premises, and it is consistent with Kant's other remarks. Kant's remark at B411 lends support to Allison's reading: "The major premise talks about a being that can be thought of in every respect, and consequently even as it might be given in intuition. But the minor premise talks about this being only insofar as it is considered as subject, relative only to thinking and the unity of consciousness" (B411). Here I follow Allison, taking the ambiguity to concern the meaning of the thinking thing, or absolute subject of judgment. Kant's claim that the argument is invalid comes down to this: the major premise predicates the concept 'substance' of the thinking subject taken as an object in general. This claim is offered as a synthetic *a priori* truth. The minor premise, however, makes an analytic or tautological claim about the logical subject of thought in

---

[9] Allison, *Kant's Transcendental Idealism*, 284.

the "I think," the transcendental unity of apperception. Since the two premises use the term differently, no valid conclusion can be drawn from them. This diagnosis applies to all four arguments.

Before looking at the details of his analysis, we should note that Kant classifies his objection as critical rather than dogmatic or skeptical. At A388–9 he distinguishes them this way. A dogmatic objection "is directed against a proposition," "requires an insight into the constitution of the nature of the object," and "claims to have better acquaintance with the constitution of the object being talked about than its opposite has." A dogmatic objection to the proof, then, would claim that the first premise is false, that the mind or thinking subject could not be a substance. Skeptical objections put "the proposition and its opposite over against one another, as objections of equal weight." This approach claims that there are equally good arguments for and against the conclusion that the mind is a substance. But in "endorsing" both claims, it ends up treating the opposing views dogmatically, presupposing that one can know the object in itself. By contrast, the critical position claims that "the assertion is groundless, not that it is incorrect." Kant rejects dogmatic knowledge of the premise, which "assumes on behalf of its assertion something that is nugatory and merely imagined" (A389). For Kant, all attempts to know the mind or soul unjustifiably take the ultimate thinking thing as an object in general. This will differ significantly from Kant's skeptical objections to the inferences in the Antinomies.

Since the doctrine of the soul belongs to metaphysics, it cannot be based on *a posteriori* knowledge: "for if the least bit of anything empirical in my thinking, any particular perception of my inner state," were used in this science, then it would be an empirical science (A342/B400). Thus the representation grounding claims about the thinking thing must be *a priori*. In fact, the arguments are based on the t.u.a.: "I think is thus the sole text of rational psychology, from which it is to develop its entire wisdom" (A343/B401). In addition to rejecting the major premise, Kant argues that the minor premise misconstrues the merely formal self-consciousness of the "I think." Let us examine this objection first.

In both editions Kant emphasizes the point from the Transcendental Deduction, that the "I think" is merely the form of all thinking, and contains no intuition of a distinct individual: "For the I is, to be sure, in all thoughts; but not the least intuition is bound up with this representation, which would distinguish it from other objects of intuition" (A350; see also A345–6/B404). The B edition similarly stresses that the "I think" represents a purely logical subject, that is, the activity rather than a substantial thing:

> Now in every judgment I am always the determining subject of the relation that constitutes the judgment. However, that the I that I think can always be considered as subject, and as something that does not depend on thinking merely as a predicate, must be valid – this is an apodictic and even an identical proposition; but it does not signify that I as object am for myself a self-subsisting being or substance. (B407)

Among their many errors, metaphysicians mistake formal consciousness of the activity of thinking for an intuition of a determinable object: "The unity of consciousness, which grounds the categories, is here taken for an intuition of the subject as an object, and the category of substance is applied to it. But this unity is only the unity of thinking, through which no object is given" (B421–2). As we saw, the minor premise (in each argument) states an analytic truth about the t.u.a. But since it is a tautology, it cannot establish any synthetic claims about whatever "object in general" underlies this self-consciousness.

This analysis leads to a second objection, that all inferences from the "I think" to the ultimate nature of the determining subject commit circular reasoning. Not only is the representation "I think" not a concept, we do not have even a problematic concept of this determining self: "since the proposition I think (taken problematically) contains the form of every judgment of understanding whatever and accompanies all categories as their vehicle . . . we can at the start form no advantageous concept [of it]" (A348/B406). Since the t.u.a. is a necessary condition of applying any concept in judging, "we therefore turn in a constant circle, since we must always already avail ourselves of the representation of it at all times in order to judge anything about it" (A346). Kant says rather than the I cognizing itself through the categories,

> it cognizes the categories, and through them all objects, in the absolute unity of apperception, and hence cognizes them **through itself**. Now it is indeed very illuminating that I cannot cognize as an object itself that which I must presuppose in order to cognize an object at all. (A402)

As Allison points out, this position is independent of the unknowability of things in themselves.[10] The transcendental nature of the "I think" provides a strong argument, independent of transcendental idealism, against attempts to know the self at the foundation of all thinking. As the form of all thinking, the "I think" is itself unconditioned (A401), although not an object of thought.

Given the analytic nature of the "I think," it is surprising to find Kant labeling it in the B edition as an "empirical proposition." In the beginning of the footnote at B422–3, he says, "The 'I think' is . . . an empirical proposition, and contains within itself the proposition 'I exist.'" But he clarifies this statement at the end of the footnote:

> if I have called the proposition "I think" an empirical proposition, I would not say by this that the I in this proposition is an empirical representation; for it is rather purely intellectual, because it belongs to thinking in general. Only without any empirical representation, which provides the material for thinking, the act I think would not take place, and the empirical is only the condition of the application, or use, of the pure intellectual faculty. (B423n)

Kant's point is subtle, but consistent with what he has established. The "I think" is empirical insofar as empirical intuition is required to recognize the unity of self-consciousness. As Kant has argued, the formal awareness in the "I think" depends on the act of synthesizing the manifold given in intuition. In other words, although the t.u.a. is not itself empirical or *a posteriori*, our access to it is via the empirically given manifold. But this is equally true of the pure forms of intuition, the pure concepts of the understanding, and even the logical rules of inference.

By contrast with the tautological nature of the second premise, the major premise makes a synthetic claim, namely that the thinking self is a substance. Here is where Kant's critical objection applies, for this claim presupposes that one can know the self as an object in itself or in general. That is the unwarranted assumption behind all rational psychology. Unlike the above objection, this one does depend on the unknowability of things in themselves. In the A edition Kant begins by noting that "pure categories . . . have in themselves no objective significance at all unless an intuition is subsumed under them, to the manifold of which they can be applied as functions of synthetic

---

[10] See Allison, *Kant's Transcendental Idealism*, 291–3.

unity. Without that they are merely functions of a judgment without content" (A349–50). The B edition says, similarly, "the concept of a thing that can exist for itself as subject but not as a mere predicate carries with it no objective reality at all, i.e., . . . one has no insight into the possibility of such a way of existing, and consequently . . . it yields absolutely no cognition" (B412). The thought of the self as the subject in which thoughts inhere implies nothing about the self as an object, because we can know ourselves only as we appear to ourselves in inner sense.

Moreover, applying the concept of substance to appearances pre-supposes the schema of permanence in time. To know that I am substance I would have to establish that "I, as a thinking being, endure for myself, that naturally I neither arise nor perish – this I can by no means infer" (A349). And in the B edition: "if that con-cept, by means of the term 'substance,' is to indicate an object that can be given . . . then it must be grounded on a persisting intuition as the indispensable condition of the objective reality of a concept" (B412). At the end of the Paralogisms he says that determining the subject of thinking as an object "cannot take place without inner sense, whose intuition always makes available the object not as a thing in itself but merely as appearance . . . It is in this latter that the thinking self must now seek the conditions of the use of its logical functions for categories of substance, cause, etc." (B429–30). Thus the major premise errs by misapplying the empirically significant concept of substance to the thinking thing taken as an object in general.

Now Kant does say at A350, "one can quite well allow the propo-sition **The soul is substance** to be valid, if only one admits that this concept . . . cannot teach us any of the usual conclusions of the rationalistic doctrine of the soul." What he means is that the concept "substance" here has no real significance, but only logical significance as the idea of a thing that can only be subject, and not predicated of another thing. As Grier points out, Kant would accept the major premise construed as follows: if x were an object of possible experi-ence, then if x cannot be thought otherwise than as subject, x can exist only as substance. In this formulation the concept of substance can be legitimately applied to whatever "cannot be thought otherwise than as subject" only because that concept is restricted to objects of possible experience.[11] But since the point of rational psychology is to get behind the self as experienced, to the subject in itself, it ignores this restriction. Kant rejects this major premise, then, both because it presupposes that things in themselves are knowable, and because it overlooks the necessary schema for applying the concept of substance.

Kant's treatment of the remaining arguments follows directly from these criticisms. Not only do they suffer from the same invalidity, but their conclusions also depend on the first conclusion that the soul is a substance.[12] In the B edition these arguments are offered to prove that the substantial soul is simple, numerically identical or a person, and immaterial. From these characteristics the rational psychologist goes on to conclude that the soul is immortal, which Kant considers the basis for religion. Let us look briefly at each of these arguments.

The Second Paralogism argues that the soul or thinking subject is a simple substance. Although Kant does not offer a separate version in the B edition, the argument appears as follows in the A edition:

[1] That thing whose action can never be regarded as the concurrence of many acting things, is **simple**.
[2] Now the soul, or the thinking I, is such a thing.
[3] Thus etc. (A351)

Following the pattern of the First Paralogism, the major premise predicates simplicity of those objects in general whose actions cannot be decomposed into parts. This is clearly a synthetic claim. The minor premise states the tautology that the action of thinking cannot be divided into parts. The argument concludes, invalidly, that the thinking "I" is a simple substance. Kant emphasizes that although it is an analytic truth that the "I" of "I think" is a logically simple subject, it does not follow that the subject in itself, whatever it is, must be absolutely simple. At A355 he concedes the second premise:

The proposition **I am simple** must be regarded as an immediate expression of apperception, just as the supposed Cartesian inference *cogito, ergo sum* is in fact tautological, since the *cogito* (*sum cogitans*) immediately asserts the reality. But **I am simple** signifies no more than that this representation **I**

---

[11] See Grier, *Kant's Doctrine of Transcendental Illusion*, 162–3.
[12] Other commentators offer different accounts of the invalidity of the arguments, and the nature of the premises. See Ameriks, *Kant's Theory of Mind*, and chapter 7 of Kitcher, *Kant's Transcendental Psychology*.

encompasses not the least manifoldness within itself, and that it is an absolute (though merely logical) unity. (A355)

The B edition points out, similarly, that although the "I" of apperception is logically simple and "cannot be resolved into a plurality," "that does not signify that the thinking I is a simple **substance**, which would be a synthetic proposition" (B407–8). As the Transcendental Deduction shows, formal self-awareness in thinking must be an absolute unity because otherwise it could not produce a single complex thought. But this unified self-awareness does not represent the thinking subject in itself. Claims about the subject or soul in itself are both synthetic and unwarranted by experience:

The proposition "A thought can be only the effect of the absolute unity of a thinking being" cannot be treated as analytic. For the unity of a thought consisting of many representations is collective, and, as far as mere concepts are concerned, it can be related to the collective unity of the substances cooperating in it (as the movement of a body is the composite movement of all its parts) just as easily as to the absolute unity of the subject. (A353)

In other words, we have no insight into the ultimate nature of whatever underlies our thinking. It is entirely possible that the logical unity of thought could be produced by things that are composites in themselves. This argument hearkens back to Locke's response to Descartes's view of personal identity in the *Essay Concerning Human Understanding*. We shall return to this point below.

The Third Paralogism attempts to establish the numerical identity of the thinking subject from the logical identity of the "I" of "I think." In the A edition the major premise of the argument is, "What is conscious of the numerical identity of its Self in different times, is to that extent a **person**" (A361). The rest of the argument follows the same pattern as the first two paralogisms, and Kant's criticism is likewise of a piece with the above. The major premise makes an unwarranted synthetic claim about the subject as an object in itself; the minor premise states the analytic truth that the logical subject of thinking is conscious of its numerical identity in different times; and the conclusion invalidly infers that the thinking subject in itself is numerically identical. As with the previous paralogism, Kant's reply to this argument also shows the affinity between his and Locke's views on personal identity.

By personality Kant means "the possibility of a continuing consciousness in an abiding subject," even if interrupted (A365). It is
not clear here exactly what Kant takes this to imply, although, like
Locke, he tends to equate personality with concern for one's interests
and one's future state.[13] This leads to the Lockean strategy mentioned
above. In the *Essay Concerning Human Understanding*, Locke rejected
Descartes's view that personal identity is based in the numerical identity of the mental substance. Although Locke's own memory theory
has serious difficulties, he argued persuasively that retaining identity
of consciousness through a change of mental substance is sufficient for
personal identity. Since we have no empirical knowledge of the soul
or substratum underlying consciousness, we have no way of knowing
whether this substratum is identical through time.[14] Now Kant makes
the same points in both the Second and Third Paralogisms. First, we
have no access to the thinking subject as such. Second, there is no
inconsistency in the idea that this substratum of the numerically identical "I think" could be composite or lack numerical identity: "despite
the logical identity of the I – a change can go on that does not allow it
to keep its identity; and this even though . . . the identical-sounding
'I' is assigned to it, which . . . still keeps in view the thought of the
previous subject, and thus could also pass it along to the following
one" (A363). Like Locke, Kant envisages the possibility of a "mind-
swap" which maintains continuity of consciousness. In a footnote
he compares this idea to the way composite substances can communicate motion in a unified way in impact: "a whole series of these
substances may be thought, of which the first would communicate
its state, together with its consciousness, to the second [and so on].
The last substance would thus be conscious of all the states of all the
previously altered substances as its own states" (A363–4n). Thus Kant
agrees with Locke that continuity of consciousness constituting personal identity does not require numerical identity of the substratum
underlying the thinking subject.

In the B edition the Fourth Paralogism argues for the immateriality of the soul given that as a merely thinking thing I distinguish
myself from things outside me, including my own body. Traditionally,

---

[13] See Ameriks's discussion of the notion of personality in *Kant's Theory of Mind*, chapter 4,
especially 130–7.
[14] See book II, chapter 27, "Of Identity and Diversity," sections 11–19, in the *Essay Concerning
Human Understanding*, 336–42.

immaterialism is considered necessary for immortality, since if the thinking subject were material, the soul would die with the body. In criticizing the argument at B409 Kant remarks briefly that although it is an analytic truth that I can distinguish myself as a thinking thing from things outside me, I cannot know whether "this consciousness of myself would even be possible without things outside me through which representations are given to me, and thus whether I could exist merely as a thinking being (without being a human being)." In other words, based on experience I can separate myself as a thinking self from other things, including my own body, only in the sense that I can distinguish inner sense from outer sense. But the fact that these two forms of sense are different entails nothing about the nature of the thinking subject in itself. Because both inner and outer sense yield only appearances, "through the analysis of the consciousness of myself in thinking in general not the least is won in regard to the cognition of myself as object" (B409).

At B419–20 he points out that neither materialism nor spiritualism (i.e., immaterialism) can explain how I exist as a merely thinking subject. Materialism fails because nothing real given in space is simple. Thus matter as it appears to us cannot be the source of the logically simple thinking self. But based on our representations of the self in inner sense, neither can one conclude that the self is immaterial. This is because nothing persisting is given in inner sense. As the Refutation argues, inner intuition yields no access to the soul or persisting substratum of the thinking thing.

In the A edition Kant makes extended remarks on the debates over immaterialism and the problem of interaction. In the section titled Observation on the Sum of the Pure Doctrine of the Soul, Following these Paralogisms, he argues that the problem of interaction, apparently intractable for the realist who espouses substance dualism, dissolves when one admits that matter is only appearance. From A390–2, Kant discusses the three "solutions" traditionally offered to explain interaction between minds and bodies, namely physical influence, pre-established harmony, and "supernatural assistance" (A390). Physical influence is the theory that bodies and minds directly interact with one another. The classic argument against this position is Descartes's Sixth Meditation argument, that minds and bodies cannot interact causally because the essence of mind is thinking, that of body extension. Substances with distinct essences can share no properties in common, and therefore cannot exert causal influence on one another.[15] Now Kant remarks that this argument is the basis for the remaining two explanations, pre-established harmony and "supernatural assistance." Descartes himself embraces a form of "supernatural assistance," since he argues that the union of the mind with the body in humans is established by "divine institution." For Leibniz, pre-established harmony operates between all monadic substances, as well as between the system of corporeal nature and the system of final causes.[16]

From the point of view of transcendental idealism, there is no problem of mind–body interaction precisely because the empirically meaningful concept of substance does not apply to the thinking subject. Since we do not know ourselves as mental substances, there is in experience no heterogeneity between matter and the thinking subject. For Kant, the "opposition" between mind and body translates into the distinction between inner and outer sense. In consequence the problem of interaction becomes the question, "How is outer intuition – namely, that of space (the filling of it by shape and motion) – possible at all in a thinking subject?" (A393). In other words, how can the self that represents itself through inner sense be affected by external things through outer sense? And the only answer is that we cannot know:

But it is not possible for any human being to find an answer to this question, and no one will ever fill this gap in our knowledge, but rather only indicate it, by ascribing outer appearances to a transcendental object that is the cause of this species of representations, with which cause, however, we have no acquaintance at all, nor will we ever get a concept of it. (A393)

Just as we have no way of explaining why the human understanding thinks according to our forms of judgment, and why spatial intuition is three-dimensional and Euclidean, we cannot explain why humans have both inner and outer sense, or the ways their objects "interact."

Finally, given both the invalidity of the paralogisms and the unknowability of things in themselves, it follows that all speculation about the pre-existence or immortality of the soul is merely that,

---

[15] See the Sixth Meditation, *Philosophical Writings*, 2:54–5.
[16] For Leibniz, see *Monadology* and *Theodicy*, cited in Adams, *Leibniz: Determinist, Theist, Idealist*, 83–4.

speculation. "Thus every dispute about the nature of our thinking being and its conjunction with the corporeal world is merely a consequence of the fact that one fills the gaps regarding what one does not know with paralogisms of reason, making thoughts into things and hypostatizing them" (A395).

4. SUMMARY

This analysis supports Grier's view that there is no inconsistency in Kant's diagnosis of the failures of traditional metaphysics. Reason's transcendent principle P_2, that where the conditioned is given, the unconditioned is given, leads to the idea of the soul as the underlying subject of thinking. The attempt to discover the "objective" nature of this being in turn leads to the misuse of concepts of the understanding. Thus transcendental illusion engenders fallacies of the understanding. In misapplying the concept of substance, the Paralogisms confuse analytic truths about the logical subject of thought with synthetic claims about the subject in itself. As in all cases of transcendental realism, the doctrine of the soul ignores the distinction between appearances and things in themselves. As we have seen, Kant's resolution of these arguments is based on his "critical" rejection of the major premise as unwarranted. The next two chapters examine how transcendental illusion leads to the arguments of rational cosmology and theology.

CHAPTER 9

Transcendental illusion II: rational cosmology

In contrast to rational psychology, rational cosmology and rational theology apply the transcendent idea of the unconditioned to the object of thought. Rational cosmology concerns objects taken as appearances; rational theology argues for God as the explanation of things in themselves. All three spurious sciences assume as objectively valid the illusory principle P_2, that if the conditioned is given, the entire series of conditions is given. Despite their similar origin, the arguments and their resolutions differ in the three cases. In particular, the cosmological arguments have the form of antinomies, or pairs of opposing claims. Consequently, their solution involves the "skeptical method" mentioned in chapter 8. Kant attributes these differences to the fact that the ideas of the soul and God are "supersensible," ideas of things that are not objects of experience. By contrast, the cosmological idea of the world-whole in space and time is based on experience. For this reason, Kant also claims that the Antinomies offer an indirect proof of transcendental idealism. The first part of this chapter introduces the Antinomies and their importance to the critical philosophy. The second examines the arguments in detail, discussing their strengths and weaknesses. The last section discusses the relation between the conflicts and transcendental idealism.

I. INTRODUCTION TO THE ANTINOMIES

In both the *Prolegomena* and a letter to Garve of 1798, Kant explains the significance of the Antinomies for his critical philosophy. In paragraph 50 of the *Prolegomena*, echoing his earlier remark about Hume, Kant says that the transcendent use of pure reason is most effective "to awaken philosophy from its dogmatic slumber," and prompting it "toward the critique of reason itself."[1] More than the problems of God and the soul, the disputes over rational cosmology shaped Kant's theory of the inherent conflict in reason.

The Antinomies arise when reason attempts to explain the ultimate conditions underlying the world of appearances. The transcendent idea of the world represents "the sum total of all appearances," or "the absolute totality of the sum total of existing things" (A419–20/ B447–8). Although this idea concerns the sensible world, it "transcends all possible experience." This has several important implications. First, the cosmological arguments concern the world in space and time, and not space and time themselves.[2] Second, the idea of the world-whole has a basis in experience, unlike the ideas of the soul and God. Nevertheless, this cosmological idea is one "whose object can never be adequately given in any experience whatsoever." As Michelle Grier puts it, the idea of the world of appearance is "pseudoempirical," by contrast with the "pseudorational" ideas of the soul and God.[3]

This "pseudoempirical" character gives rise to the antithetic nature of the Antinomies, which brings into conflict competing claims of reason and the understanding. As we saw in chapter 8, reason supplies the idea of the unconditioned, driving the attempt to know appearances as a whole. But since reason produces no concepts, it must apply the concepts of the understanding to the world-whole. The opposition between the idea of reason and the concepts of the understanding generates contradictions: the thesis of each argument sides with reason and the antithesis with the understanding. In this broad sense reason contains a conflict within itself.

This analysis helps clarify the origins of the first two Antinomies. A standard interpretation, based on textual remarks, identifies the theses with rationalism, and the antitheses with empiricism.[4] In response, Sadik Al-Azm argues persuasively that the debates arise

---

[1] See *Prolegomena, Theoretical Philosophy after 1781*, 129. The letter to Christian Garve of September 21, 1798 also says the Antinomies "first aroused me from my dogmatic slumber and drove me to the critique of reason itself, in order to resolve the scandal of ostensible contradiction of reason with itself." *Kant, Correspondence*, 552.

[2] This point has been misunderstood by several commentators. See Kemp Smith, *Commentary*, 483–8; Prichard, *Kant's Theory of Knowledge*, 101; and Guyer, *Kant and the Claims of Knowledge*, 386.

[3] Grier, *Kant's Doctrine of Transcendental Illusion*, 176.

[4] Walsh claims this view prevailed among English commentators. See *Kant's Criticism of Metaphysics*, 198.

in the *Leibniz–Clarke Correspondence*. He attributes the thesis arguments to the Newtonian Samuel Clarke and the antithesis arguments
to Leibniz.[5] Now it is true that Kant assigns the theses to "dogmatism
of pure reason" and the antitheses to "a principle of pure empiricism" (A466/B494). But these labels refer to general positions rather
than to particular philosophical figures. Kant's point is that "empiricism" demands "the dissolution of the transcendental ideas of the
world-whole itself" (A466/B494), in favor of the continuing regress
postulated by the understanding. By contrast, the "dogmatic" thesis
positions apply the transcendental idea, seeking an end to the regressive series. In fact, Kant cites "the opposition of Epicureanism and Pla-
tonism" (A471/B499) as representative of the competing viewpoints.
Thus I agree with Grier that the description refers not to historical
figures, but to the conflict between reason's demand for closure and
the regress conceived by the understanding.[6]

In the first section, A409–13/B436–40, Kant reviews the idea of the
conditions of the world of appearance. He reiterates that the search
for the unconditioned involves only the "ascending" or regressive
series of subordinate conditions. This is because neither coordinated
conditions nor the "descending" consequences are presupposed by
the conditioned. An example of a regressive series is the series of past
states up to the present; the series of future states is a "progressive"
series. Because the present depends only on the past and not on the
future, reason seeks to explain it by the series of past states.

The table at A415/B443 summarizes the four Antinomies. Each
of the four categorical headings – quantity, quality, relation, and
modality – gives rise to a conflict. The quantitative regress involves
"**The absolute completeness** of the **composition** of a given whole
of all appearances." The issue is whether the world is finite or infinite
in space and time. Now Kant admits that unlike time, the parts of
space are coordinated with rather than subordinated to one another
(A412/B439), apparently deviating from his description of the regress

---

[5] See Al-Azm, *The Origins of Kant's Arguments in the Antinomies.* I agree with Walsh that Kant
likely saw "what began as an argument between Newton and Leibniz . . . in a very different
light" (*Kant's Criticism of Metaphysics*, 198). Al-Azm's interpretation in some cases obscures
Kant's approach to the issues.
[6] See Grier, *Kant's Doctrine of Transcendental Illusion*, 182–3.

of conditions. But although spatial parts are simultaneous, Kant will argue that we can represent them only through a successive synthesis, requiring a regress.

The second, qualitative Antinomy concerns "The **absolute completeness** of the **division** of a given whole in appearance" (A415/B443). At issue here is the nature of the part–whole relation for the real or substance. The real is conditioned by its parts, represented through division. But this process involves a regress to ever smaller parts. Thus the conflict is whether substance is infinitely divisible or has simple parts. Although the discussion focuses primarily on matter, Kant briefly addresses arguments concerning mental substance.

The third, relational, Antinomy regards "The **absolute completeness** of the **arising** of an appearance in general" (A415/B443). Only cause–effect gives rise to a regressive series of conditions; substance–accident and causal interaction are not relevant here. Accidents are not subordinated to substance "but are rather the way substance itself exists" (A414/B441). Similarly, causal interaction involves the idea of substances in community, not subordinated to one another. Thus the issue is whether the causal series is complete or not. If it is, then there must be a first, uncaused cause, which can initiate the series spontaneously through transcendental freedom. If there is no first cause, then the series extends infinitely. The Third Antinomy, then, represents a version of the traditional dispute over freedom and determinism.

Finally, the Fourth Antinomy concerns "The absolute completeness of the **dependence** of the **existence** of the alterable in appearance" (A415/B443). The question is whether something in appearance exists necessarily. The relevant modal concept is contingency, because "the contingent in existence always has to be seen as conditioned," since it refers "to a condition under which it is necessary" (A415/B442). Because the contingent is dependent, only the absolutely necessary could explain all contingency. So the Fourth Antinomy concerns whether there is some absolutely necessary being in appearance.

Now the reader might wonder how the third and fourth arguments differ from the proofs in rational theology. After all, the Third Antinomy concerns an unmoved mover, and the Fourth Antinomy the idea of a necessary existence, ideas employed in the cosmological and ontological proofs. The cosmological arguments differ from the theological proofs, however, because the "first cause" and "necessary being" of the Antinomies, unlike God, are located in the sensible world.

Kant adopts a "skeptical" resolution of the Antinomies, as opposed to the "critical" solution of the Paralogisms. The antinomial disputes draw apparently contradictory conclusions. The skeptical method resolves the debates by showing that the conflict is "dialectical," that the conclusions are only apparent contradictories. Following the distinction between mathematical and dynamical categories, Kant adopts one mode of resolution for the first two "mathematical" Antinomies and another for the "dynamical" Antinomies. For the former, Kant adopts a "both false" solution, claiming that the conclusions are actually contraries. For the latter his solution takes a modified "both true" position, with the thesis possibly true of things in themselves, and the antithesis necessarily true of appearances.

Given this skeptical resolution, Kant claims that the first two Antinomies yield indirect support for transcendental idealism. He could not do this with the Paralogisms, because the critical method assumes that things in themselves or objects in general are unknowable. In the Antinomies, Kant argues that if transcendental realism were true, then the disjunctions at issue would have to be true. That is, the world of appearances must be either infinite or finite in space and time, and the real would have to be either infinitely divisible or composed of ultimate indivisible parts. From the realist standpoint the conclusions are clearly contradictories and must have opposing truth values. But Kant also believes the conflicting conclusions are each supported by a valid argument. Thus contradictory conclusions would apply to the world in itself. Reasoning by *modus tollens*, since no object can have contradictory properties, the world of appearance cannot be the world in itself. Hence transcendental realism is false, and transcendental idealism is true.

Some commentators reject this reasoning, interpreting the arguments as depending on "verificationist" claims concerning what can be known.[7] If this were correct, the arguments could not support

---

[7] For commentators reading at least some of Kant's arguments this way see Strawson, *The Bounds of Sense*, 155–61 and 200; Posy, "Dancing to the Antinomy," 83ff; Allison, *Kant's Transcendental Idealism*, 46–7, 312–13; and Guyer, *Kant and the Claims of Knowledge*, 407. I address this issue below.

transcendental idealism, for the following reason. If the premises concerned only what we could know about appearances, then they could not establish *what the conditions of appearance must in fact be.* The conclusions, then, would not be realist in nature, but only epistemological. Now inherent contradictions in reason could support transcendental idealism only if they follow from realist claims. From Kant's point of view, the arguments cannot be verificationist in nature.

A verificationist reading appears plausible because the premises refer to the empirical regress involved in synthesis. And we have seen that Kant's theory of synthesis explains cognition of spatiotemporal objects. I agree with several commentators, however, that this is misleading.[8] I will argue that claims about synthesis here refer to the intellectual procedure for *thinking* the world-whole, which presupposes Kant's distinction between "analytic" and "synthetic" wholes. Kant believes realists must assume that things in themselves are synthetic wholes, composed of independently existing parts. If statements about synthesis refer to manner of *thinking* the totality of appearances rather than knowing them, then the arguments are not verificationist in nature.

2. THE ARGUMENTS OF THE ANTINOMIES

The Antinomies concern what must be true of the world of appearances as a whole in itself. Transcendental realists assume that this world is "given" or exists independently of the process of knowing or thinking it. All the arguments employ the *reductio* method, claiming that the truth of the opposing view leads to a contradiction. This is an effective way of highlighting the internal conflict of reason. As Sebastian Gardner points out, if transcendental realism were true, exactly one of the contradictory conclusions must be true. But since both arguments are valid, even if we knew that a thesis were true, we could not see "how it is *possible* for the antithesis to be false."[9] Here I follow Kant's order, discussing the arguments first and then their resolutions.

---

[8] Commentators who reject the verificationist reading include Melnick, *Space, Time, and Thought*, Grier, *Kant's Doctrine of Transcendental Illusion*, and Gardner, *Routledge Philosophy Guidebook to Kant*.

[9] See Gardner, *Routledge Philosophy Guidebook to Kant*, 251.

A. The First Antinomy: the composition of the world in time and space

The First Antinomy concerns whether the world is finite or infinite in time and space. The thesis argues for finitude: that there was a first state of the world in infinite time, and that the world is bounded in infinite space. The antithesis denies both conclusions, maintaining that the world extends infinitely in both time and space. Kant offers separate arguments on each side for the temporal and spatial nature of the world. Here are the thesis arguments.

Thesis: "The world has a beginning in time, and in space it is also enclosed in boundaries" (A426/B454). The first paragraph argues for the first part as follows:

1. Assume the contradictory, that the world has no beginning in time.
2. By hypothesis, at any given time "an eternity has elapsed, and hence an infinite series of states of things in the world . . . has passed."
3. The idea of an infinite series is the idea of a succession that cannot be completed.
4. By 3, "an infinitely elapsed world-series is impossible . . ."
5. By 4, the series of past states of the world in time must be finite.
6. Therefore, by 1, 2, and 5, "a beginning of the world is a necessary condition of its existence."

The argument that the world is finite in space follows in the next paragraph at A427–8/B455–6:

1. Assume the contradictory, that the world is "an infinite given whole of simultaneously existing things" in space.
2. The only way to think "the magnitude of a quantum that is not given" as bounded in intuition is "through the completed synthesis, or through the repeated addition of units to each other."
3. By 2, to think the whole world filling space would require completing "the successive synthesis of the parts of an infinite world," which entails that "an infinite time would have to be regarded as having elapsed."
4. But it is impossible to think of an infinite time as having elapsed.
5. Therefore, by 3 and 4, "an infinite aggregate of actual things cannot be regarded as a given whole, hence cannot be regarded as given **simultaneously**."
6. "Consequently, a world is **not infinite** in its extension in space, but is rather enclosed within its boundaries."

Clearly the second argument incorporates the first by translating the idea of a spatial whole in terms of a temporal series. Both arguments reject an actually infinite world-whole because *the idea of a completed infinite series is impossible*. Contrary to some interpreters, the alleged impossibility is not psychological (nor epistemological) but logical.[10] The main questions are why an infinite spatial world must be thought through an infinite temporal series, and why an infinite completed series is logically impossible. Answers to these questions will explain why this argument does not apply to Kant's theory of space and time, as well as responding to some objections to the argument.

Kant explains his notion of the infinite by contrasting his "true (transcendental) concept of infinity" (A432/B460) with the dogmatist's "defective concept of the infinity of a given magnitude" (A430/B458). According to the latter, "a magnitude is infinite if none greater than it . . . is possible." That is, the defective concept of infinity represents a maximally great magnitude. But because there is no limit to the addition of units, there is no greatest multiplicity. The true or mathematical notion of infinity, by contrast, "thinks only of the relation to an arbitrarily assumed unit, in respect of which it is greater than any number" (A432/B460). Unlike the defective idea of a maximum magnitude, the true notion is of a magnitude that surpasses any finite number. Now this (true) notion is not in itself logically incoherent. The contradiction in the notion of an infinite whole arises only when it is represented as a *completed series*: "The true (transcendental) concept of infinity is that the successive synthesis of unity in the traversal of a quantum can never be completed" (A432/B460). That is, the successive enumeration of an infinite series (such as the natural numbers) can never be completed, because no matter where one stops, there is always an additional member of the series to be thought.

As Melnick points out "Kant is here defending the concept of an actually infinite whole (= a whole encompassed by units only if these units are together 'greater than all number')."[11] He notes that Kant made the same distinction between true and defective notions in the Inaugural Dissertation of 1770. There, in a footnote in section 1,

---

[10] Two commentators who take the impossibility as epistemological or psychological are Guyer, *Kant and the Claims of Knowledge*, 407, and Kemp Smith, *Commentary*, 485.

[11] Melnick, *Space, Time, and Thought in Kant*, 331. I am heavily indebted to Melnick's interpretation of the mathematical Antinomies.

Kant says a non-human understanding "might distinctly apprehend a multiplicity at a single glance, without the successive application of a measure."[12] In short, there is nothing inherently contradictory in the idea of an actual infinite whole; the contradiction is in the idea of a completed infinite series.

Since time is by its nature successive, the true notion of the infinite entails that an infinite series of times cannot be thought as completed. But it is not clear why the spatial parts of the world-whole must be represented successively. In the last paragraph of the remark, Kant says to think the totality of a simultaneous infinite extension, where the boundaries are not given in intuition, requires having a concept that "must establish the possibility of a whole through the successive synthesis of the parts. Now since this synthesis has to constitute a series that is never to be completed, one can never think a totality prior to it and thus also through it" (A432/B460). Here Kant claims that the idea of a whole composed of parts could arise in only two ways: either through intuition or through thinking its relation to its parts. Because we cannot intuit the whole of appearances, that leaves only the second option, representing the whole by thinking its relation to the parts. Further, Kant assumes that the thought of the world in itself must represent the whole as composed of previously given parts. In Kant's terms, the world-whole in itself is a synthetic whole, a *totum syntheticum* rather than an analytic whole, a *totum analyticum*. As Allison puts it, "the concept of a totum syntheticum is here operationally defined in terms of the intellectual procedure through which it is conceived . . . The problem, then, is that the rule or procedure for thinking a totum syntheticum clashes with the rule or procedure for thinking an infinite quantity."[13] Nevertheless, Allison questions why it is necessary to conceive the series of states of the universe as a *totum syntheticum*.

Melnick defends Kant by emphasizing the realist view of the *marking procedures* for synthetic wholes.[14] Regardless of how the parts are

---

[12] *On the Form and Principles of the Sensible and Intelligible World, Theoretical Philosophy, 1755–1770*, 379.

[13] Other commentators refer to Kant's distinction between a *totum syntheticum* and a *totum analyticum*. See Kemp Smith, *Commentary*, 94–7, and Al-Azm, *The Origins of Kant's Arguments in the Antinomies*, 11. Allison locates the original terminology in Erdmann, *Reflexionen*, 393. See Allison, *Kant's Transcendental Idealism*, 43 and 338n26.

[14] Melnick's main discussion of the First Antinomy is in chapter 2 of *Space, Time, and Thought in Kant*, 329–53.

individuated, a transcendental realist could not conceive the totality of either temporal or spatial parts of the world as an analytic whole. Analytic wholes are those in which the whole is prior to the parts. This means the parts have no real existence *in themselves* independently of the whole, but come into existence (as parts) only as constructed by the marking process. The Aesthetic showed that our space and time are analytic wholes. Now consider what it would mean to claim that the world is an analytic whole. For temporal states, the existence of each state of the world would depend on the existence of *all* the others, entailing that the present depends also on the future as well as the past. For spatial parts this means, similarly, that no particle of matter could exist without the existence of all particles of matter. It is hard to see how a realist could defend such a conception of the world.

Melnick argues that transcendental realists must accept Kant's view that the world-whole in space and time is a synthetic whole, precisely because they represent spatiotemporal things as self-subsistent "*by representing them as all there to be met with by our procedures.*"[15] Because the world is *there to be encountered* by the subject, the parts must be thought as *given independently of the constructive process*. Since humans do not intuit the world as a whole, Kant seems justified in claiming that the idea of the world-whole arises by synthesis of the parts. Now since all synthesis is successive for humans, whether the parts exist successively or simultaneously, the *thought* of its composition requires a successive synthesis. And since representing an infinite series as completed is impossible, "this completion, hence also its concept, is impossible" (A432/B460). Thus the thesis argument concludes: "Therefore an infinite *given* magnitude, and hence also an infinite world (regarding either the past series or extension), is impossible" (emphasis mine; A430/B458).

This reading highlights both strengths and weaknesses of Kant's argument. The weak points are the theoretical assumptions that the idea of the whole must arise by synthesis from the parts, and that human synthetic thought is successive. On the other hand, this interpretation shows the argument to escape some standard criticisms. Allison discusses several common objections by different commentators.[16] Bertrand Russell raises two of them, one to Kant's concept

---

[15] *Space, Time, and Thought in Kant*, 322.
[16] See Allison, *Kant's Transcendental Idealism*, 40–5.

of infinity, and the other to the argument itself. First Russell objects to introducing the notion of synthesis in the idea of infinity, since by the Cantorian mathematical concept of infinity, "classes which are infinite are given all at once by the defining property of their members."[17] This objection is misguided, however, for as we have seen, Kant claims not that the concept of the infinite requires synthesis, but rather that thinking of an infinite whole made of given parts requires a synthesis. Kant has no objection to the mathematical concept of an infinite set of members.

Strawson shares Russell's second objection to the idea that an infinite series cannot be completed. Russell says, "all that [Kant] has even conceivably a right to say is that it cannot be completed *in a finite time*. Thus what he really proves is, at most, that if the world had no beginning, it must have already existed for an infinite time."[18] That is, either the world begins in time or it has existed infinitely. If Kant is entitled to assume only that an infinite series cannot be completed in a finite time, then the argument proves, contrary to its purpose, that the first alternative is false, and that the world is infinite in time. Both Russell and Strawson apparently assume that it makes sense to say that an infinite series can be "completed" in an infinite time. But if the idea of an infinite is the idea of a number greater than any finite number, then, regardless of the time allotted, it appears no such series could be *thought* (successively) as a completed whole.[19] Both objections miss the target as interpreted here.

Antithesis: "The world has no beginning and no bounds in space, but is infinite with regard to both time and space" (A427/B455). Again Kant offers separate proofs for time and space. The first paragraph contains the argument for time:

[17] Russell, *Our Knowledge of the External World*, 123.
[18] Russell, *Our Knowledge of the External World*, 123, and Strawson, *The Bounds of Sense*, 176.
[19] The same response can be made to a related objection by G. E. Moore and Jonathan Bennett, that Kant wrongly inferred the impossibility of an infinite series with one bound from the impossibility of an infinite series bounded at both ends. Allison points out the irrelevance, since Kant "does not claim that a series cannot be infinite if it has one end . . . His point is rather that since, as infinite, the series has only one end, it cannot constitute a totality" (44). The issue is whether it is possible to *think a totality as composed of an infinity of parts through a successive synthesis.*

1. Suppose the world has a beginning in (infinite) time.
2. "Since the beginning is an existence preceded by a time in which the thing is not, there must be a preceding time in which the world was not, i.e., an empty time."
3. But time is homogeneous: no part of time has "any distinguishing condition of its existence rather than its non-existence."
4. By 3, "no arising of any sort of thing is possible in an empty time."
5. "Thus many series of things may begin in the world, but the world itself cannot have any beginning, and so in past time it is infinite."

In this case, the antithesis argument for space appears to differ from the argument for time:

1. Assume the opposite, "namely that the world is finite and bounded in space; then it exists in an empty space, which is not bounded."
2. By 1, there would be not only relations "between things in **space**, but also a relation of things **to space**."
3. But "the world is an absolute whole, besides which there is encountered no object of intuition," and therefore nothing else to which the world could be related.
4. Hence "the relation of the world to empty space would be a relation of the world to **no object**. Such a **relation**, however, and hence also the boundedness of the world by empty space, is nothing."
5. Therefore "the world is not bounded at all in space, i.e., in its extension it is infinite."

These proofs are aimed against the view that the world is finite in absolute time and absolute space. On this conception, the world would begin at a time preceded by (infinite) empty time, and be surrounded by (infinite) empty space. Both proofs argue that these are incoherent conceptions. The first proof explicitly invokes the Principle of Sufficient Reason, claiming that there is no sufficient basis in time for the world to begin at one particular moment rather than another. Clearly this same argument applies to space: absolute space provides no sufficient basis for locating the world in one region rather than another. But if the world were temporally and spatially finite, then it would occupy determinate regions of absolute time and absolute space.

The second argument makes a different point concerning space: if the world is finite in absolute space, then it has what Melnick calls "multiple situatability."[20] That is, if it is bounded at S_1, then it has the determinate relation of being 10 feet away from some empty space S_2 distinct from S_1, and so on for all its relations to all other empty spaces. Because space is homogeneous, there is no possible way to think the difference in that situation, and one in which the world is shifted exactly 20 feet away from S_2. Yet for the absolutist they must be distinct. Kant puts the point in terms of the *correlates* of the relation: because the world encompasses all that is real in space, there is nothing real against the world on which to ground its determinate relation to space. "Such a relation, however, and hence also the boundedness of the world by empty space, is nothing" (A429/B457). Therefore, "the world is not bounded at all in space, i.e., in its extension it is infinite." If these determinate locations are not thinkable, then the realist conception of a finite world is incoherent.

In his remark on the antithesis Kant considers an alternative finitism, based on a relational theory of space and time. This is the Leibnizian view discussed earlier in chapter 3, according to which space and time are not independent of the real, but are derived from the relations among real things. As Kant explains, a relationist must think of a finite world abstracted from spatial and temporal limits, since the boundaries of the world precede its "location" in space and time: "instead of a first beginning . . . one thinks of an existence in general that **presupposes no other condition** in the world, rather than the boundary of extension one thinks of the **limits** of the world-whole, and thus one gets time and space out of the way" (A433/B461). In thinking the limits of the world as non-temporal and non-spatial, the relationist must think "surreptitiously of who knows what intelligible world in place of a **world of sense**." But cosmology concerns the nature of appearances in space and time. Thus a *mundus intelligibilis* "is nothing but the concept of a world in general, and in regard to which, consequently, no synthetic proposition at all, whether affirmative or negative, is possible" (A433/B461).

These antithesis arguments, based on the Principle of Sufficient Reason, appear stronger than the thesis arguments. First, both

---

[20] Melnick discusses the antithesis of the First Antinomy at *Space, Time, and Thought in Kant*, 329–44; the discussion of "multiple situatability" begins at 335.

Leibniz and Clarke accept this principle.[21] And second, since the unconditioned is the set of conditions jointly necessary and sufficient for the given, accepting the demand of reason implicitly commits one to some version of the Principle of Sufficient Reason. The proofs also infer the impossibility of a bounded world from the impossibility of thinking its location in absolute space and time. Without some logical basis for giving the world a determinate location in absolute space and time, the realist would be hard pressed to reject the antithesis arguments.

B. The Second Antinomy: the nature of substance

Thesis: "Every composite substance in the world consists of simple parts, and nothing exists anywhere except the simple or what is composed of simples" (A434–6/B462–4).

The first paragraph contains the argument for the thesis:

1. Assume the opposite, that "composite substances do not consist of simple parts."
2. By 1, "if all composition is removed in thought, no composite part, and (since there are no simple parts) no simple part, thus nothing at all would be left over."
3. If nothing at all would be left over, "no substance would be given."
4. Implied: substance is given.
5. Therefore, either (a) "it is impossible to remove all composition in thought" or (b) "after its removal something must be left over that subsists without any composition, i.e., the simple."
6. For substances, "composition is only a contingent relation, apart from which, as beings persisting by themselves, they must subsist" (A435–6/B463–4).
7. Therefore for substances it must be possible to remove all composition in thought: "the composite would once again not consist of substances."
8. By 6 and 7, (a) is impossible.
9. By 5 and 8 it follows that "what is a substantial composite in the world consists of simple parts."

In the remark on this argument Kant points out that the conclusion applies neither to space and time, nor to accidents of substances. First,

---

[21] For Leibniz and Clarke, see Al-Azm, *The Origins of Kant's Arguments in the Antinomies*, 30–5.

space and time are not substances. Second, as the Aesthetic showed, although they are composed of parts, the "parts are possible only in the whole" (A438/B466). Here he classifies them as *ideal* as opposed to *real* composites.[22] For space and time "if I remove all composition from it, then nothing, not even a point, might be left over; for a point is possible only as the boundary of a space (hence of a composite)" (A438–40/B466–8). The conclusion also does not apply to states or accidents of substances, since they "do not subsist by themselves" (A440/B468).

This argument is based on conceiving a substance as a self-subsistent being and, I suspect, on the view that relations are based on non-relational properties of things. Despite the various theories of substance, substances were generally conceived as independent entities. This implies that where a being is composed of substances, the existence of the composite depends on the existence of the parts. This is Kant's point in line 6, where he claims that for composite substances, composition is a "contingent relation." Now if the composition of composite substances is only a contingent property, then it must be possible "to remove all composition in thought," that is, to think the real in the composition independently of the composite. Once all composition is abstracted away, according to the argument, all that remains are non-composite or simple parts. Although not stated explicitly, the argument would apply to both material and mental substances.[23]

The above reasoning is valid only if being "self-subsistent" rules out all contingent properties. But this is not obvious. From the fact that *a composite of substances* must be composed of self-subsistent elements, it does not follow that these elements could not be composite in nature. Even if composition is a contingent property, substances could be irreducibly composite if one conceived of self-subsistent elements (substances) as possessing contingent properties.

[22] Grier points out that despite the similarity to the earlier distinction between analytic and synthetic wholes, Kant reserves the term "whole" or *totum* for the world as a whole, which was the subject of the First Antinomy. The term "composite" or *compositum* applies generally to anything in appearance made up of parts. See Grier, *Kant's Doctrine of Transcendental Illusion*, 196.

[23] Grier makes this point forcefully. She criticizes Al-Azm for reading the thesis and antithesis arguments as using different notions of substance, the thesis concerning only material substance and the antithesis substances generally. See Al-Azm, *The Origins of Kant's Arguments in the Antinomies*, 46ff, and Grier, *Kant's Doctrine of Transcendental Illusion*, 196–207.

A different defense is suggested by the second paragraph, where Kant says it follows that "all things in the world are simple beings, that composition is only an *external* state of these beings" (my emphasis). He continues: "reason must still think of them as the primary subjects of all composition and hence think of them prior to it as simple beings" (A436/B464). This passage appeals to the principle of the reducibility of relations discussed in the Amphiboly. On this view, all relations or "external determinations" are reducible to non-relational or "inner determinations" of things. Although Kant claims transcendental realists must endorse the reducibility of relations, he denies that it applies to appearances in space and time. Reading the thesis proof this way yields a valid argument. Given both that composition is a relation among parts and that self-subsistence implies only non-relational properties, self-subsistent substances must be simples. A rational metaphysician could avoid the conclusion by denying either the reducibility of relations or that self-subsistent entities have only necessary properties. As Grier points out, however, if one accepts reason's demand for the unconditioned, the idea of a composite that is not reducible to ultimate, simple parts fails to achieve closure.[24]

Antithesis: "No composite thing in the world consists of simple parts, and nowhere in it does there exist anything simple" (A435/B463). The first paragraph argues that composites are not composed of simple parts by locating composites in space:

1. Assume the opposite: suppose substances are composed of simple parts.
2. Because composition is an "external relation between substances," it is possible only in space.
3. By 2, the space occupied by a composite thing must have as many parts as the thing occupying it.
4. But space is infinitely divisible and does not consist of simple parts.
5. Therefore by 3 and 4 every simple part of the composite must occupy a space.
6. By virtue of occupying space, every simple part contains parts external to one another.

[24] See Grier, *Kant's Doctrine of Transcendental Illusion*, 203.

7. Hence every simple part is a composite of real substances.
8. Because 7 is self-contradictory, substances cannot be composed of simple parts.

By contrast, the proof in the second paragraph that there are no simples anywhere does not depend on their relation to space, but rather on the nature of experience in general:

1. Assume that the transcendental idea of the simple applied to appearances.
2. By 1, the empirical intuition of such an object would have to be possible.
3. Such an intuition would contain "absolutely no manifold whose elements are external to one another and bound into a unity" (A437/B465).
4. Implied: spatial and temporal intuition by its nature contains a manifold of external elements bound together in a unity.
5. But "this intuition is definitely required for absolute simplicity."
6. By 4 and 5, the simplicity of anything given in appearance "cannot be inferred from any perception, whatever it might be."
7. Therefore nothing simple is given in the world of sense "regarded as the sum total of all possible experiences."

Rather than arguing against the existence of indivisible parts, this second proof claims only that experience could in principle offer no evidence for their existence. Because appearances are given in space and time, and because empirical intuition inherently contains a manifold, intuition could offer no grounds for inferring the simplicity of anything given in appearance. This argument is aimed against both material and mental simples.

The first proof sides with the understanding in locating the world of appearance in space (and time). Although the proof does not mention matter *per se*, the first paragraph of the remark indicates that the substances under consideration are bodies (A441/B469). As Grier points out, it is a mistake to interpret the argument as relying on Kant's theory in the Aesthetic. It is true that the argument concludes that there are no simple parts of matter, based on the fact that the space matter occupies is infinitely divisible. But as we shall see, in his resolution Kant rejects that inference. Unlike Kant, the antithesis assumes that space is transcendentally real, and concludes that substance in itself is infinitely divisible.

In line 2 the proof moves from the claim that composition is an "external relation" to the claim that composite substances must exist in space. But the claim in line 6, that the mathematical divisibility of space entails the real divisibility of whatever occupies it, is not obviously true. Al-Azm offers two possible defenses. One is to read the argument as making the Leibnizian point that postulating simples violates the Principle of Sufficient Reason. That is, if one admits that the real occupying space contains a manifold of external parts, "it would be simply arbitrary" to stop at a real thing that is indivisible.[25] Since the text does not explicitly mention this principle, his second suggestion looks more promising. According to it, line 6 assumes that the hypothesized simple parts occupy space "in exactly the same sense as the composite object itself is said to be in space."[26] It would follow that all parts reached by division are "external" to each other in the same sense that the substances making up the composite are external. Suppose, for example, one explains the spatial extension of matter in terms of impenetrability. To say that one half of a body occupies a different space from the other half is to say that the parts bear this impenetrability relation to one another. If every part of matter bears this relation to every other part of matter, one can never arrive at a non-divisible "simple" that stands in no impenetrability relation to another space-occupying part.[27]

As the last paragraph of the remark indicates, the second proof is also aimed against the view that the thinking self is a simple substance. As we saw in the Paralogisms, Kant's argument against the simple soul depends on his idealistic principle that the thinking thing in itself is not given in experience. Here he wants to show, independently of transcendental idealism, that philosophers who claim to have imme-diate awareness of a simple self are mistaken. Given that conclusion, it is puzzling to find Kant claiming that nothing in inner sense "could prove a manifold of elements *external* to one another, and hence *real*

[25] Al-Azm, *The Origins of Kant's Arguments in the Antinomies*, 63–4.
[26] Al-Azm, *The Origins of Kant's Arguments in the Antinomies*, 61.
[27] In the *MFNS* of 1786, Kant argues for a dynamical theory of matter as composed of centers of repulsive force. As Michael Friedman explains in his introduction to the translation, "matter is explicitly taken to be continuous or infinitely divisible, and material *substance*, in particular, is now characterized precisely by the impossibility of elementary monadic simple elements." *Theoretical Philosophy after 1781*, 174. Contrary to the antithesis argument of the Second Antinomy, Kant's theory depends on his transcendental idealism, and the view that matter is only appearance and not a thing in itself.

composition" (A443/B471; my emphasis). I think his point, however, is that the data of inner sense cannot be used either for or against the existence of a simple self. As the stated proof points out, awareness through inner sense is inherently complex and therefore cannot support the simplicity of mental substance. On the other hand, the manifold of inner sense cannot prove anything about the subject "considered **externally**, as an object of intuition" (A443/B471). In other words, any conclusion about the real nature of mental substance must be based on its "external" existence in relation to other things, and not merely on inner intuition. The point of the second proof is to refute claims that empirical intuition could support the simplicity of mental or material substance.

C. The Third Antinomy: freedom and determinism

Thesis: "Causality in accordance with laws of nature is not the only one from which all the appearances of the world can be derived. It is also necessary to assume another causality through freedom in order to explain them" (A444/B472). The premises are contained in the first paragraph, A444–6/B472–4, and the conclusion is spelled out in the second:

1. Assume the opposite, that there is only causality "in accordance with laws of nature."
2. By 1, "everything that **happens** presupposes a previous state, upon which it follows without exception according to a rule."
3. By 2, this applies to every state of the world-series, and so on *ad infinitum*.
4. By 3, there is no first beginning, and thus "no completeness of the series on the side of the causes descending one from another."
5. But "the law of nature consists just in this, that nothing happens without a cause sufficiently determined *a priori*."
6. Thus the assumption that "all causality is possible only in accordance with laws of nature . . . contradicts itself."
7. Therefore there must be a causality "through which something happens without its cause being further determined by another previous cause, i.e., an **absolute** causal **spontaneity** beginning **from itself** . . . hence transcendental freedom."

As the remark points out, the conclusion establishes that there must be a first cause that has the spontaneous power to begin the series of world states. But it also opens up the possibility that there are spontaneous causes operating within the world-series:

because the faculty of beginning a series in time entirely on its own is thereby proved . . . now we are permitted also to allow that in the course of the world different series may begin on their own as far as their causality is concerned, and to ascribe to the substances in those series the faculty of acting from freedom. (A450/B478)

The thesis argument aims to prove the existence of transcendental freedom, or a cause having the power to initiate an event spontaneously, without prior determination. But the idea of transcendental freedom makes possible the concept of free will or practical freedom, the power of a rational agent to choose independently of sensuous determinations (A533–4/B561–2). The different series within the world that "begin on their own as far as their causality is concerned" would include consequences ensuing from such free choices. Since such actions have "natural consequences to infinity, there begins an absolutely new series, even though as far as time is concerned this occurrence is only the continuation of a previous series" (A450/B478). According to this conception, the events initiated by the original, transcendentally free occurrence could be either causally determined or undetermined.

The key to the argument is line 5, that causal determinism requires that "nothing happens without a cause sufficiently determined *a priori*." Clearly this expresses the transcendental demand that causal explanations terminate in a complete set of sufficient conditions for the given. Only on this assumption can one avoid the possibility of an infinite regress of causal states. What this does, of course, is to turn the original motive for causal explanations against itself, exploiting the "inherent tension" in the demands of reason. While admitting that transcendental freedom cannot be explained, its proponent claims that this is true of causal connections themselves: "with causality in accordance with natural laws . . . we do not in any way comprehend how it is possible for one existence to be posited through another existence" (A448/B476). So the thesis emphasizes the demand for closure in the causal series, and concludes that a sufficient account requires a cause not subject to deterministic connections. When challenged to explain that cause, the proponent claims to be no worse off than the determinist, since, as Hume demonstrated, there are no *a priori* explanations for causal connections.

Antithesis: "There is no freedom, but everything in the world happens solely in accordance with laws of nature" (A445/B473). This argument occurs in a very compressed form in the first paragraph:

1. Assume the opposite, that there is an uncaused beginning to the causal series of appearances.
2. By 1, there would exist a first state S_1, with the power to begin absolutely another state S_2, "and hence also a series of its consequences," S_3, S_4, and so on.
3. By 2, the "determination of this spontaneity itself," the causality of S_1 "will begin absolutely, so that nothing precedes it through which this occurring action is determined in accordance with constant laws."
4. But "a dynamically first beginning of action presupposes a state that has no causal connection at all with the cause of the previous one, i.e., in no way follows from it."
5. Therefore "transcendental freedom is contrary to the causal law, and is a combination between the successive states of effective causes in accordance with which no unity of experience is possible . . . and hence is an empty thought entity." (A445–7/B473–5)

Unlike Strawson, who sees the argument simply as endorsing the universal principle of causality, Al-Azm notes the subtle way it explores the notion of causal imputation. The point is to show that the idea of a spontaneously acting cause that initiates a causally determined series is incoherent. But the argument is not easy to make out. Line 3 states that, by definition, the *causal action* of the transcendentally free cause in state S_1 is not determined by its antecedent states nor is it governed by constant laws. The confusion arises with line 4, which appears to repeat the point in line 3. Al-Azm's account suggests the following reconstruction.[28] Suppose the dynamical first beginning of

---

[28] I have simplified his presentation; see Al-Azm, *The Origins of Kant's Arguments in the Antinomies*, 103–5.

action mentioned in line 4 refers to the causality of S_2 rather than S_1. Kant's point, then, is that the *deterministic causality* of the series S_2, S_3, S_4, . . . is not imputable to its antecedent condition S_1, since S_1 acts spontaneously. Thus there are really two causal first beginnings here, the spontaneous action of S_1 on S_2, and the deterministic action of S_2 on S_3. Because S_1 does not act causally by constant, deterministic laws, it cannot cause S_2 to act causally by constant, deterministic laws. Thus the concept of a spontaneous cause initiating a deterministic causal series is incoherent.

As Al-Azm sees it, the argument raises a question about the relation between the spontaneous act of origination "and the agent presumably 'responsible' for that act."[29] This suggests a tactic used by opponents of free will, who rejected the idea of undetermined choice precisely because it conflicts with moral responsibility. For a spontaneous, undetermined choice would be one not connected to antecedent conditions, including the agent's character. In that case it could not be said to be the action of the agent. The antithesis argument here makes the parallel point that to attribute causality to a state presupposes that it follows from the nature (and antecedents) of the state to act in that manner. Thus spontaneous causality cannot provide a sufficient explanation of a series of causally determined states.

In the remarks on the antithesis, Kant relates the Third Antinomy to the First Antinomy. At A449/B477 he points out that the success of the thesis argument for a first dynamical state depends on the conclusion that there is a first temporal state of the world. If one admits that substances have always existed, then "there is no difficulty in also assuming that the change of their states, i.e., the series of their alterations, has always existed, and hence that no first beginning, whether mathematical or dynamical, need be sought." Moreover, the second paragraph picks up the point stated in the proof at A447/B475, that admitting transcendental freedom destroys the unity of experience:

For alongside such a lawless faculty of freedom, nature could hardly be thought any longer, because the laws of the latter would be ceaselessly modified by the former, and this would render the play of appearances, which in accordance with mere nature would be regular and uniform, confused and disconnected. (A451/B479)

---

[29] Al-Azm, *The Origins of Kant's Arguments in the Antinomies*, 105.

In other words, the existence of transcendental freedom within appearances would make nature indeterministic. Not only would it be impossible to predict the consequences of events, but, as Kant argued in the Second Analogy, it would be impossible to distinguish between an event, an objective succession of states, and a subjective succession of perceptions. Clearly the antithesis position sides with the principles of the understanding.

On the above reading, the antithesis argument also appeals to the Principle of Sufficient Reason. Only instead of emphasizing sufficiency in a complete set of conditions, the latter emphasizes a sufficient explanation of deterministic causal connections. Corresponding to each strength is a weakness: the thesis can explain neither the source of spontaneity nor the relation between spontaneity and determinism; the antithesis cannot give closure to the causal series. These corresponding strengths and weaknesses illustrate both the tension in applying the Principle of Sufficient Reason, and the conflict between reason and the understanding.

D. The Fourth Antinomy: contingency and necessity

Thesis: "To the world there belongs something that, either as a part of it or as its cause, is an absolutely necessary being" (A452/B480). The thesis states that something absolutely necessary exists within the world. The proof consists of two parts, the first arguing for an absolutely necessary being, and the second arguing that this being must exist in the world. The first part consists of these steps:

1. The sensible world as the whole of appearances contains a series of alterations.
2. "Every alteration, however, stands under its condition, which precedes it in time, and under which it is necessary" (A452/B480).
3. Every given conditioned presupposes a complete series up to the unconditioned, "which alone is absolutely necessary."
4. "Thus there must exist something absolutely necessary, if an alteration exists as its consequence."

The second part argues that this necessary being cannot be outside the world of appearances:

5. Assume the opposite, that the absolutely necessary being is outside the world of sense.

6. By 5, the series of alterations in the world "would derive from it, without this necessary cause itself belonging to the world of sense" (A452–4/B480–2).

7. But "the beginning of a time-series can be determined only through what precedes it in time."

8. By 7, "the supreme condition of the beginning of a series of changes" must exist in the time before the series comes into existence.

9. By 8, the absolutely necessary cause of the series "belongs to time, hence to appearance (in which alone time is possible, as its form); consequently it cannot be thought as detached from the world of sense."

Although the argument seems straightforward, it turns out to be more complicated than it appears on the surface. The main issue is how it differs from the Third Antinomy argument for a transcendentally free cause. Commentators such as Kemp Smith and Bennett claim this proof is redundant, since the necessary being argued for here is just the first, uncaused cause at issue in the preceding Antinomy.[30] Although the second part suggests this reading, Grier argues persuasively that the two arguments have different purposes.[31] First, there is the obvious point that the two proofs involve different categories, the Third Antinomy causality, and the fourth the modal concepts of necessity and contingency. As Kant explains in discussing the ontological argument in the next section, the nominal definition of an absolutely necessary being is one whose non-being is impossible (A592–3/B620–1). Notice that on this definition, even if the necessary being exists in time, there could be no time at which it did not exist. That alone would rule out the idea that it is merely the first temporal state of a causal series. The natural application of this notion to appearances would be to substance: rather than taking the necessary

[30] See Kemp Smith, *Commentary*, 495, and Bennett, *Kant's Dialectic*, 241.

[31] See Grier, *Kant's Doctrine of Transcendental Illusion*, 219–27. I am not as convinced, however, by her claim that the Third Antinomy also does not involve the notion of a first causal state in time. She cites as evidence Kant's claim in the remark on the thesis that "here we are talking of an absolute beginning not, as far as time is concerned, but as far as causality is concerned" (A450/B478). See Grier, 220–1. She is right that the issue there is whether deterministic causality must be conditioned by transcendental freedom. As we saw above, however, at least the antithesis position takes the thesis argument to presuppose a first causal state in time. Whether she is right about the Third Antinomy, her point seems stronger with respect to the Fourth.

being as a first state of the series, it makes more sense to take it as something substantial existing permanently in time. In fact, in the solution Kant says, "Here we deal not with unconditioned causality, but with the unconditioned existence of the substance itself" (A559/B587).

Grier also points out that the references to cause in the Fourth Antinomy can be construed in terms of immanent rather than transitive causation. As Spinoza distinguished them, transitive causation occurs between really distinct things, for example in a collision in which one body causes another to move. An immanent cause, by contrast, is a ground of something, inseparable from its effect. The numbers 1 and 2 can be seen as the "immanent causes" of the number 4, for example, insofar as they are contained in it.[32] Thus Grier maintains the Fourth Antinomy treats necessary existence as the immanent cause of all contingent existence in appearances rather than a temporally first, transitive cause.

The first part argues directly from the contingency of appearances to an absolutely necessary being. The description of appearances as a series of alterations establishes their contingency, since, as line 2 spells out, an alteration is an event necessitated by a temporally prior condition. Although this presupposes a causal account, what is relevant to the argument is the contingency. Moreover, we should note that the necessity obtaining between empirical causes and effects is relative rather than absolute. That is, if an empirical state follows necessarily from a prior state, then its existence is not absolutely necessary in Kant's sense. Line 3 expresses the demand of reason for totality in the conditions, which can be satisfied only by something whose existence is absolutely necessary. This conclusion is stated in line 4, which describes alteration as its consequence. On Grier's reading, the term "consequence" should be understood as an ontological rather than a temporal effect.

The second part of the proof argues that this absolutely necessary ground must belong to the world "either as a part of it or as its cause." Here Kant returns to the *reductio* method, and derives a contradiction from the idea that the necessary being is outside appearances. The key is in lines 7 and 8, which argue that the "beginning" of a time-series

---

[32] See Spinoza, *Ethics*, part I, proposition 18, in *The Ethics and Selected Letters*, 46 and 25 of Shisley's introduction.

must itself exist in the time prior to the series. As I argued above, Kant intends to apply this to substance rather than to a (temporary) first state of the series. The issue is whether it has to exist temporally or can be conceived of as existing outside time. Clearly, if it exists at all in time, then it exists at all times. Kant addresses the atemporal version of "grounding" in the third paragraph of the remark. If the "condition must be taken in just the same significance as it has . . . in the series," and the series takes place in time, then "the necessary being must be regarded as the supreme member of the world-series" (A457–8/B485–6). Unfortunately it is not obvious that the relation among appearances is relevant if the issue is whether the contingency of the entire series requires an absolutely necessary ground.

The last two paragraphs of the remark respond to this objection. Here Kant argues that a shift from a cosmological to an intelligible necessary being confuses empirical and intelligible contingency (A458/B486). By empirical contingency he means "that the new state could not at all have occurred on its own, without a cause" in the previous time (A460/B488). An intelligible contingency is one "whose contradictory opposite is possible" (A458/B486). A body changing state from motion to rest is an example of empirical contingency, since motion at one time does not contradict rest at another time (A460/B488). The contradictory opposite of a state would require "that at the very time when the previous state was, its opposite could have been there in place of it." In other words, if the absolutely necessary being were outside time, it could only ground logical contingency. Because the contingency here is empirical, the necessary being must be in time, in the world of appearances.

Antithesis: "There is no absolutely necessary being existing anywhere, either in the world or outside the world as its cause" (A453/B481). The antithesis explicitly contradicts not only the thesis, but also the view rejected above, that there is an absolutely necessary being outside the world of appearances. The proof devotes a paragraph to each alternative. The argument against the thesis is this:

1. Assume the opposite, "that either the world itself is a necessary being or that there is such a being in it."
2. By 1, in the series of alterations, either (a) "there would be a beginning that is unconditionally necessary, and hence without

a cause," or (b) "the series itself would be without any beginning, and although contingent . . . it would nevertheless be absolutely necessary and unconditioned as a whole."

3. Alternative (a) conflicts with the "law of the determination of all appearances in time," and so is not possible.
4. Alternative (b) is self-contradictory "because the existence of a multiplicity cannot be necessary if no single part of it possesses an existence necessary in itself."
5. Therefore the original assumption is not possible.

The next paragraph argues that an absolutely necessary cause cannot exist outside the world, as follows:

6. Assume "there were an absolutely necessary cause of the world outside the world" (A453–5/B481–3).
7. By 6, "this cause, as the supreme member in the **series of causes** of alterations in the world, would first begin these changes and their series" (A455/B483).
8. But its action would "begin to act then, and its causality would belong in time, and for this very reason in the sum total of appearances, i.e., in the world."
9. Therefore, "this cause would not be outside the world, which contradicts what was presupposed."
10. Therefore, "neither in the world nor outside it (yet in causal connection with it) is there any absolutely necessary being."

A footnote to line 7 distinguishes two senses of "begin," one active (transitive), meaning to initiate, and the other passive, referring to a temporal commencing. Kant says, "I infer here from the former to the latter." So the inference from line 7 to line 8 appears to incorporate the argument from the thesis that by virtue of initiating a series of appearances in time, the necessary cause would also have to be in time. Here the point is used ultimately against the existence of an absolutely necessary being.

The first stage of the proof appears straightforwardly to follow the logic of the Principle of Sufficient Reason. Again, siding with the understanding, the antithesis argument first rules out an absolutely necessary being as part of the world, since its existence contradicts the principle of causality, which requires every contingency to be conditioned by a further contingency. The more interesting argument is against the second alternative, that the entire world of appearances is absolutely necessary. The proof rejects this possibility on the grounds that the idea of a necessary series composed entirely of contingent parts is incoherent. This objection thus applies the Principle of Sufficient Reason in a direction opposed to the thesis argument, claiming that the contingency of the parts does not provide a sufficient basis for the necessity of the whole.

3. KANT'S RESOLUTIONS AND TRANSCENDENTAL IDEALISM

The remainder of the chapter falls into three parts. Sections 3 through 5 contain general remarks about the arguments. In sections 6 and 7 Kant discusses their relation to transcendental idealism. He then presents his solution in section 8, and applies it in detail to each argument in section 9. The newest material here concerns the Third Antinomy debate over determinism and transcendental freedom. Kant explains at length how human actions can be subject to causal laws as appearances, and also attributed to free will as their intelligible cause. This is important as a preamble to his moral theory, presented in the *Groundwork of the Metaphysics of Morals* and *Critique of Practical Reason.*

Earlier I discussed Kant's claim that the thesis positions represent the "dogmatism" of pure reason, and the antithesis positions the "pure empiricism" of the understanding (A466/B494). Following that description in the third section, Kant evaluates the advantages and disadvantages of each position. The dogmatic theses have the advantage of supporting practical interests: Kant describes them as "so many cornerstones of morality and religion" (A466/B494). By contrast, the antithesis "robs us of all these supports," and as a consequence, "moral ideas and principles lose all validity" (A468/B496). On the other hand, in rejecting reason's demand for completion of the series, the antithesis arguments promote the interests of speculative reason by making continuing inquiry possible. By contrast, the dogmatist introduces "ideas with whose objects it has no acquaintance because, as thought-entities, they can never be given" (A469/B497). Dogmatism thereby abandons natural inquiry, "certain that it can never be refuted by facts of nature because it is not bound by their testimony." Given the nature of these conflicts, in the absence of practical and speculative interests, one "would be in a state of cease-less vacillation" (A475/B504), one day persuaded by the thesis, the next by the antithesis.

In the fourth section Kant claims that because the conflicts arise from the inherent tension within reason, they are all resolvable by rea-son. The fact that the object is the empirical cosmos implies that the resolution will derive from the empirical synthesis on which the tran-scendent idea is based (A479/B507). The fifth section gives a "skeptical representation" of the conflicts, describing them as between ideas that are either too big or too small for the concept of the understanding. For the first three Antinomies, the thesis conclusions are "too small," since they close off the series. The opposing antithesis conclusions asserting the infinity of the mathematical and dynamical series are "too big" for the concepts of the understanding. The pattern breaks with the Fourth Antinomy, where Kant says the thesis idea of an absolutely necessary being is "too big for your empirical concept," while the antithesis position that all existence is contingent "is too small for your concept" (A489/B517).

The sixth and seventh sections relate the conflict to transcendental idealism. Section 6 distinguishes transcendental idealism from both transcendental realism and empirical idealism. For transcendental idealism, "objects of experience are **never** given **in themselves**, but only in experience" (A492–3/B521). But "experience" means possible rather than actual perception:

> That there could be inhabitants of the moon, even though no human being has ever perceived them, must of course be admitted; but this means only that in the possible progress of experience we could encounter them; for everything is actual that stands in one context with a perception in accor-dance with the laws of the empirical progression. (A493/B521)

The empirical idealist, to the contrary, tries to reduce all objects to collections of actual perceptions, and has difficulty accounting for possible perceptions.

Section 7 then sketches the general form of Kant's resolution: although the conclusions of the arguments appear contradictory, they are not. Instead, the opposition is "dialectical" as opposed to "analyti-cal" (A504/B532). At A503/B532 Kant cites as examples the judgments, "every body smells good" and "every body smells not good," which are not contradictories, since they both assume that every body has some smell. If, however, there are bodies that lack an aroma, then the propositions are contraries, since they can both be false. Similarly, all the Antinomies presuppose that the world as the whole series of appearances is a thing in itself. If this were true, then the conclusions would contradict each other, with one true and the other false. But if appearances are not things in themselves, then the world "does not exist at all (independently of the regressive series of my representations)" and "by itself it is not to be met with at all" (A505/B533). And at A506–7/B534–5 Kant offers this dilemma to show how the first two Antinomies support transcendental idealism: "If the world is a whole existing in itself, then it is either finite or infinite. Now the first as well as the second alternative is false . . . Thus it is also false that the world (the sum total of appearances) is a whole existing in itself." As we shall see below, for the dynamical Antinomies, Kant offers a different resolution.

The eighth section explains the principles of Kant's resolution. He recalls that reason's idea of the unconditioned is only regulative, supplying a maxim for inquiry, rather than constitutive, making a substantive claim about the object: "Thus the principle of reason is only a **rule,** prescribing a regress in the series of conditions for given appearances, in which regress it is never allowed to stop with an absolutely unconditioned" (A509/B537). Thus the principle "cannot say **what the object is**, but only **how the empirical regress is to be instituted**" (A510/B538). The rest of the section distinguishes between two sorts of empirical regress, one to infinity (*in infinitum*), the other extending indeterminately (*in indefinitum*).

A regress to infinity applies where the whole is empirically given. For example, in dividing a body (or a line segment), the process can go on to infinity since the parts (conditions) are given with the whole. Because here "an unconditioned (indivisible) member of this series of conditions is never encountered . . . the division goes to infinity" (A513/B541). Where one is given only a member and seeks to extend the series, the regress is indefinite rather than infinite. For example, in tracing someone's ancestors, because the whole series is not given, "this regress . . . goes to an indeterminate distance, searching for more members for the given" (A523/B541). The rule for the infinite regress is, "You **ought** never to stop extending it," because one is assured that there is always a further member given empirically with the whole. By contrast, the rule for the indefinite regress is, "Extend it as far as you **want**," because no member can be given as absolutely unconditioned (A511/BH539). In neither regress, however, is the series being given "infinite in the object" (A514/B542). Since the objects of the regress are only appearances, the conditions – parts or further members – are given *only in the regress*. In sum, for appearances one cannot determine how big the series of conditions is, either finite or infinite, "for it is nothing in itself." Although we can know *a priori* that space and time are infinite, there is no determinate answer to the question, is the world infinite in space and time?

The particular solutions follow from this analysis. For the First Antinomy, the question is whether the world is bounded by empty time or space. Since experience is always of the conditioned – i.e., an empty space or time beyond the world is not a possible object of experience – one could never encounter the boundary of the world. Like the inquiry into one's ancestors, the search for the conditions goes on *in indefinitum*: one is not assured of encountering a further member of the series, but neither can one assume an unconditioned member. In consequence, as Kant puts it in a footnote: "This world-series can thus be neither bigger nor smaller than the possible empirical regress . . . And since this cannot yield a determinate infinite, nor yet something determinately finite . . . we can assume the magnitude of the world to be neither finite nor infinite" (A518/B546). Thus there is no determinate answer to the question: how big is the world? In a second footnote Kant notes the difference between his position and the antithesis view that the world is actually infinite in time and space (A521/B549). For Kant, both the thesis and antithesis are false of appearances.

The same reasoning applies to the Second Antinomy, concerning the divisibility of the real. In this case, since bodies are given in experience, the regress is *in infinitum*, meaning that one must continue seeking the condition (parts) for every member encountered. But although one can never arrive at simples, neither is one entitled to claim, with the antithesis, that the whole is composed of an infinity of parts: although all the parts are contained in the intuition, "the **whole division** is **not** contained in it; this division consists only in . . . the regress itself, which first makes the series actual" (A524/B552). Here there are also two cases, one for matter as continuous quantity (*quantum continuum*), another for matter as discrete (*quantum discretum*). In the first case matter is not articulated into parts, and the division proceeds to infinity as it does for space. In the second case matter is articulated, as in an organic body. Here, "only experience can settle how far the organization in an articulated body may go, and . . . such parts must nevertheless at least be within a possible experience" (A527/B555). In general, however, the extent to which appearances can be divided "is not a matter of experience"; it is "a principle of reason never to take the empirical regress . . . to be absolutely complete." As Melnick explains, the transcendental realist can apply the idea of infinity to a whole given of parts. For the transcendental idealist, because an infinite series cannot be completed, the idea of infinity applies only to the rule for seeking the condition.[33]

In concluding his account of the mathematical Antinomies, Kant explains that they admit of a "both false" resolution because the conditions are homogeneous with the conditioned. When investigating the temporal and spatial bounds of the universe, or the parts of the given whole, "none other than a sensible condition can enter, i.e., only one that is itself a part of the series" (A530/B558). For the dynamical Antinomies the matter is different, since "a synthesis of **things not homogeneous** . . . must be at least admitted in the case of the dynamical synthesis." In these cases the dynamic series allows for an intelligible condition that is not part of the series. In consequence, although the dialectical arguments collapse, the rational propositions "may **both be true**" if their significance is restricted to either things in themselves or appearances (A531–2/B559–60). As we shall see, however, this resolution provides no support for transcendental idealism.

The resolution of the conflict between transcendental freedom and causal determinism follows the "both true" pattern. First Kant emphasizes that the causal principle of the understanding necessarily applies to appearances (A532/B560). The idea of transcendental freedom originates in reason, and represents the power to begin a state "**from itself**, the causality of which does not in turn stand under another cause determining it in time in accordance with the law of nature"

---

[33] See Melnick, *Space, Time, and Thought in Kant*, especially 379–95.

(A533/B561). This is the basis of the idea of practical freedom or free will. Morality and religion assume that human beings can determine themselves, independently of causal necessitation (A534/B562). Whereas for the transcendental realist, causal determinism could not coexist with transcendental freedom, this is possible for the transcendental idealist. Kant then explains how "the very same effect that is determined by nature" can also allow for freedom (A536/B564).

Before looking at the details of Kant's solution, there are two issues to address briefly. One concerns the relation between Kant's views of freedom here and in his ethical theory. Allison argues that in 1781 Kant had not yet developed the notion of autonomy central to his moral theory. Thus the idea of free will here is the negative idea of the agent resisting determination by sensible impulses. Not until the *Groundwork of the Metaphysics of Morals* (1785) and the *Critique of Practical Reason* (1788) did Kant conceive of free will as autonomy, the faculty for giving the law to oneself.[34] Accordingly he also changes his stand on our knowledge of freedom. In the first *Critique* he claims only that transcendental freedom is conceivable; the moral theory argues that transcendental freedom can be deduced from the existence of the moral law.

A second issue is whether the Dialectic account of the relation between transcendental and practical freedom is inconsistent with remarks in the later Canon of Pure Reason. As we have seen, the Antinomies treat practical freedom as in some sense dependent on transcendental freedom. By contrast, in the Canon Kant says whether, in actions of practical freedom, "reason is not itself determined by further influences," does not concern us in the practical sphere, since "we ask of reason only a **precept** for conduct; it is rather a merely speculative question, which we can set aside as long as our aim is directed to action or omission" (A803/B831). Here he allows the possibility that the spontaneity exhibited in free will might not be the absolute spontaneity of transcendental freedom. This implies that transcendental freedom is not presupposed by practical freedom.

Allison thinks the apparent contradiction between the texts can be dispelled. First he claims Kant takes the dependence of practical

---

[34] See Allison, *Kant's Transcendental Idealism*, chapter 15, especially 315–17. I am indebted to Allison's explanation of transcendental and practical freedom.

on transcendental freedom as conceptual rather than real: "it is this **transcendental** idea of **freedom** on which the practical concept of freedom is grounded" (A533/B561). Since confusing transcendental ideas for ideas of objects involves transcendental illusion, Kant could not consistently claim that the reality of practical freedom presupposes the reality of transcendental freedom. This introduces the possibility mentioned in the Canon, that practical freedom is not the absolute spontaneity conceived in the idea of transcendental freedom.[35] But as Kant claims, the speculative basis of practical reason is not an issue for morality.

The "both true" resolution of the Third Antinomy begins with Kant reaffirming that "if all causality in the world of sense were mere nature, then every occurrence would be determined in time," and so abolishing "transcendental freedom would also simultaneously eliminate all practical freedom" (A534/B562). Moreover, if appearances were things in themselves, then "freedom cannot be saved," for nature would be a "determining cause, sufficient in itself, of every occurrence" (A536/B564). But because appearances are not things in themselves, "they themselves must have grounds that are not appearances." Although these "intelligible" grounds are outside appearances, they nevertheless give rise to effects in the series. "The effect can therefore be regarded as free in regard to its intelligible cause," and yet the result of necessary laws in regard to appearances (A537/B565). The remainder of this section explains how transcendental freedom and determinism can coexist by distinguishing the intelligible from the empirical character of action.

At A538/B566 Kant defines the intelligible as "that in an object of sense which is not itself appearance." The "clarification" applies this definition to human intellectual faculties. Through the t.u.a., one recognizes that acts of understanding and reason "cannot be accounted at all among impressions of sense." In consequence, subjects identify themselves as partly phenomenal, and partly merely intelligible (A546–7/B575). Human actions, then, can have both an empirical and an intelligible character, where "character" refers to the "law of its causality" (A539/B567). In its empirical character, as subject to sensible conditions, the action is connected to other appearances "in

[35] See Allison, *Kant's Transcendental Idealism*, 315–19.

accordance with constant natural laws." By virtue of its intelligible character the action would not stand under temporal conditions, for time is only a condition of appearances. Considered as an effect of an intelligible cause, "no **action** would **arise** or **perish**," and so, not being part of the empirical series that makes its necessary, the action would be free of all causal determination (A541/B569). Thus intelligible causality "begins its effects in the sensible world **from itself**, without its action beginning **in it** itself." Kant concludes that "freedom and nature . . . would both be found in the same actions, simultaneously and without any contradiction, according to whether one compares them with their intelligible or their sensible cause" (A541/B569).

As Allison explains, this is a "compatibilism" in which the empirical and intelligible characters represent alternative ways of explaining the action.[36] The empirical account views the action as emanating from an agent's desires, themselves understood as determined by physiological, psychological, and sociological causes. In presupposing that an individual's character develops as an effect of these conditions, empirical explanations accord with the causal principle. Explanations by intelligible causes appeal to the agent's reasons for acting rather than to natural causes. This "causality of reason" is expressed through imperatives, both moral and non-moral: "The **ought** expresses a species of necessity and a connection with grounds which does not occur anywhere else in the whole of nature" (A547/B575). Whereas there is no room in nature for the idea that something ought to exist, this 'ought' expresses an action whose ground "is nothing other than a mere concept." Explanations in terms of reasons assume that choices are governed by rational principles relating the action to the agent's purposes.

The question, of course, is how both types of causation can work together. Kant believes that when we exercise practical reason, our desires function as incentives rather than causes of action. As Allison explains, for beings with free will, an incentive can determine an action only "insofar as the agent incorporates that incentive into his rule or maxim of action."[37] When an agent acts freely on a desire, the action is based on a maxim licensing the action on that

---

[36] Allison, *Kant's Transcendental Idealism*, 325–9.   [37] *Kant's Transcendental Idealism*, 327.

desire: "In circumstances C, it is permissible (or obligatory) to act on my desire D." According to this model of rational agency, desires are effective only insofar as agents subsume them under rules they endorse. The intelligible character of free action consists in this act of incorporation.[38]

Kant uses the example of the malicious liar to illustrate his view. An explanation in terms of the person's empirical character seeks its sources in upbringing and environment as well as natural temperament, that is, "the occasioning causes" (A554/B582). Nevertheless, we hold the agent responsible: "This blame is grounded on the law of reason, which regards reason as a cause" that, independently of conditions, ought to have determined the person to act otherwise (A555/B583). This is possible because "one regards the causality of reason not as a mere concurrence with other causes, but as *complete in itself* . . . [R]eason, regardless of all empirical conditions of the deed, is fully free, and this deed is to be attributed entirely to its failure to act" (A555/B583, emphasis added). On this model, the empirical and intelligible accounts of action do not conflict, since the former is incomplete and subject to temporal conditions. Reason is atemporal because the "act of incorporation" is timeless. Kant says, "In regard to the intelligible character . . . no **before** or **after** applies" (A553/B581). That is, although the imperatives under which one acts apply to temporal events, one's adherence to them is not part of the causal series.

It follows that in judging free actions, "we can get only as far as the intelligible cause, but we cannot get **beyond** it . . . But why the intelligible character gives us exactly these appearances and this empirical character" cannot be explained (A557/B585). In keeping with transcendental idealism, Kant claims that this resolution proves only the possibility of practical or transcendental freedom in the noumenal realm. He ends the section by noting that his resolution demonstrates that freedom and causal necessity are compatible: "since in freedom a relation is possible to conditions of a kind entirely different from those in natural necessity, the law of the latter does not affect the former; hence each is independent of the other" (A557/B585).

---

[38] For a discussion of this view, see Allison, *Kant's Theory of Freedom*, part I: "Freedom and rational agency in the *Critique of Pure Reason*," 11–82.

Transcendental illusion II

Compared to this discussion, Kant's resolution of the Fourth Antinomy is mercifully short, following the pattern of the above resolution. First he points out that because every member in the series of
appearances is contingent, there is no unconditioned or absolutely
necessary member anywhere (A559/B587). So if appearances were
things in themselves, then there could be no absolutely necessary
being as their condition. But because the dynamic regress can postulate a heterogeneous condition, one outside the spatiotemporal order,
it is possible for contingent appearances to be grounded in an absolutely necessary intelligible being. This "both true" resolution differs
from that of the previous Antinomy since "in the case of freedom,
the thing itself as cause (*substantia phaenomenon*) would nevertheless
belong to the series of conditions, and only **its causality** would be
thought as intelligible" (A561/B589). An absolutely necessary being,
however, could not exist in the sensible world, although it could be
"the ground of the possibility of all these appearances" (A562/B590).
In his concluding remark Kant notes that this transcendental idea of
an absolutely necessary intelligible ground of all existence is the basis
of rational theology, the subject of the next chapter.

4. SUMMARY

In the Antinomies Kant examines the arguments of rational cosmology, those concerning the nature of the world considered as the sum
total of appearances. The four metaphysical disputes, following the
four categorical heads, debate whether the world is infinite in space
and time, whether matter is infinitely divisible, whether all events
are causally determined, and whether there is an absolutely necessary
existence. Kant's analysis shows how each thesis position endorses the
demand of reason for the unconditioned, while its antithesis presupposes the principles of the understanding. Kant offers a "skeptical"
resolution of the disputes, arguing that in no case are the conclusions
true contradictories. These disputes are significant for providing indirect support for transcendental idealism. This applies most clearly to
the first two, mathematical, Antinomies. If appearances were things in
themselves, either the thesis or antithesis would have to be true. Since
in the mathematical Antinomies both conclusions are false of appearances, appearances cannot be things in themselves. For the last two,

dynamical, Antinomies, Kant offers a "both true" resolution, which presupposes the truth of transcendental idealism. In these cases the thesis is possibly true of things in themselves, with the antithesis true of appearances. This analysis of the metaphysical disputes reinforces the critical theory that the synthetic *a priori* principles of the understanding apply only to appearances, and not to things in themselves, and thus exposes the illusion in attempting to take the regulative demand of reason for constitutive concepts of objects.

CHAPTER 10

Transcendental illusion III: rational theology

Kant has a complex attitude toward religion. One one hand he consistently rejects religious belief based on superstition, fanaticism, and anthropomorphism. He especially opposes faith that appeals to emotion at the expense of reason. As Allen Wood explains, "Kant is willing to condone a faith which bases itself on special divine revelation only insofar as the content of its revelation accords with the precepts revealed naturally to every human being through the faculty of reason."[1] And in keeping with transcendental idealism, Kant rejects the possibility of metaphysical knowledge of God. As he famously puts it in the 1787 Preface: "Thus I had to deny **knowledge** in order to make room for **faith**" (Bxxx). On the other hand, although rational theology is a pseudoscience, the idea of God serves two legitimate purposes. First, it is necessary for moral faith. As rational moral agents, we recognize the moral law to pursue the highest good. But we can realize our purposes only within the world of nature. Thus moral action makes sense only on the assumption that nature is in harmony with morality. For Kant, this implies that nature is governed by a supremely perfect being. Kant elaborates on this point in the *Lectures on the Philosophical Doctrine of Religion* as well as his ethical writings. In its second role, the idea of God has a regulative function promoting the inquiry into natural purposive systems in empirical science. *The Critique of the Power of Judgment* contains the detailed explanation of this role. Here his main purpose is to critique the assumptions of rational theology. The first part of the chapter presents a rather dense account of the origin of the idea of God. In the remainder Kant makes his penetrating analyses of the three traditional proofs of the existence of God.

[1] Wood, *Kant's Rational Theology*, 16.

I. THE IDEAL OF PURE REASON

In sections 1–3 Kant explains how the idea of God arises as an ideal of reason. His account distinguishes two transcendental ideas: first, the idea of the sum total of all reality, as all possible predicates of things, and second, the idea of the *ens realissimum*, the individual having the highest degree of reality. Kant calls the latter the ideal of reason. Both ideas represent the unconditioned, in this case that underlying all objects in general.

In section 1 Kant compares these ideas to Plato's Forms. The idea of "Humanity in its entire perfection" (A568/B596), for example, is the idea of the properties essential to human nature as well as contingent properties consistent with this idea. Like Plato's Form of humanity, this idea is a perfect exemplar of its type and the ground of all (imperfect) copies in appearance. Now the idea of the individual embodying all these perfections would be the idea of a divine human being, such as the sage of the Stoics. Because no appearance satisfies either the idea or the ideal of reason, neither has objective reality. Nonetheless, like Plato's Forms, they have regulative significance as standards of action and evaluation.

Section 2 explains how these ideas arise in the logical processes involved in thinking determinate objects. Kant discusses two principles of determination, one concerning concepts, and the other existing things. All concepts are subject to the Principle of Determinability (PD): to determine the content of a concept is to apply one of a pair of opposing predicates to it. This procedure is governed by the principle of contradiction, according to which at most one of two opposed predicates can be contained in a concept. The logical principle makes consistency a necessary condition for the form of concepts. The second principle, that of "thoroughgoing determination" (Principle of Thoroughgoing Determinability or PTD), applies to existing things. This is the traditional view that every existing thing is completely determined with respect to "every pair of **possible** predicates" (A573/B601). More formally, for every possible existent and for every pair of possible predicates, one (and only one) predicate must apply to the thing. This principle underlies the idea of the complete cognition of a thing. But since a complete cognition is not attainable, the PTD can never be exhibited *in concreto*, and thus is a transcendental idea of reason. Rather than representing an object, it actually represents a *procedure* for cognizing an object.

This procedure can be carried out only against the backdrop of "the idea of an All of reality (*omnitudo realitatis*)" (A575–6/B604). To affirm a predicate of something requires conceiving the predicate as a kind of reality. Conceiving the absence of a reality logically presupposes the positive concept of the reality. Thus the idea of the sum total of possible predicates constitutes "a transcendental substratum" grounding all concepts of existing things. From here it is a short step to the transcendental ideal of an individual having the highest reality. This occurs by thinking the collective unity of all possible realities as an individual. All concepts of individuals presuppose this ideal – the *ens realissimum* – as the ground of "thoroughgoing determination that is necessarily encountered in everything existing." Kant explains this process in terms of the disjunctive syllogism, in which reason presupposes only the idea of the being answering to the ideal, not its existence.[2]

Under the influence of transcendental illusion, reason hypostatizes the *ens realissimum* as an actual being having all possible reality, the *ens originarium, ens summum, ens entium* (original being, highest being, being of all beings) (A579/B607). When personalized "as a being that is singular, simple, all-sufficient, eternal," a divine intelligence and will, this becomes the theological idea of God. Like the ideas of the world as a whole and the soul, however, the idea of God oversteps all bounds of experience, and thus does not represent an object of knowledge. Kant says, "we dialectically transform the **distributive** unity of the use of the understanding in experience, into the **collective** unity of a whole of experience" (A583/B661). In other words, the legitimate thought of the totality of predicates distributed among possible objects of experience becomes the idea of the collection of properties to be predicated of a single individual.

In section 3 Kant explains how reason then hypostatizes this ideal by means of the transcendental illusion underlying the Paralogisms and the Antinomies. In seeking the unconditioned, reason applies the

---

[2] In the *New Elucidation* (1755) and *The Only Possible Argument* (1763) Kant made this argument for the existence of God (*Theoretical Philosophy, 1755–1770*, 1–45 and 107–201). Wood calls it the "possibility proof" and discusses both its pre-critical and critical uses at *Kant's Rational Theology*, 64–71.

illusory principle P_2, "If the conditioned is given, the entire series of conditions is given," to objects in general. Here reason searches for an absolutely necessary being underlying all contingency: "For the contingent exists only under the condition of something else as its cause . . . necessarily without condition" (A584/B612). As opposed to the Fourth Antinomy cosmological idea of a necessary being in appearances, the theological idea represents a necessary thing in itself underlying objects in general. Because this latter idea represents only something whose non-being is impossible (A592/B620), it is indeterminate with respect to perfection, and is equally applicable to a limited being. Nonetheless, reason naturally takes the *ens realissimum* as the best candidate for an absolutely necessary being since "it satisfies the concept of unconditioned necessity on at least one point . . . since every other concept is defective and in need of completion" (A585–6/B613–14). A reinforcing motive resides in the demands of practical reason, since the existence of a highest being would provide a subjective basis for obeying the moral law. In this way the natural demand of reason for closure in the series of conditions leads humans to argue for the necessary existence of God as the *ens realissimum*.

At A590–1/B618–9 Kant classifies the three traditional proofs for the existence of God in terms of their evidence. The physico-theological proof, better known as the argument from design, is based on observations of "the special constitution of our world," and argues that God must exist as the author of the order experienced in nature. The cosmological argument that God exists as the creator of the world is also empirically based, but on an "indeterminate" experience of existence. The ontological proof differs in inferring "the existence of a highest cause entirely *a priori* from mere concepts." Because Kant believes the two empirical arguments covertly presuppose the ontological proof, he begins his criticism with that argument. In all three cases, he argues that the proofs fail to demonstrate that God exists as an absolutely necessary being.

2. THE ONTOLOGICAL ARGUMENT

Oddly enough, Kant's discussion lacks a detailed account of the ontological argument, beginning abruptly with his criticisms of it. (He only briefly sketches the other two proofs.) So it may be helpful to present the most famous versions. The argument was originally formulated by St. Anselm (1033–1109), Archbishop of Canterbury. Anselm bases the existence of God on the idea of God as that than which nothing greater can be conceived. The argument as it appears in the *Proslogion* is this:

> For, it is possible to conceive of a being which cannot be conceived not to exist, and this is greater than one which can be conceived not to exist. Hence, if that, than which nothing greater can be conceived, can be conceived not to exist, it is not that, than which nothing greater can be conceived. But this is an irreconcilable contradiction. There is, then, so truly a being than which nothing greater can be conceived to exist, that it cannot even be conceived not to exist; and this being thou art, O Lord, our God.[3]

In his Fifth Meditation, Descartes offers a similar proof for the existence of God as a supremely perfect being:

> it is quite evident that existence can no more be separated from the essence of God than the fact that its three angles equal two right angles can be separated from the essence of a triangle, or than the idea of a mountain can be separated from the idea of a valley. Hence it is just as much of a contradiction to think of God (that is, a supremely perfect being) lacking existence (that is, lacking a perfection), as it is to think of a mountain without a valley.[4]

Both versions argue by *reductio ad absurdum* that there is a contradiction in conceiving the nonexistence of the *ens realissimum*; the argument can be schematized as follows:[5]

1. It is possible to conceive of an *ens realissimum* (that than which nothing greater can be conceived or the supremely perfect being).
2. Assume that this being can be conceived not to exist (that the idea of existence can be separated from its essence).
3. A being that cannot be conceived not to exist is greater than one that can be conceived not to exist. (Existence is a perfection.)
4. By 3, if the *ens realissimum* can be conceived not to exist, then one can conceive of something greater than it. (If existence can be separated from its essence, then it is possible to conceive a being more perfect than it.)

---

[3] *Anselm's Basic Writings*, 6–9.   [4] Descartes, *Philosophical Writings*, 2:46.
[5] As Van Cleve points out, Kant is probably responding directly to Descartes's version; cf. A602/B603. Van Cleve also discusses both modal and non-modal versions of the argument, in *Problems from Kant*, chapter 12.

5. The concept of something greater than the *ens realissimum* is self-contradictory.
6. Therefore, the assumption in 2 is false: the *ens realissimum* cannot be conceived not to exist. (Existence cannot be separated from its essence.)
7. Therefore, the *ens realissimum* exists necessarily.

Because both arguments claim that existence is contained in the mere concept of the *ens realissimum*, the necessity attributed to God's being is absolute or logical necessity.

Kant raises two main objections to the proof: first, that the idea of an absolutely or logically necessary being is not a determinate concept of an object; and second, that the proof errs by treating existence as a real property or determination of objects. Most of the discussion focuses on the second point, which Kant defends in a variety of ways. This criticism has traditionally been taken more seriously, both for its independence of transcendental idealism, and for anticipating the analysis of existence in modern logic.

Kant first attacks the notion of an absolutely necessary being. Beyond the nominal definition as "something whose non-being is impossible" (A592/B620), we have no determinate concept of such a thing. The idea of unconditional or absolute necessity is an idea of reason and not a concept of the understanding. Moreover, logical necessity properly applies only to analytic judgments, which presuppose the conditional or possible existence of things. For example, from the logical necessity of the judgment "a triangle has three angles," one cannot infer the existence of triangles, but only that if triangles exist, then they must have three angles. The power of transcendental illusion leads us to think that one is entitled to infer that something exists necessarily whose concept is arbitrarily defined to include existence (A594/B622). From this criticism it follows that attempts to prove that such a being is an *ens realissimum* are doubly suspect, since the latter idea is also devoid of objective meaning.

The more fundamental error is treating existence as a real property of things. Kant argues that although in existential judgments (i.e., "x exists"), existence functions as a grammatical or "logical" predicate, it nevertheless is not a real predicate representing a property of objects. He develops this point in three interrelated arguments: first, that all existential judgments are synthetic, so existence claims can never be analytic; second, that concepts of objects can contain only possible existence and never actual existence; and third, that existence claims "posit" an object rather than determining its concept. As we shall see, commentators disagree on the success of Kant's attack.

First Kant claims that although judgments that predicate real properties of objects are analytic when the property is essential, existential judgments are always synthetic: "is the proposition, **This or that thing . . . exists** . . . an analytic or a synthetic proposition? If it is the former, then with existence you add nothing to your thought of the thing" (A597/B625). His point is that whereas analytic judgments are only ampliative, existential judgments must be synthetic because they are informative. If one concedes this point, then negative existential judgments (e.g., "God does not exist") can never be self-contradictory, ruling out an *a priori* proof for the existence of any being.

At A598/B626 Kant says that rather than representing a real predicate, "a concept of something that could add to the concept of a thing," the concept of existence "posits" the object represented by the concept. The (coherent) concept of a thing implies possible but not actual existence. In general, Kant says, "if I cancel the predicate in an identical [i.e., analytic] judgment and keep the subject, then a contradiction arises . . . But if I cancel the subject together with the predicate, then no contradiction arises" (A594/B622). Thus a contradiction arises if one "posits" God (asserts his existence) but denies omnipotence, but there is no contradiction in failing to "posit" God. The judgments "God is omnipotent" and "God exists" have the same subject concept, but only the latter judgment "posits" the object satisfying the concept. Kant reinforces this point with his famous example of the concept of a hundred dollars:

A hundred actual dollars do not contain the least bit more than a hundred possible ones. For since the latter signifies the concept and the former its object and its positing in itself, then, in case the former contained more than the latter, my concept would not express the entire object and thus would not be the suitable concept of it. But in my financial condition there is more with a hundred actual dollars than with the mere concept of them (i.e., their possibility). (A599/B627)

In other words, the concept of the hundred dollars is the same whether I judge that I actually have a hundred dollars or merely think that I might have a hundred dollars. But the two judgments make different assertions: the world in which I own a hundred dollars is objectively different from one in which I do not. Therefore, the actual existence attributed to the hundred dollars cannot be included as a property in its concept. If it were, then I could improve my financial condition simply by including the concept of existence in the concept of large sums of money.

This echoes a criticism made of both Anselm's and Descartes's arguments. In replying to Anselm, Gaunilo argues that one could equally claim that because one has a concept of a perfect island, such an island necessarily exists. And in the *First Objections to the Meditations*, the Dutch theologian Caterus similarly answers Descartes that although "the complex 'existing lion' includes both 'lion' and 'existence,' and it includes them essentially," it is absurd to conclude that some lion necessarily exists. These counter-examples illustrate Kant's point at A594/B622 that if existence were a real property or determination of things, it could be arbitrarily added to any concept, with absurd results.[6]

In the next paragraph Kant makes the stronger claim that existence *cannot* be a property of an object. He says,

[a] Even if I think in a thing every reality except one, then the missing reality does not get added when I say the thing exists, but it exists encumbered with just the same defect as I have thought in it; otherwise something other than what I thought would exist. [b] Now if I think of a being as the highest reality (without defect), the question still remains whether it exists or not. For although nothing at all is missing in my concept of the possible real content of a thing in general, something is still missing in the relation to my entire state of thinking, namely that the cognition should also be possible *a posteriori*. (A600/B628; [a] and [b] designations added)

I have divided the passage into two parts, because critics make two distinct objections to it. The standard response to part [b] is just that it begs the question. Kant merely presupposes that (actual) existence is not contained in the concept of the *ens realissimum*. While it may be true of all other beings that their essence is distinct from existence, the question is whether the *ens realissimum* is an exception to this rule.

---

[6] For Gaunilo see *Anselm's Basic Writings*, 149–51. For Caterus see Descartes, *Philosophical Writings*, 2:72.

The criticism of part [a] is more complex. Commentators such as Allen Wood claim that if this argument were valid, then it would prove that nothing could be a real predicate.[7] They apparently interpret the argument this way:

1. Suppose I conceive of something having every reality (real predicate) except one under the (complex) concept C.
2. Suppose I predicate existence of this object, "C exists."
3. If existence were a real predicate, then my assertion would change the concept of the thing [i.e., to "the existing C"].
4. [Implied] Thus I could never succeed in asserting the existence of an object C.

According to Wood, this argument works for any real predicate:

1'. Suppose I conceive of something under the concept C having every reality except F.
2'. Suppose I predicate F of this C.
3'. If F were a real predicate, then my assertion would change the concept of the thing by adding F to it, and thus the concept of the thing would become $C' = \{C, F\}$.
4'. Thus I could never predicate anything outside the concept of C to the C.

This criticism raises the thorny issues of the nature of predication, and the meaning of singular terms and definite descriptions. Despite lacking a theory of language, Kant's analysis of analytic and synthetic judgments implies a distinction between what is essentially contained in the subject-concept, and what is predicated of it synthetically (or contingently). It is apparent that informative contingent predications cannot add a property to a thing's essence. But then Wood's point is just that in distinguishing existence from other predicates, this argument also begs the question.

When all these points are taken together, the question comes down to whether Kant is right that existential judgments "posit" the object of the concept rather than predicating a property of it. Modern logic formalizes this view in analyzing the existential quantifier as a second-order rather than first-order predicate of things. Here I follow Colin

7 See Wood, *Kant's Rational Theology*, 112.

McGinn's admirably clear summary of the contemporary view and its weaknesses.[8] While disagreeing with Kant's claim that existence is not a real or first-order predicate, McGinn himself rejects the ontological argument on distinctly Kantian grounds.

The "orthodox" view of existence, championed by Russell and Frege, consists of three theses. The ontological thesis has two sub-theses: negatively, that existence is not a property that individuals instantiate; and positively, that it is a property instantiated by proper-ties of individuals. The semantic thesis maintains that "statements of existence are really higher-order statements involving reference to a property or . . . propositional function. The subject of the statement is never a term for an individual but always a term for a property."[9] Thus the assertion "Tigers exist" predicates existence of the property or predicate 'being a tiger' rather than of individual tigers.[10] This leads to the definitional thesis that 'exists' can always be defined in terms of the notions of a first-order predicate or property of individuals and 'sometimes true' or 'possible.'[11]

McGinn claims that despite its general acceptance, this orthodox view is riddled with difficulties. He outlines four serious problems. First is what it means for a property F to have instances. He argues that defining existence in terms of instantiating a property ends up in circularity, since "it must be *existent* things that instantiate the property."[12] Thus the orthodox view gives an inadequate account of existence. The second objection is stronger, namely that the view is not coherent. Consider statements attributing existence to properties: they would themselves have to be interpreted as referring to a prop-erty instantiated by the property said to exist. Thus this account of assertions that properties exist presupposes a vicious infinite regress of properties. The third problem concerns existence claims whose sub-jects are proper names or demonstratives, such as "Venus exists," as well as the general claim, "Something exists." For singular sentences, the orthodox view pushes one toward a problematic description the-ory of singular reference. The latter case is worse, since there is no good candidate for a property to be instantiated. Finally, McGinn claims that the orthodox view requires every object to have some unique property, and entails as analytic the substantive claim that there are

[8] See McGinn, *Logical Properties*, chapter 2.   [9] *Logical Properties*, 20.
[10] *Logical Properties*, 19.   [11] *Logical Properties*, 20.   [12] *Logical Properties*, 22.

no bare existents. For these reasons he prefers the analysis of existence as a property of objects, universal to existing things. Semantically the term operates like standard predicates 'blue' and 'man,' although he also maintains that the existential quantifier can be retained for general existence claims.[13]

Although McGinn rejects Kant's logical criticism of the ontological argument, he ends up agreeing on the idea of the *ens realissimum*. First he points out that even if existence were a second-order predicate, one could reformulate the argument to claim that the concept of the supremely perfect being contains the property of (necessarily) having an instance. The real problem, however, lies in the notion of the most perfect conceivable being of any type: "We just don't know what it would *be* to be the most perfect conceivable meal or piece of music. Similarly, the notion of, say, the most powerful conceivable mouse makes little sense." The problem is that the argument "trades on notions of the maximal forms of certain attributes, particularly perfection, that are inherently ill-defined."[14] This agrees with Kant that the concept of the *ens realissimum* is an idea of reason rather than a determinate concept of the understanding.

We have seen, then, that although Kant may not conclusively refute the ontological argument, his criticisms pinpoint two key issues that philosophers continue to debate today: first, whether existence is a first-order property, and second, whether the concepts of a necessary being and an *ens realissimum* are objectively meaningful. Both issues touch on complex questions in logic and philosophy of language, and thus cannot be easily resolved. Like modern logicians, and unlike traditional defenders of the ontological argument, Kant firmly believes that logic must have a unified account of existence: it will not do to say that the concept of the *ens realissimum* differs from all others in containing existence in its essence. Whatever one's position on the issues, one has to appreciate the significance of Kant's contribution.

3. THE COSMOLOGICAL ARGUMENT

Kant opens his discussion of the cosmological argument by contrasting it with the ontological argument. The latter, he thinks, "contrives" an arbitrary concept of an object – the *ens realissimum* – and then proceeds *a priori* by extracting existence from this concept. The strategy

---

[13] *Logical Properties*, 50–1.   [14] *Logical Properties*, 50.

of the cosmological proof works in the opposite direction. First it infers the existence of an absolutely necessary being from the existence of a contingent world. Then, in a second step, it argues that this necessary being must be the *ens realissimum*. This second step, Kant claims, implicitly assumes the validity of the ontological argument.

The classic versions of the cosmological argument were formulated by St. Thomas Aquinas (1225–74), the Dominican theologian credited with synthesizing Aristotelianism with Christian doctrine. In the *Summa Theologiae*, Aquinas details "five ways" to prove the existence of God, the first three of which are cosmological. The proofs argue for the existence of God, first, as a "first mover" at the source of all motion (change); second, as the "first cause" at the origin of all efficient causality; and finally, as the necessary being underlying all contingent existence. This third argument proceeds as follows:

We find in nature things that are possible to be and not to be, since they are found to be generated, and to be corrupted . . . But it is impossible for these always to exist, for that which can not-be at some time is not. Therefore, if everything can not-be, then at one time there was nothing in existence. Now if this were true, even now there would be nothing in existence, because that which does not exist begins to exist only through something already existing. Now it is impossible to go on to infinity in necessary things which have their necessity caused by another, as has been already proved in regard to efficient causes. Therefore, not all beings are merely possible, but there must exist something the existence of which is necessary . . . Therefore we cannot but admit the existence of some being having of itself its own necessity, and not receiving it from another, but rather causing in others their necessity. This all men speak of as God.[15]

Although the first two proofs proceed somewhat differently, all three arguments conclude that God exists as the necessary being at the source of the contingent world.

As with most arguments, Kant's own characterization is highly abstract: "If something exists, then an absolutely necessary being also has to exist. Now I myself, at least, exist; therefore, an absolutely necessary being exists" (A604/B632). The argument is *a posteriori* because it is based on the contingent existence of something; Kant says the proof is called "cosmological" because "the object of all possible experience is called 'world'" (A605/B633). But unlike the argument from

---

[15] Aquinas, *The Basic Writings of St. Thomas Aquinas*, 25–7.

design, the particular nature of the world is irrelevant to this proof. What makes the cosmological proof an argument for the existence of God, according to Kant, is a second inference, that this absolutely necessary being is the *ens realissimum*, or God. Although he later details several objections to the first stage, Kant primarily attacks the second stage. His main point, often misunderstood, is that this step, if valid, would imply the validity of the ontological proof. Since he previously rejected that proof, it follows that the second stage of the cosmological proof must also be invalid.

In an obscure argument at A605/B633 Kant explains the second stage thus:

The necessary being can be determined only in one single way, i.e., in regard to all possible predicates, it can be determined by only one of them, so consequently it must be **thoroughly** determined through its concept. Now only one single concept of a thing is possible that thoroughly determines the thing *a priori*, namely that of an *ens realissimum*.

Kant apparently assumes that the necessary being can be determined only through one *a priori* concept, because all limited concepts of reality are logically contingent. This reading is also suggested by Kant's gloss at A606–7/B634–5: "What this being might have in the way of properties, the empirical ground of proof cannot teach; rather here reason . . . turns its inquiry back to mere concepts: namely, to what kinds of properties in general an absolutely necessary being would have to have." In any case, the only candidate for an *a priori* concept determining the absolutely necessary being is the rational ideal of the *ens realissimum*. Whether proponents of the cosmological argument actually reason this way, Kant is certainly correct that the last step of the argument must connect the absolutely necessary first cause with a supremely perfect being. (In fact, Aquinas offers no reason for taking the absolutely necessary being as God.) Without this inference the argument would differ from the Fourth Antinomy argument only in locating the necessary being outside the world.

Kant then argues that this inference implies the validity of the ontological argument. The conclusion, "Every absolutely necessary being is at the same time the most real being," can be converted *per accidens* to the claim, "Some most real beings are at the same time absolutely necessary beings" (A608/B636). But since it is not possible for more than one *ens realissimum* to exist, the conversion proceeds to the universal, "Every most real being is a necessary being." In other words, the above reasoning entails that the concept of the most real being contains the concept of existence, which is the crux of the ontological argument.

Because Kant concentrates his criticism on this second stage, some commentators mistakenly assume he considers the first stage to be valid. But nothing could be further from the truth. In fact, the first three of four objections detailed at A609–10/B637–8 are aimed at the first stage. First he objects to the attempt to prove an intelligible cause outside the world in general, since "the principle of causality has no significance at all and no mark of its use except in the world of sense." Similarly, he rejects the reasoning to a "first" cause to avoid an infinite series of causes, both within and without experience. As he argued in the Antinomies, an uncaused cause is neither a possible object of experience nor a justifiable postulation of reason. Third, Kant reiterates the false satisfaction of reason in trying to explain the conditioned (the contingent) by reference to an absolutely necessary unconditioned, an idea having no determinate content. And finally, he attacks the second stage for confusing "the logical possibility of a concept of all reality . . . with its transcendental possibility." As we saw earlier, the idea of all possible reality represents only the "transcendental substratum" for the process of forming determinate concepts of individuals.

Considered more traditionally, then, Kant rejects the cosmological argument for misapplying the principle of causality beyond the legitimate field of experience, for illegitimately assuming that an infinite series of causes is impossible, for mistakenly thinking that the (undefined) idea of an absolutely necessary being can "explain" the existence of the contingent universe, and for hypostatizing the logical idea of a collection of all real properties as an individual, the *ens realissimum*. Clearly Kant accepts no part of the cosmological argument. As he puts it near the end of this section:

The ideal of the highest being is, according to these considerations, nothing other than a **regulative principle** of reason, to regard all combination in the world **as if it** arose from an all-sufficient necessary cause, so as to ground on that cause the rule of a unity that is systematic and necessary according to universal laws; but it is not an assertion of an existence that is necessary in itself. (A619/B647)

In the next chapter we shall see how this ideal regulates the search for empirical knowledge.

4. THE ARGUMENT FROM DESIGN

The physico-theological proof, better known as the argument from design, also makes an *a posteriori* argument for the existence of God. Whereas the cosmological proof argues from the fact that something exists contingently, this argument depends on a "**determinate experience**," namely of order in nature. It concludes that God must exist as the infinite intelligence responsible for such order. This argument also enjoys a long history: Aquinas's fifth proof represents one version. In the modern period, a more familiar version appeared in the *Natural Theology* (1802) of William Paley (1743–1805), Archdeacon of Carlisle. Even before Paley's work appeared, however, David Hume presented a concise formulation in his *Dialogues Concerning Natural Religion*, published posthumously in 1779. Of course Hume's purpose was the opposite of Paley's; rather than accepting the proof, he set out to refute it. Not only are his criticisms devastating, they are among the most humorous in the history of philosophy. As we shall see, although Kant raises many of the same objections he made to the cosmological argument, he shares Hume's view of other weaknesses in the argument.

Hume's *Dialogues* concern the possibility of natural theology, that is, defending the existence of God on grounds available to humans. They take place between three characters, representing different positions: Cleanthes, who advocates the argument from design, Demea, an "orthodox" believer who defends the ontological proof, and Philo, the skeptic. Cleanthes states the argument from design as follows:

Look round the world, contemplate the whole and every part of it: you will find it to be nothing but one great machine, subdivided into an infinite number of lesser machines, which again admit of subdivisions to a degree beyond what human senses and faculties can trace and explain . . . The curious adapting of means to ends, throughout all nature, resembles exactly, though it much exceeds, the productions of human contrivance – of human design, thought, wisdom, and intelligence. Since therefore the effects resemble each other, we are led to infer, by all the rules of analogy, that the causes also resemble, and that the Author of nature is somewhat similar to the mind of man, though possessed of much larger faculties, proportioned to the grandeur of the work which he has executed.[16]

The argument compares the order exhibited in nature with that possessed by machines designed by humans. In standard form it proceeds this way:

1. Machines created by humans are things whose parts are ordered so as to produce a result; the whole serves a purpose, and each part is related to achieve this purpose.
2. The universe as a whole is composed of parts that fit together to achieve results.
3. Therefore, the universe resembles machines.
4. Rule of analogy: whenever two effects resemble each other, their causes also resemble each other.
5. Therefore, the cause of the universe resembles the cause of machines.
6. Machines are produced by (human) design and intelligence.
7. Therefore, the universe was produced by design or intelligence.
8. This cause is proportionately greater as the effect is proportionately greater, so that the cause of the universe is much more intelligent than the cause of machines.
9. Therefore, God exists as the intelligent cause of the universe.

Kant's version at A625–6/B653–4 consists of four statements, combining the analogy from steps 2 through 6 above into the premise: "This purposive order is quite foreign to the things of the world, and pertains to them only contingently, i.e., . . . through a principle of rational order grounded on ideas" (A625/B653). Although this proof is "the oldest, clearest and most appropriate to common human reason" (A623/B651), Kant nevertheless rejects it as no more successful than the other two arguments for the existence of God.

Like the cosmological argument, Kant divides this proof into two parts: the first concluding that the cause of the universe is an intelligent being (line 7), and the second identifying this cause with God or the *ens realissimum* (line 9). Here too he objects that the second

---

[16] Hume, *Dialogues Concerning Natural Religion*, part II.

inference assumes the validity of the ontological argument. Thus neither *a posteriori* proof succeeds in avoiding the transcendental argument.

But this is not Kant's only criticism; like Hume, he raises several objections to the analogy. Despite their different theories of knowledge, both attack the argument for making indefensible empirical claims, and question the comparison between human machines and the universe. In part II of the *Dialogues*, Philo points out that we have no experience of the universe as a whole, so in fact premise 2 is questionable, since we cannot say whether the order we observe in nature is typical of the whole. Kant echoes this point at A622–3/B650–1: "We are not acquainted with the world in its whole content, still less do we know how to estimate its magnitude by comparison with everything possible." In other words, we have no basis for making empirical claims about the degree of order in the universe or its degree of perfection, since we have no standard of comparison. He also criticizes the idea of an *ens realissimum* for lacking determinate content. At A628/B656 he rejects the inference to a divine intelligence, since "the predicates **very great**, or 'astonishing' or 'immeasurable power' and 'excellence' do not give any determinate concept at all, and really say nothing about what the thing in itself is, but are rather only relative representations" based on a comparison to human attributes.

Both philosophers also formulate a dilemma involved in attempting to use God's existence or design as an explanation of the universe. In part IV of the *Dialogues*, Hume points out that, for any explanatory item (in this case God's design), either that item requires an explanation or it does not. If it needs an explanation, then something else must be the cause of it. On the other hand, if it is permissible to stop the explanation at that item, then it seems just as permissible to stop it at a prior step, for example, postulating an inherent order in matter. Thus from the explanatory standpoint, the argument only adds steps to the series, but does not offer an ultimate explanation. At A621–2/B649–50 Kant constructs a similar dilemma for attempts to explain the causal series by an intelligible being. As he puts it, if one stays within the series of natural causes, then one cannot cut off the explanation at any point. On the other hand, if one jumps to the intelligible order, then we are outside the realm of cognition, which is the only domain in which causal connections have any significance.

Moreover, both Hume and Kant point out that it is logically possible that order could arise from the nature of matter itself, so design is not the only possible explanation. Hume says in fact that experience shows that there are other sources of order, such as gravitation, magnetism, heat, and so on, which all produce effects in a lawlike fashion. Kant also cites the failure of the analogy to support the view that God created the world, certainly a principle of natural theology. As he says at A626–7/B654–5, "the purposiveness and well-adaptedness of so many natural arrangements would have to prove merely the contingency of the form, but not of the matter." That is, the best the proof can show is that God is "the highest **architect of the world** . . . but not a **creator of the world**, to whose idea everything is subject, which is far from sufficient for . . . proving an all-sufficient original being." The analogy with human creation, then, can establish at best that the order in nature is caused by a divine plan, but not that God created the matter so ordered.

Although Kant questions the inference to a divine architect, he does not push the analogical reasoning as Hume does. In fact, Hume's arguments in part V of the *Dialogues* are among the most entertaining in the history of philosophy. Since the success of analogical reasoning is a matter of degree, depending on how similar the compared items are, any dissimilarity is a weakness in the reasoning. Hume points out that, based on our experience of the manner in which humans design and create machines, the conclusion to a single, infinitely perfect architect of the universe is not warranted. First, as we saw above, our limited experience gives us no basis for judging the perfection of the order in the universe. Moreover, since human creation proceeds by trial and error, this universe could be one in a series of universes that were discarded as failures. It is also true that human machines generally result from collaborative efforts. Analogical reasoning, then, gives better support for the conclusion that the universe was planned by a committee of imperfect, bumbling designers rather than the *ens realissimum* of traditional theology.

Kant ends the chapter by briefly contrasting two types of theology based on the idea of the absolutely necessary being. Deism conceives of this being only as an impersonal cause of the world; Kant calls this a mere "transcendental theology" (A631/B659). By contrast, the theist personalizes this original being as a divine intelligence, the author of the world. This is the basis of natural theology. Although he rejects both forms of theology as fruitless speculation, Kant foreshadows his argument in the Canon of Pure Reason and in the *Critique of Practical Reason* that the idea of God as the author of nature is a necessary postulate of practical reason: "In the future we will show about the moral laws that they not only presuppose the existence of a highest being, but also . . . they postulate this existence rightfully but, of course, only practically" (A634/B662). We shall see how he develops this point in chapter 11.

5. SUMMARY

In this chapter, Kant completes his discussion of the transcendental illusion motivating reason's search for the unconditioned. In rational theology, reason attempts to prove the existence of God as the absolutely necessary being conditioning all objects in general. As Kant sees it, the attempt begins with the logical idea of the collection of all possible predicates. This "transcendental substratum" for thinking the real becomes hypostatized as an *ens realissimum*, a being having the highest degree of reality. The illusion is completed when this absolutely necessary being is identified with the *ens realissimum*, or God. The proofs mistakenly treat the regulative idea of the *ens realissimum* as a concept of a determinate object.

Kant criticizes the three traditional proofs – the ontological, cosmological, and physico-theological arguments – for embodying this transcendental illusion. Although the latter two make *a posteriori* arguments, Kant believes they implicitly presuppose the validity of the *a priori* ontological argument. This occurs in the assumption that the only possible candidate for the absolutely necessary being is a being with the highest reality. Although thinkers before Kant made some of his objections, his evaluation of the ontological argument is noteworthy for anticipating developments in modern logic. In arguing that existence is not a real predicate of individuals, Kant foreshadows Frege's and Russell's treatment of the existential quantifier as a second-order predicate or propositional function. Thus Kant makes a significant contribution, independent of the critical philosophy, to the debate over the ontological argument. Despite rejecting claims to theoretical knowledge of God, Kant maintains that the idea of God is significant for practical reason, as a foundation for moral faith, as well as a regulative idea promoting empirical inquiry.

CHAPTER II

Reason and the critical philosophy

As we saw in chapter 10, Kant believes the transcendental ideas of reason perform two positive functions: first, the idea of the unconditioned generates regulative principles for scientific explanations; second, the ideal of the *ens realissimum* provides a basis of moral faith for practical reason. The last part of the *Critique* sketches an account of both functions. Despite the brevity of his account here, Kant claims that reason is essential to the operations of the understanding. In spelling out this relation, Kant completes his revolutionary theory of the intellect. As we saw earlier in the Analytic, in analyzing concepts as predicates of possible judgments, Kant overturned the traditional view that judging presupposes conceiving. Here he completes the reversal by showing how judgment presupposes the higher-order functions of reason.

The final section of the *Critique* is the Transcendental Doctrine of Method. Although this contains four chapters, only the first two offer substantive discussions. In chapter I, the Discipline of Pure Reason, Kant contrasts the methods of philosophy and mathematics. The significant aspects here concern his theory of mathematical construction, and his views on definitions, axioms, and demonstrations. In chapter II, the Canon of Pure Reason, Kant outlines the moral theology required by practical reason, sketching his conceptions of the good and the morally ideal world. Here he argues that the moral law requires us to postulate the existence of God and the immortality of the soul.

I. THE APPENDIX: THE REGULATIVE USE OF REASON

Kant explains the positive role of transcendental ideas in an Appendix to the critique of speculative theology. First, he says, "Everything grounded in the nature of our powers must be purposive and consistent with their correct use" (A642/B670). Ideas of reason, then, must have a positive real function, analogous to their logical use. This function has two aspects. First, the speculative interest of reason to seek the unconditioned provides the understanding a motive to inquire into nature. Second, reason supplies methodological principles guiding the understanding in creating empirical theories. By now it is clear that transcendental ideas of reason are regulative only and not constitutive. Because regulative principles function as imperatives rather than assertions, they do not make cognitive claims, but merely give directions for systematizing empirical knowledge. Despite their "subjective" character, these ideas have a "necessary regulative use . . . directing the understanding to a certain goal . . . which, although it is only an idea (*focus imaginarius*), . . . serves to obtain for these concepts the greatest unity alongside the greatest extension" (A644/B672). Regulative ideas transcend experience and consequently represent only ends to strive for in science, rather than features of objects. But without them, the understanding could not produce empirical cognitions, since it would lack a motivation to explain the phenomena, as well as maxims for proceeding.

At A646/B674 Kant describes reason as the faculty of deriving the particular from the universal. In logical inferences, the use of reason is "apodictic," since the universal is certain and given, and the particular can be subsumed under it. In its real, explanatory use, by contrast, reason operates "hypothetically," by proposing problematic ideas to fit the given particulars. Because one can never be certain that the idea applies to all possible instances, these hypotheses can only approximate universal rules. In general, the task of reason is to supply unity to the judgments of the understanding. It does this by "projecting" the idea of an interconnected whole – a complete explanation of nature – as a goal. Kant uses the example of the concept of power: experience shows that substances have diverse powers. He actually cites the mental powers, "sensation, consciousness, imagination, memory, wit, the power to distinguish, pleasure, desire, etc." (A649/B677). Reason produces the "logical maxim" to combine these powers under general headings, and, ultimately, to seek "**a fundamental power**" at the origin of all mental abilities.

But reason supplies more than the stimulus to explain natural phenomena: in fact the understanding could not function without reason. In a cryptic comment at A647/B675 Kant says, "The hypothetical use of reason is therefore directed at the systematic unity of the understanding's cognitions, which, however, is the **touchstone of truth** for its rules." He remarks below that without the law of reason there would be "no coherent use of the understanding, and, lacking that, no sufficient mark of empirical truth; thus in regard to the latter we simply have to presuppose the systematic unity of nature as objectively valid and necessary" (A651/B679). Kant's point is that the truth values of empirical judgments can be determined only by testing them for evidence against a system of empirical judgments. In particular, empirical generalizations can attain the status of laws only by being subsumed under higher-order laws. Thus empirical cognition presupposes both the logical (justificatory) and the real (explanatory) functions of reason. Although the ideas of reason are not constitutive, they are necessary for the understanding to produce cognitive claims.

In addition to motivating the understanding, reason supplies three methodological principles guiding scientific inquiry, the logical principles of genera, species, and the affinity or continuity of forms. Although all three principles were traditionally recognized as presuppositions of scientific explanation, until Kant no philosopher offered a systematic justification.

The first, logical principle of genera is known as Occam's razor, or the law of parsimony. It was expressed in the "scholastic rule that one should not multiply beginnings (principles) without necessity" (A652/B680). In other words, the simpler the explanation, the better. Scientists apply the principle whenever they seek commonalities among diverse forms: here Kant adds to his example of mental powers the attempt to find common principles for the varieties of salts and earths. This requires comparing distinct individuals or species to identify their common characteristics. Rather than representing merely an aesthetic value, however, the principle has a transcendental basis. If this law did not obtain, there could be no empirical concepts:

no concept of a genus, nor any other universal concept, indeed no understanding at all would obtain . . . The logical principle of genera therefore presupposes a transcendental one if it is to be applied to nature . . . According to that principle sameness of kind is necessarily presupposed in the manifold of a possible experience (even though we cannot determine its degree *a priori*). (A653–4/B681–2)

That is, if we could not presuppose some degree of unity in experience, concepts of the understanding would have no application. Thus empirical concept formation presupposes reason's maxim to seek unity in the phenomena.

The second principle aims at completeness through specificity. This "law of specification" balances Occam's razor by demanding subspecies for every species. Like the first law, the second also has a transcendental ground in the function of the understanding. For the logical structure of concepts requires that they be not only subsumable under higher-order concepts, but also subject to partition into lower-level concepts. These two laws together constitute a tension in reason, expressing interests both "in the **domain** (universality) in regard to genera" and "in **content** (determinacy) in respect of the manifoldness of species" (A654/B682).

Finally, Kant derives from these two principles a third, "the law of the **affinity** of all concepts." It postulates "a continuous transition from every species to every other through a graduated increase of varieties" (A657–8/B685–6). That is, the demands for unity and completeness rule out ending the search for both similarities and differences at any point. Kant says the principle that "there are no different original and primary genera, which would be, as it were, isolated and separated from one another" entails that "intervening species are always possible, whose difference from the first and second species is smaller than their difference from each other" (A659–60/B687–8). This idea was traditionally expressed as the principle that "nature makes no leaps." Recognized by Leibniz, it was most fruitfully expressed as the Law of Least Action by Pierre-Louis Moreau de Maupertuis (1698–1759). Maupertuis's version states that whenever changes occur in nature, the quantity of action is always the smallest possible, where quantity of action is proportional to the product of a body's mass and its velocity and the distance it travels. Kant explains how the law applies to planetary orbits. If we find that there are variations in the circular orbits of planets, "we suppose that the movements of the planets that are not a circle will more or less approximate to its properties, and then we come upon the ellipse" (A662–3/B690–1). Although Kant does not say so explicitly, all three principles formally codify his solution to the Antinomies, namely that the world of appearances is given only in the empirical regress. For if appearances do not have their nature independently of the regress, then one cannot presuppose limits to the search for genera or species.

These principles enable the understanding to produce empirical theories and laws explaining the phenomena. From the Analytic, we know that from its functions the understanding supplies only *a priori* concepts such as substance and causality, which are too abstract to yield empirical concepts. For example, the First Analogy requires that all events be thought as changes of substance, but leaves the nature of substance undetermined. Similarly, although the Second Analogy guarantees the existence of empirical causal laws, it cannot provide them. From Kant's cryptic examples, empirical concept formation involves comparing individuals (or species) and abstracting from their differences to identify their similarities. (In effect this is the process empiricists such as Locke thought gave rise to all concepts.) These similar features then are represented by empirical concepts, which the understanding orders in genus–species relations.

In the *Critique of the Power of Judgment* of 1790 Kant takes a more systematic approach to empirical explanations. In this work he emphasizes two uses of judgment, determining and reflective. As the First Introduction explains, in determining judgment one applies a given concept to an individual, thereby making a cognitive claim. In reflection one is given an individual, and seeks a concept under which to subsume it.[1] Kant assigns both empirical concept formation and aesthetic judgment to reflective judgment. The factor unifying these two accounts is the transcendental principle of purposiveness, to which Kant alludes in the Appendix and the Canon of Pure Reason.

The remainder of the Appendix emphasizes the regulative nature of the principles of reason. In places Kant appears to contradict himself, sometimes calling them "objective," and at other times "subjective." As Grier points out, however, a charitable reading can resolve the difficulties.[2] There are two related senses in which the principles are "subjective." First, Kant consistently maintains that they do not provide determinate concepts of objects, but only guide the understanding in securing such concepts. In that sense they lack objective validity. And second, because they function as imperatives rather than

---

[1] See *Critique of the Power of Judgment*, 15.
[2] See *Kant's Doctrine of Transcendental Illusion*, 268–79, for her discussion of this issue.

assertions, they serve as "subjective maxims" for this activity: "I call all subjective principles that are taken not from the constitution of the object but from the interest of reason in regard to . . . the cognition of this object, **maxims** of reason. Thus there are maxims of speculative reason . . . even though it may seem as if they were objective principles" (A666/B694). Here Kant explicitly compares the principles of reason to the "subjective" practical maxims on which agents act. He attributes the subjectivity of both types of maxims to their origin in the interests of reason. Despite their "subjectivity" as maxims, as Grier points out, the principles are "objective" insofar as they project an object for the understanding, namely a complete system of cognition. More telling is Kant's view that the coherent function of the understanding presupposes both logical and real functions of reason. Thus the regulative principles of reason are "indispensably necessary": without them there could be no determinate cognition of objects.

The Appendix ends with remarks "On the final aim of the natural dialectic of human reason." This adds little, primarily emphasizing the illusion resulting from misusing regulative principles. Of psychological interest is his analysis of two mental failings: "lazy" and "perverted" reason. Lazy reason occurs when one takes the idea of God constitutively, thus bypassing the search for natural causes, "so that instead of seeking them in the universal laws of the mechanism of matter, we appeal right away to the inscrutable decree of the highest wisdom" (A691/B719). Perverted reason, similarly, takes place when one reverses the relation between natural phenomena and the ideal of systematic unity. Here "the concept of such a highest intelligence is determined anthropomorphically, and then one imposes ends on nature forcibly and dictatorially" (A692/B720). In assuming that all natural systems are teleological, one effectively destroys the unity of nature, making it "entirely foreign and contingent in relation to the nature of things" (A693/B721).

More substantive are Kant's views of the relation between the ideas of God and purposive unity in nature. At A686–7/B714–15 he remarks: "This highest formal unity that alone rests on concepts of reason is the **purposive** unity of things, and the **speculative** interest of reason makes it necessary to regard every ordinance in the world as if it had sprouted from the intention of a highest reason." Such a principle opens up "entirely new prospects for connecting up things in the world in accordance with teleological laws, and thereby attaining to the greatest systematic unity among them." And he returns to the idea at A694/B722, asserting that "Complete purposive unity is perfection" and that "The greatest systematic unity . . . is . . . the ground of the possibility of the greatest use of human reason." Because this idea "is legislative for us, . . . it is very natural to assume a corresponding legislative reason (*intellectus archetypus*) from which all systematic unity of nature, as the object of our reason, is to be derived." As I indicated above, this notion becomes the basis for Kant's theory of reflective judgment in the third *Critique*, as well as the key to Kant's moral theology.

2. THE DOCTRINE OF METHOD: THE DISCIPLINE OF REASON

Although "discipline," positively, means a form of instruction, Kant's concern here is with the negative sense, as a corrective: "The **compulsion** through which the constant propensity to stray from certain rules is limited and finally eradicated is called **discipline**" (A709/B737 and note at A710/B738). His discussion of transcendental illusion so far has concerned the discipline of the "content" of reason. Here he addresses the discipline of the method of pure reason (A712/B740). He divides the chapter into four sections, of which the first is the most important. Kant's strategy is to criticize the traditional "analytic" methods of philosophy by contrasting them with the "synthetic" method of mathematics. In particular, he argues that dogmatic metaphysicians are mistaken to think that philosophy can attain synthetic *a priori* truths having the immediate certainty of mathematical cognition. Here he both develops the theory of mathematical construction and presents a sophisticated theory of definition. The remaining sections discuss the polemical use of reason, and its use with regard to hypotheses and proofs, emphasizing Kant's enlightenment attitude toward knowledge.

Kant's main point is that the formal methods of philosophy and mathematics differ because of the nature of their concepts. Although both employ *a priori* concepts, philosophical concepts originate in the understanding, whereas mathematical concepts derive from pure intuition. In consequence, the objects of mathematics can be constructed *a priori*, unlike the objects of philosophy. Corresponding to this distinction are differences in the status and evidence of their principles. On Kant's view, only mathematics begins with axioms, produces demonstrations, and can succeed in defining its concepts. Philosophy can produce neither complete definitions of concepts nor axiomatic principles. Although Kant's original distinction between analytic and synthetic judgments depends on the notion of "concept containment," in fact neither pure concepts of the understanding nor empirical concepts can, strictly speaking, be defined.

Kant begins by characterizing philosophical cognition as rational cognition from concepts, and mathematical cognition as "from the **construction** of concepts." To construct a concept is "to exhibit *a priori* the intuition corresponding to it." Although this requires a non-empirical intuition of an individual object, the construction must "express in the representation universal validity for all possible intuitions that belong under the same concept" (A713/B741). Mathematical construction represents in pure intuition an individual object, which, in spite of its particularity, has universal validity. Although the construction may take place empirically, for example on paper, it need not, since figures can be exhibited *a priori* "through mere imagination, in pure intuition" (A714/B742). Even when the figure is represented empirically, features such as the actual lengths of sides or sizes of angles are irrelevant to the spatial relations being represented. In either case it proceeds *a priori*, and thus exhibits synthetic *a priori* propositions.[3]

It is tempting to think mathematics and philosophy concern different objects, the former quantity, the latter quality. This is a mistake, however, since philosophy deals with magnitudes such as totality and infinity, and mathematics concerns qualitative features such as "the continuity of extension" (A715/B743). The difference is not in the object, but in the manner of representing it: "only the concept of magnitudes can be constructed, i.e., exhibited *a priori* in intuition, while qualities cannot be exhibited in anything but empirical intuition . . . Thus no one can ever derive an intuition corresponding to the concept of reality from anywhere except

---

[3] Friedman agrees with Thompson, Parsons, and Brittan that empirical intuition is required to establish the *real possibility* of mathematical concepts. It is not, however, required for pure mathematics. See Friedman, *Kant and the Exact Sciences*, 101–2.

experience" (A714–15/B742–3). Consider the difference between the shape and the color of a cone: colors are given only in empirical intuition, whereas the pure intuition of space affords everything required to describe the region delineated by a cone. Thus colors cannot be constructed *a priori* (although their degree of intensity can be).

The key is the relation between concepts and their objects. At A719–20/B747–8 he reminds us that all cognition is ultimately related to possible intuitions: "for through these alone is an object given." Mathematics can construct its concepts *a priori* because the intuition of space provides the objects of geometry along with their concepts.[4] Philosophical concepts make claims about real properties given only empirically: "I cannot exhibit the concept of a cause in general in intuition in any way except in an example given to me by experience, etc." (A715/B743). Put technically, the synthetic *a priori* cognition of the "**thing** in general . . . can never yield *a priori* more than the mere rule of the synthesis of that which perception may give *a posteriori*, but never the intuition of the real object, since this must necessarily be empirical" (A720/B749). So although extensive and intensive measurements of real properties are constructible in intuition, the properties themselves are not.

So far we have been treating mathematical construction as if there were only one kind. In fact Kant distinguishes ostensive constructions of geometry from symbolic constructions of arithmetic and algebra. Although the latter also contain synthetic *a priori* judgments, they are more abstract, lacking their own object:

> But mathematics does not merely construct magnitudes (*quanta*), as in geometry, but also mere magnitude (*quantitas*), as in algebra, where it entirely abstracts from the constitution of the object that is to be thought . . . In this case it chooses a certain notation for all construction of magnitudes in general (numbers), as well as addition, subtraction, extraction of roots, etc., and . . . it then exhibits all the procedures through which magnitude is generated and altered in accordance with certain rules in intuition. (A717/B745)

Friedman explains this clearly.[5] First he remarks that, based on Kant's theory in the Aesthetic, one would expect time to provide an object

[4] Emily Carson emphasizes this point in "Kant on the Method of Mathematics," 645–51.
[5] *Kant and the Exact Sciences*; see especially 104–14.

for arithmetic as space does for geometry. But in fact, numbers are not temporal "objects," and arithmetic does not have its own object. Time comes into play in the science of mechanics: at B49 Kant says, "our concept of time therefore explains the possibility of as much synthetic *a priori* cognition as is presented by the general theory of motion." The key is Kant's distinction between a magnitude as an object (*quanta*), and a mere magnitude as a quantity (*quantitas*).

Friedman says *quanta* refers to "the particular magnitudes there happen to be. These are given, in the first instance, by the axioms of Euclid's geometry, which postulate the construction (from the modern point of view, the existence) of all the relevant spatial magnitudes."[6] In other words, geometry is the science of existing magnitudes given in space. The numerical formulas of arithmetic and algebra, by contrast, are based on *quantity*, "the concept of a thing in general through the determination of magnitude." Arithmetic and algebra make no existence assumptions. Rather, their formulas express "the operations and concepts . . . for manipulating, and thereby calculating the specific magnitude of any magnitudes which happen to exist."[7] As Kant puts it, symbolic construction "entirely abstracts from the constitution of the object that is to be thought." Rather than presenting the object in intuition, "it chooses a certain notation for all construction of magnitudes in general (numbers)," and "then exhibits all the procedures through which magnitude is generated and altered in accordance with certain rules in intuition" (A717/B745). The formulas of arithmetic and algebra are not principles for constructing objects, then, but rules for operating with whatever magnitudes are given in experience.[8] As we shall see, Kant also denies these formulas the character of axioms.

At A718/B746 Kant elaborates two types of spatial (geometrical) construction. An empirical procedure "would yield only an empirical proposition (through measurement of its angles), which would contain no universality, let alone necessity." In the second procedure, "I put together in a pure intuition . . . the manifold that belongs to the schema of a triangle in general and thus to its concept,

---

[6] Friedman, *Kant and the Exact Sciences*, 114.   [7] *Kant and the Exact Sciences*, 114.
[8] Friedman explains that for Kant, arithmetic is concerned with rational magnitudes, whereas "algebra is also concerned with irrational or incommensurable magnitudes," produced by the extraction of roots. See *Kant and the Exact Sciences*, 108–12.

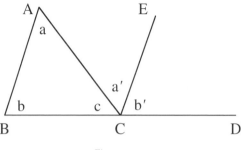

Figure 11.1

through which general synthetic propositions must be constructed." Lisa Shabel explains his point.[9] She argues that the empirical procedure is modeled in Christian Wolff's "mechanical" demonstration of the angle-sum theorem (that the sum of the angles of a triangle equals 180°), in his *Mathematisches Lexicon*. There Wolff constructs the triangle ABC with angles a, b, c. (See Figure 11.1.)

He then uses a compass to "carry" the arcs describing angles a and b along the line BD, creating angle a′ equal to a, and angle b′ equal to b. He then concludes that the three interior angles equal 180°. As Shabel explains, this "demonstration" amounts to a measurement of the interior angles by fallible tools, and depends on visual inspection to determine equality of the angles. The resulting judgment "is an empirical assessment based on the features of the particular constructed triangle; the skill of the geometer who 'carries' the arcs; and the precision of the tools used to do so."[10] In consequence, the conclusion that the interior angles sum to two right angles is only a "metric judgment" concerning a particular empirical triangle, lacking the universality and necessity required for a mathematical demonstration.

Euclid's own demonstration, by contrast, represents the *a priori* method establishing the necessity and universality of the angle-sum theorem. In it, the geometer

extends one side of his triangle, and obtains two adjacent angles that together are equal to two right ones. Now he divides the external one of these angles by drawing a line parallel to the opposite side of the triangle, and sees that here there arises an external adjacent angle which is equal to an internal one, etc. (A716/B744)

[9] See Shabel, "Kant's 'Argument from Geometry'," 209–13.
[10] Shabel, "Kant's 'Argument from Geometry'," 211.

That is, Euclid proceeds by first extending line BC to D, then constructing line CE parallel to line AB. Since AC is a transversal, angle a′ is equal to angle a, and since BD is a transversal, angle b′ is equal to angle b. Thus the demonstration shows that the interior angles of triangle ABC are equal to the three angles lying on BCD, and consequently to two right angles or 180°. As Shabel points out, this proof depends not on visual inspection or empirical procedures, but only on the judgment of "containments among spatial regions" which depends on "prior stipulations for constructing spatial regions," available only through the pure intuition of space.[11] Thus the diagram represents only the *a priori* act, which, Kant says, "considers the concept *in concreto*, although not empirically" (A715/B743).

Owing to the constructibility of concepts in pure intuition, "Mathematics is thoroughly grounded on definitions, axioms, and demonstrations" (A726/B754). In all three respects it differs from philosophy, which, as we have seen, cannot exhibit its objects *a priori* in intuition. At A722/B750 Kant characterizes a transcendental proposition of philosophy as "a synthetic rational cognition in accordance with mere concepts, and thus discursive, since . . . no intuition is given by it *a priori*." Not only can philosophy not demonstrate its propositions from the mere analysis of concepts, it cannot even provide clear definitions of its terms.

The most original part of Kant's analysis is his theory of definition. At A728/B756 he contrasts real definition, analyzing the concept of a thing, with nominal definition, defining a word or "designation."[12] Now "**to define** properly means just to exhibit originally the exhaustive concept of a thing within its boundaries" (A727/B755). By contrast, the "explication" or "exposition" of a concept merely identifies some marks thought in the concept of a thing. It is no surprise to find that empirical concepts cannot be defined exhaustively; not only do different persons think different marks with respect to the concept, but an exhaustive analysis depends on experience:

Thus in the concept of **gold** one person might think, besides its weight, color, and ductility, its property of not rusting, while another might know nothing about this . . . And in any case what would be the point of defining such a

---

[11] Shabel, "Kant's 'Argument from Geometry'," 212.
[12] See Carson for a helpful discussion of real and nominal definition, "Kant on the Method of Mathematics," 648.

concept? – since when, e.g., water and its properties are under discussion, one will not stop at what is intended by the word "water" but rather advance to experiments. (A727–8/B755–6)

Despite their *a priori* origin, philosophical concepts are also not definable, because pure concepts of the understanding and reason are "given" rather than made arbitrarily:

> Strictly speaking no concept given *a priori* can be defined, e.g., substance, cause, right, equity, etc. . . . But since the concept . . . as it is given, can contain many obscure representations, . . . the exhaustiveness of the analysis of my concept is always doubtful, and . . . can only be made **probably** but never **apodictically** certain. (A728–9/B756–7)

Pure concepts arise in the activity of judging, and are "given" as concepts of synthetic functions. The concepts, like these functions, are too indeterminate to specify their objects.

This leaves only arbitrary concepts that can be defined, since "I must know what I wanted to think, since I deliberately made it up, and it was not given to me either through the nature of the understanding or through experience" (A729/B757). But even here there are limitations, for "if the concept depends upon empirical conditions," one cannot be certain that it has an object. For example, my ability to define the concept of a spiritual substance does not guarantee its existence. The only arbitrary concepts that guarantee the existence of their objects are geometric, precisely because they can be constructed *a priori*, "and thus only mathematics has definitions. For the object that it thinks it also exhibits *a priori* in intuition, and this can surely contain neither more nor less than the concept, since through the explanation of the concept the object is originally given" (A729–30/B757–8). Mathematical concepts are definable because they are constructible *a priori* in pure intuition. The form of intuition constrains the arbitrariness of the concept, while its construction ensures the existence of the object. As Emily Carson points out, because construction is a synthetic process, mathematical definitions are synthetic rather than analytic.[13] On Kant's view, definition is the beginning point in mathematics, whereas in philosophy, definition "must conclude rather than begin the work" (A730–1/B759–60).

---

[13] See Carson, "Kant on the Method of Mathematics," 648.

The constructibility of mathematical concepts also confers the status of axioms on fundamental mathematical propositions. Axioms "are synthetic *a priori* principles, insofar as they are immediately certain" (A732/B760). Now although philosophy has synthetic *a priori* principles, these are discursive, i.e., "rational cognition in accordance with concepts" (A732/B760). But synthetic judgments are always based on a "third, mediating cognition," since they cannot be obtained from mere concepts. The principle that everything that happens has a cause, for example, can be justified only in relation to "the condition of time-determination in an experience" (A733/B761). For mathematics, construction in pure intuition allows connecting the predicates both *a priori* and immediately (A732/B761). The axioms of geometry are just the fundamental principles of construction, such as "three points always lie in a plane" (A733/B761). Kant also remarks that the principles of extensive measurement labeled the Axioms of Intuition are not themselves axioms, but principles demonstrating the applicability of mathematical axioms to objects of experience (A733/B761). Although he does not say so here, Kant also claims in that section of the Analytic that arithmetic and algebra lack axioms. There, at A163–4/B204, he says "the self-evident propositions of numerical relation . . . are, to be sure, synthetic, but not general, like those of geometry, and for that reason also cannot be called axioms." This is related to the view discussed above, that arithmetic and algebraic formulas are rules for calculating quantities in general.

Finally, only mathematical principles can be demonstrated. A demonstration is "an apodictic proof, insofar as it is intuitive" (A734/B762). Because mathematics derives its cognition from the construction of concepts, "i.e., from the intuition that can be given *a priori* corresponding to the concepts" (A734/B762), its non-axiomatic principles deserve the title of theorems. As we saw above, philosophical principles such as the principle of causality cannot be presented in intuition *a priori*, but require a transcendental deduction which must appeal to the necessary conditions of experience. In consequence, Kant says, philosophical principles should be labeled "dogmata" rather than theorems (A736/B764). Despite this label, there is no room for dogmatic methods in philosophy, since the attempt to prove speculative principles directly "merely masks mistakes and errors, and deceives philosophy" (A737/B765).

This last point becomes the focus of the second section of the Discipline of Pure Reason, where Kant argues eloquently for the critical method based on the autonomy of reason. Just as citizens of a free state legislate for themselves, the "very existence of reason depends upon this freedom" (A738/B766), since any external constraint effectively negates the function of reason. Although reason cannot establish its claims dogmatically, it can use polemics to defend itself against dogmatic claims to the contrary. Kant briefly returns to the worry that reason could be divided against itself, reminding us that even the antithetical claims of the Antinomies are not genuine contradictories, since the transcendental distinction between appearances and things in themselves dissolves the apparent contradiction. Similarly, the illusory arguments concerning God and the soul violate the conclusion that knowledge is only of appearances. Thus the debates of dogmatic metaphysics are resolved by the critical power of reason to correct itself. As for skepticism, Kant reiterates many of his criticisms of Hume, and particularly Hume's failure to recognize the *a priori* contributions of the sensibility and the understanding. Any parent will appreciate Kant's clever comparison of dogmatism and skepticism to the psychological stages of childhood and adolescence: "The first step in matters of pure reason, which characterizes its childhood, is **dogmatic**. The just mentioned second step is **skeptical**, and gives evidence of the caution of the power of judgment sharpened by experience." The critical method characterizes mature reason, which "subjects to evaluation not the *facta* of reason but reason itself, as concerns its entire capacity and suitability for pure *a priori* cognition" (A761/B789). The final two sections apply Kant's conclusions on the power of reason to the use of hypotheses and proofs.

3. THE DOCTRINE OF METHOD: THE CANON OF PURE REASON

The last section deserving discussion is the Canon, originally intended as a metaphysics of morals. A canon is "the sum total of the *a priori* principles of the correct use" of cognitive faculties (A796/B824). Here he places his analysis of theoretical reason in the context of reason in general, emphasizing the primacy of practical reason. Through a discussion of the interests of reason, Kant sketches his conception of the highest good, explaining the relations between morality, happiness, and the ideas of God and the immortality of the soul. This account presupposes the role of transcendental idealism in making the realm of nature compatible with the demands of the moral law.

In the first section Kant inquires about the origin of the natural tendency of reason "to venture to the outermost bounds of all cognition by means of mere ideas in a pure use" (A797/B825). Assuming a unified function and purpose of natural faculties, the highest ends of reason must be practical, and its theoretical use subordinated to its practical use. The final aim of speculation, he says "concerns three objects: the freedom of the will, the immortality of the soul, and the existence of God" (A798/B826). But as Kant has shown, theoretical reason cannot achieve cognition of any of these objects. Empirical investigation must proceed on the assumptions that all phenomena are caused, that substances are material, and that the only necessities are changes of phenomenal states in accordance with causal laws. With respect to speculative reason, these three propositions are transcendent, that is, "considered in themselves, entirely idle" (A799/B827).

Only practical reason can produce "pure laws determined completely *a priori*," having more than merely regulative status, "which do not command under empirical conditions but absolutely" (A800/B828). These, of course, are the moral laws, which "concern our conduct in relation to the highest end." Thus the ultimate aim of reason concerns "**what is to be done** if the will is free, if there is a God, and if there is a future world." It follows that "the ultimate aim of nature which provides for us wisely in the disposition of reason is properly directed only to what is moral" (A801/B829). In the final analysis, because reason itself is a unity, and its highest ends are practical, the value of theoretical reason resides in its service to practical reason.

Kant next sketches the idea of practical freedom as the capacity to choose independently of necessitation by sensible impulses or desires. At A802/B830 he contrasts the animal will (*arbitrium brutum*), whose power of choice is causally determined by "sensible impulses," i.e., instincts or desires, with the free will (*arbitrium liberum*), which can choose based on a concept of the good. Experience proves that humans have free will, and can exercise practical freedom, since they can conceive of an objective good, and evaluate their desires accordingly. In recognizing the necessity of the moral law, in conceiving how one ought to act, the human will demonstrates its independence from natural necessitation and thus practical freedom.

Now at A803/B831 Kant makes the claim discussed in chapter 9, that the existence of practical freedom does not prove the reality of transcendental freedom, the power to initiate a series spontaneously, independent of all causal influences. This is because the speculative question remains, "whether in these actions, through which it prescribes laws, reason is not itself determined by further influences, and whether that which with respect to sensory impulses is called freedom might not in turn with regard to higher and more remote efficient causes be nature." Here in the Canon Kant characterizes practical freedom "as one of the natural causes, namely a causality of reason in the determination of the will." So although transcendental freedom is "contrary to the law of nature," it is a problem only for theoretical reason. We saw in the Fourth Antinomy how transcendental idealism provides the solution.

In the second section Kant lays out his conception of the highest good, and the relation between morality and happiness. He begins at A804–5/B832–3 with the three questions addressing the interests of reason:

1. What can I know?
2. What should I do?
3. What may I hope?

The first question concerns only speculative reason, and is answered in the critical theory of knowledge. The second is a question for practical reason; the third, which "is simultaneously practical and theoretical," introduces the notion of happiness. Defining happiness as "the satisfaction of all our inclinations," Kant distinguishes between "pragmatic" laws aiming at happiness and the moral law, which is motivated by "**the worthiness to be happy**" (A806/B834). Whereas pragmatic laws are empirically based, depending on both the agent's subjective inclinations and experience of causal connections, the moral law "abstracts from inclinations and natural means of satisfying them, and considers only the freedom of a rational being in general and the necessary conditions under which alone it is in agreement with the distribution of happiness in accordance with principles." Thus only the moral law can be known *a priori* and commands absolutely.

In the remainder of this section Kant introduces the foundation of a "moral theology" in order to solve two problems. First is the general problem of systematic unity mentioned in chapter 10: what guarantees that the world of nature will permit moral action? The other is how to provide an incentive to the rational agent to act morally: what guarantees that doing the right thing will result in happiness? The solution requires postulating the existence of a morally perfect being, whose divine wisdom and benevolence ensure the efficacy of moral action as well as a morally just distribution of happiness in a future world.

In the ideal moral world, free rational agents all act in conformity to the moral law. Each action has a "thoroughgoing systematic unity in itself as well as with the freedom of everyone else" (A808/B836). Although this intelligible notion abstracts entirely from empirical conditions, it nonetheless has objective reality as a standard for human action in the sensible world. Thus it answers the question, "What should I do?" and so provides a model for worthiness to be happy. But it does not explain what guarantees that moral choices will be effective or why one should hope to be happy. The solution to these problems lies in the "**ideal of the highest good**" (A810/B838). This is the idea of a divine intelligence, God, who ensures that the natural order will be consistent with the moral order, and that those who are worthy attain the happiness they deserve. Kant says that moral ends would not be attainable unless some efficient cause determined for moral conduct "an outcome precisely corresponding to our highest ends, whether in this or in another life. Thus without a God and a world that is now not visible to us but is hoped for, the majestic ideas of morality are, to be sure, objects of approbation and admiration but not incentives for resolve and realization" (A812–13/B840–1). On Kant's view, the "complete" good for rational agents requires both moral conduct and the happiness a worthy agent deserves: neither the happy immoral agent nor the unhappy moral agent satisfies our conception of a just world. And, obviously, happiness is not distributed according to moral worth in the world of appearances. But the moral law is absolutely necessary. Consequently, to avoid regarding moral laws "as empty figments of the brain" (A811/B839), the rational agent must presuppose first, that moral action is efficacious in the present, and second, that it will be rewarded in a future life, if not in this one.

In this moral theology, God is the "**single, most perfect,** and **rational** primordial being" whose supreme will is the source of natural as well as moral laws. God has the traditional attributes of omnipotence, omniscience, omnipresence, and is eternal. Because the systematic unity of ends requires us to regard the laws of nature as if they were commands of this divine will, we are also justified in representing nature as "a system of ends," having a purposiveness "inseparably connected *a priori* to the inner possibility of things" (A816/B844). Although we must postulate a divine intelligence as the source of both natural and moral orders, it is a mistake to regard moral obligation as grounded in God's commands: "we will not hold actions to be obligatory because they are God's commands, but will rather regard them as divine commands because we are internally obligated to them" (A819/B847). Effectively responding to the dilemma in Plato's *Euthyphro*, Kant maintains that we must regard the goodness of moral action as independent of God's will, based rather in the conception of a rational agent.

The Canon ends by characterizing the nature of belief in this moral theology. First Kant classifies different ways of believing or "taking to be true." Conviction occurs when belief has objectively sufficient grounds, persuasion when the grounds are only subjectively sufficient. Whereas the former has public validity, allowing "the possibility of communicating it and finding it to be valid for the reason of every human being," the latter has only private validity (A820/B849). This distinction gives rise to three stages in relation to conviction: "**having an opinion, believing,** and **knowing**" (A822/B850). In having an opinion, one is conscious that its grounds are both "subjectively **as well as** objectively insufficient"; i.e., one cannot defend the view. Believing occurs when one has only subjectively sufficient grounds which one recognizes as objectively insufficient. Knowing, of course, requires both subjectively and objectively sufficient grounds. Kant's point is to differentiate moral and theological belief from theoretical claims to knowledge. Since theoretical claims allow of objectively sufficient grounds, judgments of theoretical reason make claims to knowledge. But despite Kant's defense of his moral theology, "no one will be able to boast that he **knows** that there is a God and a future life; for if he knows that, then he is precisely the man I have long sought" (A828–9/B856–7). Nevertheless, "the belief in a God and another world is so interwoven with my moral disposition that I am in as little danger of ever surrendering the former as I am worried that the latter can ever be torn away from me" (A829/B857). In this way Kant resists the temptation to conflate practical assumptions with the cognitive claims of theoretical reason.

4. SUMMARY

The final sections of the *Critique* – the Appendix to the Critique of Speculative Theology and the Transcendental Doctrine of Method – highlight the positive role of the ideas of reason, and the relation between theoretical and practical reason. Kant also elaborates his theory of mathematics in his critique of philosophical methods. In the Appendix, Kant explains the regulative function of theoretical reason in providing both a stimulus and methodological guidelines for empirical inquiry. This analysis completes his revolutionary theory of the intellect, rejecting the traditional views that conceiving is prior to judging, and judging prior to reasoning. In contrasting philosophical and mathematical methods in the Discipline of Pure Reason, Kant fills in the theory of mathematical construction sketched in the Aesthetic. Because mathematical concepts originate in pure intuition, they allow of *a priori* construction. As a result, mathematics begins with definitions, contains axioms, and produces demonstrations of its theorems. Philosophy, by contrast, operates with discursive concepts, which cannot be constructed or even defined. As a result, philosophical principles lack the character of axioms and theorems; they can be justified only indirectly, through transcendental deductions. Thus dogmatic metaphysicians who claim immediate certainty for their principles are mistaken.

Kant originally intended the final substantive discussion, in part II of the Canon, as a metaphysics of morals, parallel to the transcendental doctrine of theoretical reason. Here he argues that experience proves that humans have practical freedom, the ability to choose independently of sensuous impulses and desires. Connecting morality

with the transcendental ideas of reason, he argues that practical freedom requires us to postulate the existence of God and the immortality
of the soul, to guarantee that moral action will be effective in the sensible world, and that the morally worthy agent will find happiness
in a future life. Recognizing the shortcomings of this account, Kant
published the *Groundwork of the Metaphysics of Morals* in 1785, and
the *Critique of Practical Reason* in 1788, containing his mature theory
of the autonomy of practical freedom.

Conclusion: Kant's transcendental idealism

To finish, let us return to the questions raised in chapter 3 about the coherence and defense of Kant's idealism. Since in section 4 of chapter 3 I discussed Kant's justification for the non-spatiotemporality thesis (NST) and the unknowability thesis (UT), here I shall focus on the consistency of his position. I shall not attempt to survey the literature, which is far too vast, nor to spell out in detail the prevailing interpretations. My bibliography contains enough references to point the reader in the right direction.[1] Rather, my aim is to indicate briefly what I take to be the most charitable interpretation of Kant's position, expanding on my remarks on the B edition Preface in chapter 2.

Beginning with F. H. Jacobi in 1787, the most severe critics claimed that Kant is not justified in asserting that things in themselves exist, and that this claim, along with NST, violates UT. The merit of these charges, of course, depends on how one interprets the distinction between appearances and things in themselves. Historically, the two main contenders have been the "two worlds" and "double aspect" views. From Kant's time to the early twentieth century, commentators favored the "two worlds" view, according to which appearances and things in themselves are ontologically distinct. This view has generally lost ground, primarily because it is hard to support textually. If the two worlds are ontologically distinct, then it is difficult to understand in what sense appearances are *of* things in themselves, or how things in themselves could "ground" appearances. From an internal point of view, I find nothing to recommend the "two worlds" interpretation.

---

[1] Chapter 8 of Sebastian Gardner's *Guidebook* contains a concise discussion of the different positions and their strengths and weaknesses. Hoke Robinson also explores the issues in detail in "Two Perspectives on Kant's Appearances and Things in Themselves."

The main competitor, the "two aspect" view, has been most force-fully defended by Henry Allison, following the influential work of Gerold Prauss.[2] It takes seriously Kant's references to appearances as *of* things in themselves, and regards the distinction as marking two ways of considering objects: as they appear to perceivers, and as they are independently of them. But because of difficulties in explaining how these "two aspects" are related, many philosophers, and espe-cially Paul Guyer, have rejected this view.[3] More recently, in *Kantian Humility*, Rae Langton denies that Kant is an idealist, and offers a third interpretation. Thus there is no clear consensus on how to read Kant's distinction between appearances and things in themselves.

My own view developed out of my defense of NST in *Space and Incongruence*, where I traced Kant's idealism to the development of his critical theory of space. Since then I have found Allison's read-ing largely persuasive, and so I classified my position under the "two aspect" interpretation. But some recent literature suggests that I may be mistaken, since my position is similar to alternatives Sebastian Gardner and Hoke Robinson distinguish from the "two aspects" view.[4] In any case, here I shall simply outline the approach offer-ing the most charitable account of the critical philosophy.

The Prefaces to the *Critique* indicate that the distinction between appearances and things in themselves arises by critical reflection on some (pre-reflective) axioms basic to philosophy. These are:

1. Something exists that has an intrinsic nature of its own.
2. Cognition (representation) is a relation between a subject and an object.
3. In sensation human subjects are affected by existing things.

As we saw in chapter 8 on the Amphiboly, one pair of concepts reason employs in transcendental reflection is the distinction between the inner and the outer: "In an object of the pure understanding only that is internal that has no relation (as far as the existence is

---

[2] See Allison's recently revised *Kant's Transcendental Idealism*, chapters 2 and 3, as well as "Transcendental Idealism: The 'Two Aspect' View."
[3] See *Kant and the Claims of Knowledge*, chapter 15.
[4] See Gardner's discussion of the "indeterminacy" view at *Guidebook*, 295–8; Robinson also distinguishes a "two Perspectives" position from the "two aspect" view, "Two Perspectives on Kant's Appearances and Things in Themselves," at 428–32.

concerned) to anything that is different from it" (A265/B321). I take this to be the basis of Kant's distinction between things in themselves and appearances. Things in themselves are whatever exists (taken collectively) considered *non-relationally*. Appearances are this same collection in their relation to human subjects. These definitions are neutral with respect to idealism and realism. Transcendental realists maintain that perceptual or other cognitive processes give access to things in themselves, so that, to some extent, appearances represent things in themselves. Transcendental idealists deny that humans have such access; although appearances are *of* things in themselves, they do not *represent* them. I agree with Allison and Gardner that Kant's idealism results primarily from his doctrine of sensible intuition, and secondarily from the theory of discursive judgment. These analyses lead Kant to conclude that objects of human intuition are not things in themselves, but only appearances.

This explains why at Bxxvi–xxvii Kant says it is absurd to think there could be appearances without anything that appears (cited in chapter 2). The absurdity is in maintaining that anything could exist without an intrinsic, non-relational nature (whether known or not). In Kant's critical terms, this is equivalent to the absurdity that the conditioned (appearance) can exist without its conditions (the thing in itself). The view that things in themselves are the non-relational conditions of existing things as they appear to human perceivers provides no basis for a "two worlds" interpretation. Kant recognizes, however, that "there may even be beings of understanding to which our sensible faculty of intuition has no relation at all" (B308–9). That is, it is entirely possible that some things in themselves do not appear to humans, e.g., God.[5] But given UT, this possibility lacks cognitive significance.

The next questions are how appearances relate to things in themselves, and how to understand the notion of "affection." Kant's theory of intuition depends on axiom 3: sensation arises through outer sense insofar as external things affect the subject. It is natural to construe this as a relation between the subject in itself and things in themselves. In *Kant und das Ding an sich*, Erich Adickes developed this interpretation as the doctrine of "double affection." As Gardner explains, on

[5] See Gardner, *Guidebook*, 294–5.

this view "the subject is originally affected transcendentally by things in themselves, and then reaffected – this time as an empirical being endowed with sense organs – by the empirical objects which are the products of the first affection."[6] But this model clearly violates UT: affection is a causal relation, and all concepts, including causality, apply only within experience.

Transcendental idealism entails that affection of subjects by objects can be ascribed only on the empirical level, because it is a causal relation. Thus despite its intuitive appeal, it is an error to think of whatever relation obtains between subjects and things in themselves as causal. Given UT, we cannot know how the subject in itself relates to other things. The theory of double affection represents a form of transcendental illusion: it arises from an attempt to make meaningful cognitive claims about the unconditioned. On the empirical level, by contrast, there is no difficulty in representing the relation between subjects and objects causally. As I argued in chapter 7, the Second Analogy requires us to recognize sensations as physical states caused in perceivers by external, physical objects. So there is no "double affection." We have no way to represent how we as subjects in ourselves are related to things in themselves.

This same reasoning can be used to answer a similar criticism of the "double aspect" view. Several philosophers claim that any attempt to identify appearances ontologically with things in themselves also violates UT. After all, numerical identity is defined in part by the principle of the indiscernibility of identicals: two things are numerically identical if and only if they share all properties. But NST denies that appearances and things in themselves share *any* properties. Thus it is nonsensical to assert that things in themselves *are* appearances taken non-relationally. The solution here echoes that given above. On my view, things in themselves are the ontological *ground* of appearances. But we have only a minimal *logical* conception of this relation, an indeterminate notion of condition to conditioned. That cannot be the notion of *numerical identity* defined by the indiscernibility of identicals, since concepts of number do not apply beyond experience. Thus I find myself sympathetic to the "indeterminacy" view described by Gardner, according to which "transcendental reflection is incapable

---

[6] Gardner, *Guidebook*, 291–2.

of making out determinately the relation between appearances and things in themselves."[7] Attempts to define that relation precisely do not take transcendental idealism seriously.

Kant's idealism raises many more questions I have not touched on. Interested readers will find no lack of discussion in the literature.[8] My hope here is to sketch an answer to some of the more serious charges against transcendental idealism. I have argued that it is not blatantly incoherent. In chapter 3 we saw how Kant's theory of space and time supports NST. In chapter 2 I explained why NST and the claim that things in themselves exist do not contradict UT, since neither view ascribes any properties to things in themselves. As I have insisted throughout this book, whatever the difficulties with Kant's critical theory, it offers a powerful and systematic alternative to the philosophies that preceded it, and continues to set the stage for philosophical debate.

[7] Gardner, *Guidebook*, 297.
[8] See chapter 10 of Van Cleve's *Problems from Kant* for a helpful discussion of many issues.

Works cited

BIOGRAPHIES

Cassirer, Ernst. *Kant's Life and Thought.* Trans. James Haden. New Haven: Yale University Press, 1981.

Kuehn, Manfred. *Kant: A Biography.* Cambridge: Cambridge University Press, 2001.

WORKS BY KANT CITED IN THE TEXT

Unless otherwise noted, all quotations and references are to translations available in the Cambridge Edition of the Works of Immanuel Kant. Volumes from which works are cited are:

Correspondence. Trans. and ed. Arnulf Zweig. Cambridge: Cambridge University Press, 1999.

Critique of Pure Reason. Trans. and ed. Paul Guyer and Allen W. Wood. Cambridge: Cambridge University Press, 1997. As is customary, citations are to the A (1781) and B (1787) pagination of the Akademie edition.

Critique of the Power of Judgment. Trans. and ed. Paul Guyer and Eric Matthews. Cambridge: Cambridge University Press, 2000.

Lectures on Logic. Trans. and ed. J. Michael Young. Cambridge: Cambridge University Press, 1992. Contains the following works cited:

The Blomberg Logic, 1–246.

The Dohna-Wundlacken Logic, 427–516.

The Jäsche Logic, 519–640.

The Vienna Logic, 249–377.

Lectures on Metaphysics. Trans. and ed. Karl Ameriks and Steve Naragon. Cambridge: Cambridge University Press, 1997. Contains the following works cited:

Metaphysik Mrongovius, 107–283.

Metaphysik Vigilantius, 415–506.

Practical Philosophy. Trans. and ed. Mary J. Gregor. Cambridge: Cambridge
   University Press, 1996. Contains the following works cited:
   Groundwork of the Metaphysics of Morals, 37–108.
   Critique of Practical Reason, 133–271.
Theoretical Philosophy, 1755–1770. Trans. and ed. David Walford. Cambridge:
   Cambridge University Press, 1992. Contains the following works cited:
   A New Elucidation of the First Principles of Metaphysical Cognition, 1–45.
   Concerning the Ultimate Ground of the Differentiation of Directions in Space,
   361–72.
   On the Form and Principles of the Sensible and the Intelligible World
   [Inaugural Dissertation], 373–416.
   *The Only Possible Argument in Support of a Demonstration of the Existence
   of God*, 107–201.
Theoretical Philosophy after 1781. Trans. and ed. Henry Allison and Peter
   Heath, trans. Gary Hatfield and Michael Friedman. Cambridge: Cam-
   bridge University Press, 2002. Contains the following works cited:
   *Prolegomena to Any Future Metaphysics that Will be Able to Come Forward
   as Science*, 49–169.
   Metaphysical Foundations of Natural Science, 171–270.
   *On a Discovery Whereby Any New Critique of Pure Reason Is To be Made
   Superfluous by an Older One*, 281–336.

Other editions of Kant's works:
Nachträge zu Kants Kritik der reinen Vernunft. Ed. Benno Erdmann. Kiel:
   Lipsius & Tischer, 1881.
Reflexionen Kants zur kritischen Philosophie. Ed. Benno Erdmann. Leipzig:
   Feuss Verlag, 1882.
The standard German edition of Kant's works is *Kants gesammelte Schriften*.
   Ed. Royal Prussian (later German) Academy of Sciences. Berlin: Georg
   Reimer, later Walter de Gruyter & Co., 1900–. The marginal numbers
   in works in the Cambridge edition are to volumes and pages of this
   edition.

OTHER WORKS CITED

Adams, Robert. *Leibniz: Determinist, Theist, Idealist*. Oxford: Oxford Uni-
   versity Press, 1994.
Adickes, Erich. *Kant und das Ding an sich*. Berlin: Pan Verlag, 1924.
Al-Azm, Sadik J. *The Origins of Kant's Arguments in the Antinomies*. Oxford:
   Oxford University Press, 1972.
Allison, Henry E. *Kant's Theory of Freedom*. Cambridge: Cambridge Uni-
   versity Press, 1990.

Kant's Transcendental Idealism. New Haven: Yale University Press, 1983, rev. ed. 2004.

"Transcendental Idealism: The 'Two Aspect' View." In *New Essays on Kant*, ed. Bernard den Ouden. New York: Peter Lang, 1987, 155–78.

Ameriks, Karl. *Kant's Theory of Mind*. Oxford: Clarendon Press, 1982.

Anselm, St. *Anselm's Basic Writings*. Trans. S. W. Deane. La Salle, Ill.: Open Court Publishing Co., 1962.

Aquinas, St. Thomas. *The Basic Writings of St. Thomas Aquinas*. Trans. Anton C. Pegis. New York: Random House, 1945.

Arnauld, Antoine and Pierre Nicole. *Logic or the Art of Thinking: The Port-Royal Logic*. Trans. and ed. Jill Vance Buroker. Cambridge: Cambridge University Press, 1996.

Bennett, Jonathan. *Kant's Analytic*. Cambridge: Cambridge University Press, 1966.

Kant's Dialectic. Cambridge: Cambridge University Press, 1974.

Berkeley, George. *De Motu*. In *The Works of George Berkeley Bishop of Cloyne*, 4:1–52. Ed. A. A. Luce and T. E. Jessop. London: Thomas Nelson and Sons, 1951.

Three Dialogues Between Hylas and Philonous. Ed. Robert M. Adams. Indianapolis: Hackett, 1979.

A Treatise Concerning the Principles of Human Knowledge. Ed. Kenneth P. Winkler. Indianapolis: Hackett, 1982.

Bird, Graham. *Kant's Theory of Knowledge*. London: Routledge & Kegan Paul, 1962.

Brittan, Gordon G., Jr. *Kant's Theory of Science*. Princeton: Princeton University Press, 1978.

Broad, C. D. *Kant: An Introduction*. Ed. C. Lewy. Cambridge: Cambridge University Press, 1978.

Brook, Andrew. *Kant and the Mind*. Cambridge: Cambridge University Press, 1994.

Buroker, Jill Vance. "Descartes on Sensible Qualities." *Journal of the History of Philosophy* 29 (1991): 585–611.

"On Kant's Proof of the Existence of Material Objects." *Proceedings of the Sixth International Kant Congress*, ed. Gerhard Funke and Thomas M. Seebohm, 2.1:183–97. Washington, D.C.: Center for Advanced Research in Phenomenology and University Press of America, 1989.

"The Role of Incongruent Counterparts in Kant's Transcendental Idealism." In James Van Cleve and Robert E. Frederick, eds., *The Philosophy of Right and Left* (see below), 315–39.

Space and Incongruence: The Origin of Kant's Idealism. Dordrecht: D. Reidel, 1981.

Carson, Emily. "Kant on the Method of Mathematics." *Journal of the History of Philosophy* 37 (1999): 629–52.

Chipman, Lachlan. "Kant's Categories and their Schematism." In *Kant on Pure Reason*, ed. Ralph C. S. Walker, 100–16.

Descartes, René. *Meditations on First Philosophy*. In *The Philosophical Writings of Descartes*, ed. J. Cottingham, R. Stoothoff, and D. Murdoch. 3 vols. Cambridge: Cambridge University Press, 1985.

Dörflinger, Bernd. "The Underlying Teleology of the First *Critique*." *Proceedings of the Eighth International Kant Congress*, 1.2: 813–26.

Dummett, Michael. "The Significance of Quine's Indeterminacy Thesis." In *Truth and Other Enigmas*. Cambridge, Mass.: Harvard University Press, 1978.

Falkenstein, Lorne. *Kant's Intuitionism*. Toronto: University of Toronto Press, 1995.

Frege, Gottlob. *The Foundations of Arithmetic*. Trans. J. L. Austin. Oxford: Basil Blackwell, 1959.

"The Thought." In G. Frege, *Logical Investigations*. Trans. and ed. P. T. Geach and R. H. Stoothoff. Oxford: Oxford University Press, 1977.

Friedman, Michael. "Causal Laws and the Foundations of Natural Science." In *The Cambridge Companion to Kant*, ed. Paul Guyer (see below), 161–97.

Kant and the Exact Sciences. Cambridge, Mass.: Harvard University Press, 1982.

Gardner, Sebastian. *Routledge Philosophy Guidebook to Kant and the Critique of Pure Reason*. London: Routledge, 1999.

Gibbons, Sarah. *Kant's Theory of Imagination*. Oxford: Oxford University Press, 1994.

Gochnauer, Myron. "Kant's Refutation of Idealism." *Journal of the History of Philosophy* 12 (1974): 195–206.

Grice, H. P. and P. F. Strawson. "In Defense of a Dogma." *Philosophical Review* 45 (1956): 141–58.

Grier, Michelle. *Kant's Doctrine of Transcendental Illusion*. Cambridge: Cambridge University Press, 2001.

Guyer, Paul, ed. *The Cambridge Companion to Kant*. Cambridge: Cambridge University Press, 1992. Contains an extensive bibliography.

Kant and the Claims of Knowledge. Cambridge: Cambridge University Press, 1987.

"Kant's Intentions in the Refutation of Idealism." *Philosophical Review* 92 (1983): 329–83.

Henrich, Dieter. "The Proof-Structure of Kant's Transcendental Deduction." *Review of Metaphysics* 22 (1969): 640–59.

Hintikka, Jaakko. "On Kant's Notion of Intuition (Anschauung)." In *The First Critique: Reflections on Kant's Critique of Pure Reason*, ed. T. Penelhum and J. J. MacIntosh (see below), 38–53.

Hume, David. *Dialogues Concerning Natural Religion*. Ed. Richard H. Popkin. Indianapolis: Hackett, 1998.

Enquiry Concerning Human Understanding. Ed. L. A. Selby-Bigge, rev. P. H. Nidditch. Oxford: Oxford University Press, 1975.

A Treatise of Human Nature. Ed. L. A. Selby-Bigge, rev. P. H. Nidditch. Oxford: Oxford University Press, 1978.

Kemp Smith, Norman. *A Commentary to Kant's Critique of Pure Reason*. New York: Humanities Press, 1962.

Kitcher, Patricia. *Kant's Transcendental Psychology*. Oxford: Oxford University Press, 1990.

Langton, Rae. *Kantian Humility: Our Ignorance of Things in Themselves*. Oxford: Clarendon Press, 1998.

Leibniz, Gottfried Wilhelm. *Discourse on Metaphysics, Correspondence with Arnauld and Monadology*. Trans. George R. Montgomery. La Salle, Ill.: Open Court, 1968.

The Leibniz–Clarke Correspondence. Ed. H. G. Alexander. Manchester: Manchester University Press, 1965.

New Essays on Human Understanding. Ed. Peter Remnant and Jonathan Bennett. Cambridge: Cambridge University Press, 1996.

Philosophical Papers and Letters. Trans. and ed. Leroy E. Loemker. Dordrecht: D. Reidel, 1969.

Locke, John. *An Essay Concerning Human Understanding*, ed. P. H. Nidditch. Oxford: Oxford University Press, 1975.

Longuenesse, Béatrice. *Kant and the Capacity to Judge*. Princeton: Princeton University Press, 1998.

Lovejoy, Arthur O. "On Kant's Reply to Hume." In *Kant: Disputed Questions*, ed. M. Gram, 284–308. Chicago: Quadrangle Books, 1967.

McGinn, Colin. *Logical Properties*. Oxford: Clarendon Press, 2000.

Melnick, Arthur. *Kant's Analogies of Experience*. Chicago: University of Chicago Press, 1973.

Space, Time and Thought in Kant. Dordrecht: Kluwer Academic Publishers, 1989.

Naragon, Steven. "Kant on Descartes and the Brutes." *Kantstudien* 81 (1990): 1–23.

Newton, Isaac. *Mathematical Principles of Natural Philosophy and his System of the World*. Trans. Florian Cajori. 2 vols. Berkeley: University of California Press, 1966.

Parsons, Charles. "Kant's Philosophy of Arithmetic." In *Kant on Pure Reason*, ed. Ralph C. S. Walker (see below), 13–40.

"The Transcendental Aesthetic." In *The Cambridge Companion to Kant*, ed. Paul Guyer (see above), 62–100.

Paton, H. J. *Kant's Metaphysic of Experience*. 2 vols. New York: Macmillan, 1936.

Penelhum, T. and J. J. MacIntosh, eds. *The First Critique: Reflections on Kant's Critique of Pure Reason*. Belmont, Calif.: Wadsworth, 1969.

Posy, Carl. "Dancing to the Antinomy: A Proposal for Transcendental Idealism." *American Philosophical Quarterly* 20 (1983): 81–94.

Prauss, Gerold. *Erscheinung bei Kant*. Berlin: De Gruyter, 1971.

Kant und das Problem der Dinge an sich. Bonn: Bouvier, 1974.

Prichard, H. A. *Kant's Theory of Knowledge*. Oxford: Clarendon Press, 1929.

Quine, Willard Van Orman. "Two Dogmas of Empiricism." In *From a Logical Point of View*. New York: Harper and Row, 1961.

Word and Object. Cambridge, Mass.: MIT Press, 1960.

Robinson, Hoke. "Two Perspectives on Kant's Appearances and Things in Themselves." *Journal of the History of Philosophy* 32 (1994): 411–41.

Russell, Bertrand. *Our Knowledge of the External World*. New York: New American Library, 1956.

Russell, Bertrand and Alfred North Whitehead. *Principia Mathematica*. 3 vols. New York: Cambridge University Press, 1910–13.

Shabel, Lisa. "Kant's 'Argument from Geometry'." *Journal of the History of Philosophy* 42 (2004): 195–215.

Spinoza, Baruch. *The Ethics and Selected Letters*. Trans. Samuel Shirley. Indianapolis: Hackett, 1982.

Strawson, P. F. *The Bounds of Sense*. London: Methuen, 1966.

Thompson, Manley. "Singular Terms and Intuitions in Kant's Epistemology." *Review of Metaphysics* 26 (1972): 314–43

Vaihinger, Hans. *Commentar zu Kants Kritik der reinen Vernunft*. 2 vols. Stuttgart: W. Spemann and Union Deutsche Verlagsgesellschaft, 1881–92.

Van Cleve, James. "Four Recent Interpretations of Kant's Second Analogy." *Kantstudien* 64 (1973): 69–87.

Problems from Kant. Oxford: Oxford University Press, 1999.

Van Cleve, James and Robert E. Frederick, eds. *The Philosophy of Right and Left*. Dordrecht: Kluwer, 1991.

Walker, Ralph C. S., ed. *Kant on Pure Reason*. Oxford: Oxford University Press, 1982.

Walsh, W. H. *Kant's Criticism of Metaphysics*. Edinburgh: Edinburgh University Press, 1975.

White, Morton. "The Analytic and the Synthetic: An Untenable Dualism." Reprinted in *Semantics and the Philosophy of Language*, ed. Leonard Linsky, 272–86. Urbana: University of Illinois Press, 1952. (First published 1950.)

Wolff, Robert Paul. *Kant's Theory of Mental Activity*. Cambridge, Mass.: Harvard University Press, 1963.

Wood, Allen. *Kant's Rational Theology*. Ithaca: Cornell University Press, 1978.

Young, J. Michael. "Kant's View of Imagination." *Kantstudien* 79 (1988): 140–64.

GENERAL WORKS NOT CITED

Beck, Lewis White. *Studies in the Philosophy of Kant*. Indianapolis: Bobbs-Merrill, 1965.
Dicker, Georges. *Kant's Theory of Knowledge: An Analytical Introduction*. Oxford: Oxford University Press, 2005.
Höffe, Otfried. *Immanuel Kant*. Trans. Marshall Farrier. Albany: State University of New York Press, 1994.
Nagel, Gordon. *The Structure of Experience: Kant's System of Principles*. Chicago: University of Chicago Press, 1983.
Pippin, Robert B. *Kant's Theory of Form: An Essay on the Critique of Pure Reason*. New Haven: Yale University Press, 1982.
Walker, Ralph C. S. *Kant*. London: Routledge & Kegan Paul, 1978.

ANTHOLOGIES NOT CITED

Förster, Eckart, ed. *Kant's Transcendental Deductions: The Three 'Critiques' and the 'Opus postumum'*. Stanford: Stanford University Press, 1989.
Harper, William A. and Ralph Meerbote, eds. *Kant on Causality, Freedom, and Objectivity*. Minneapolis: University of Minnesota Press, 1984.
Kitcher, Patricia, ed. *Kant's "Critique of Pure Reason": Critical Essays*. Lanham, Md.: Rowman & Littlefield, 1998.
Wolff, Robert Paul, ed. *Kant: A Collection of Critical Essays*. Garden City, N.Y.: Doubleday Anchor, 1967.

BIBLIOGRAPHIES

Ameriks, Karl. "Recent Work on Kant's Theoretical Philosophy." *American Philosophical Quarterly* 19 (1982): 1–24. Contains an extensive bibliography of works before 1982.

The North American Kant Society (NAKS) maintains comprehensive on-line bibliographies of works on Kant, from 1986 to the present, intended for use by members of the Society. They may be accessed at www.naks.ucsd.edu. The website also has information for those wishing to join NAKS.

Index